RUSSIAN REFERENCE GRAMMAR

RUSSIAN Reference Grammar

A Complete Guide for Students and Professionals

NICHOLAS MALTZOFF

NATIONAL TEXTBOOK COMPANY • Skokie, Illinois 60077 U.S.A.

NTC RUSSIAN SERIES

Basic Russian, Book I (2nd Edition)
Basic Russian, Book II
Simplified Russian Grammar (3rd Edition)
Russian Reference Grammar
Pronounce Russian Correctly
Roots of Russian Language
Reading and Translating Contemporary Russian
Business Russian
Russian Composition and Conversation: A Guidebook
Russian Conversations for Beginners Accompanying Cassette
Six Soviet One-Act Plays
Trio: Intermediate Level Adaptations of Pushkin, Lermontov and Gogol
Quartet: Intermediate Level Adaptations of Turgenyev, Tolstoy, Dostoyevsky and Checkhov
The Inspector General
The Queen of Spades
Asya
Dear Comrade
Beginner's Russian Reader (3rd Edition)
Russian Intermediate Reader
Russian Area Reader
Modern Russian Reader for Intermediate Classes

For further information or a current catalogue, write:
National Textbook Company, 8259 Niles Center Rd., Skokie, IL 60077 U.S.A.

*This edition first published in 1981 by National Textbook Company.
8259 Niles Center Rd., Skokie, IL 60077.
All rights reserved. No part of this book may be reproduced, stored in a retrieval system, or transmitted into any form or by any means, electronic, mechanical, photocopy, recording or otherwise, without the prior permission of National Textbook Company. Manufactured in the United States of America. Originally published © 1965 by Fearon • Pitman Publishers.*

1234567890PP 987654321

PREFACE

THE AIM OF this book is to serve as a reference text for those engaged in the study of Russian. In addition to standard rules of grammar, tables, and lists of exceptions, every section includes a paragraph on usage, containing, as a rule, some of the more special points. The sections on usage incorporate elements of syntax and stylistics, in order to guide the student in the proper application of given rules. This procedure, we believe, will be found particularly valuable in the chapters on Adverbs, Prepositions, Conjunctions, and Particles, which have been treated in detail.

Russian Reference Grammar will be found most useful by students who are familiar with basic rules and who have reached a certain degree of proficiency in speaking. It has been deemed advisable, however, to supply translations of practically all Russian words or sentences.

In order to include in a book of this size the greatest amount of desirable information, the explanations pertaining to each paragraph have been kept brief. Rules given in this book have frequently been illustrated with examples taken from authoritative sources, especially when dealing with the more delicate points of grammar.

To facilitate reference, the contents has been organized according to main sections, divisions, and sub-divisions.

A list of principal sources consulted in the preparation of this book is included.

N. MALTZOFF

пожалуйста – p. 178
пожалуй – p. 326.
спасибо – p. 329
здравствуйте – p. 329, 10

BIBLIOGRAPHY

Грамматика русского языка. Том I. Фонетика и морфология.
    Академия наук СССР.
Грамматика русского языка. Том II. Синтаксис.
    Академия наук СССР.
Современный русский язык. Грамматическое учение о слове.
    В. В. Виноградов.
Современный русский язык. Морфология.
    В. В. Виноградов.
Очерк современного русского литературного языка.
    А. А. Шахматов.
Современный русский язык. Синтаксис.
    Под редакцией Е. М. Галкиной-Федорук.
Современный русский язык. Лексикология, Фонетика, Морфология.
    Е. М. Галкина-Федорук, К. В. Горшкова, Н. М. Шанский.
Современный русский язык. Синтаксис.
    Е. М. Галкина-Федорук, К. В. Горшкова, Н. М. Шанский.
Трудные вопросы грамматики и правописания.
    В. А. Добромыслов и Д. Э. Розенталь.
Методические разработки по грамматике. Сборник статей.
    Под редакцией С. Г. Бархударова.
Очерк грамматики русского литературного языка.
    Р. И. Аванесов и В. Н. Сидоров.
Учебник русского языка для студентов-иностранцев.
    И. М. Пулькина и Е. Б. Захава-Некрасова.
Очерки по стилистике русского языка.
    А. Н. Гвоздёв.
Очерки по синтаксису русской разговорной речи.
    Н. Ю. Шведова.
Краткий справочник по русской грамматике.
    И. М. Пулькина.
Справочник по русской грамматике для иностранцев.
    Н. Г. Хромец, А. П. Вейсман.

Словарь русского языка.
> Академия наук СССР.

Толковый словарь русского языка.
> Под редакцией Д. Н. Ушакова.

Этимологический словарь русского языка.
> А. Преображенский.

Russian Syntax.
> F. M. Borras and R. F. Christian.

Russian Grammar.
> B. O. Unbegaun.

Russian Grammar.
> Nevill Forbes.

Grammaire de la langue russe.
> André Mazon.

Emplois des aspects du verbe russe.
> André Mazon.

Russische Grammatik.
> Erich Berneker. Max Vasmer.

CONTENTS

CHAPTER 1 ALPHABET AND PRONUNCIATION

The Alphabet   1
Handwriting   2
    Variations in Handwriting   2
    "Hooks" in Certain Letters   3
    Connecting of Letters   3
Capitalization   3
Pronunciation of Hard and Soft Sounds   4
Vowels   4
Consonants   4
Hard and Soft Signs   5
Pronunciation of Vowels   6
Jotation   6
Stressed and Unstressed Vowels   6
    о and а   7
    е, э and я   7
    и, у, ю and ы   7
Open and Closed Vowels   7
Pronunciation of Consonants   8
Voiced and Voiceless Consonants   8
    Voiced Pronounced Voiceless   8
    Voiceless Pronounced Voiced   9
The Ending го   9
Unpronounced Consonants   10
Isolated Cases   10
The Letter й   10
Stress   10
  Nouns   10
  Adjectives   11
  Verbs   11
Spelling Rule   11

CHAPTER 2 NOUNS

Gender: Rules   12
Nouns Ending in ь   12
Additional Rules for Determining Gender   13
   Masculine Nouns Ending in а, я, о, or е   13
   Common Gender Nouns:
      Masculine and Feminine Ending in а   13
   Gender of Nouns of Foreign Origin   14
   Gender of Nouns Ending in мя   14
   Substantivized Adjectives   15
Usage of the Gender   15
   Nouns Indicating Professions and Occupations   15
   Common Gender Nouns   16
   The Nouns человéк, друг, товáрищ, враг   16
   Nouns of Foreign Origin Ending in о, е, и, у, ю, á   16
   Foreign Geographical Nouns   17
Number   17
Rules for the Plural of Nouns   17
Basic Plural Endings   17
Plural of Nouns with Stems Ending in г, к, х, ж, ч, ш, щ, ц   18
Irregular Plural Endings   18
   Masculine Nouns   19
      Nouns Ending in Stressed а or я   19
      Nouns Ending in á, я́, or ы́, и́   19
      Plural of Nouns Ending in -анин or -янин   20
      Other Hard Nouns Ending in the Plural in и or а   21
      Nouns Ending in -ья   21
   Neuter Nouns   22
      Nouns Ending in -мя   22
      Nouns Ending in -ко   22
      Plural Ending -ья   22
      Isolated Cases of Irregularities   22
   Feminine Nouns   23
      Plurals of мать, дочь, and кýрица   23
   The Fleeting о or е   23
Nouns Having Only One Number   23
   Nouns Used Only in the Singular   23
   Nouns Found Only in the Plural   24
Usage of the Singular and Plural   25
   Nouns Used Normally in the Singular, and Occasionally in the Plural   25
      Nouns Which Express Long Duration or Repetition   25
      Nouns Which Express Large Quantities   25
      Collective Nouns   25
   Abstract Nouns   25
   Names of Vegetables and Berries   26
   Singular Used to Imply Plurality   26

CHAPTER 3 DECLENSION OF NOUNS

Introductory Remarks: Nouns and Cases   27
DECLENSION OF MASCULINE NOUNS, SINGULAR   27
Special Rules Pertaining to Masculine Nouns   28
   Rules for the Genitive Case   28
   Rules for the Accusative Case   30
   Rules for the Instrumental Case   30
   Rules for the Prepositional Case   30
     Endings у or ю   30
     Ending ии   31
   The Fleeting o and e   32
   Declension of the Noun путь   33
DECLENSION OF NEUTER NOUNS, SINGULAR   33
Special Rules Pertaining to Neuter Nouns   33
   Nouns of Foreign Origin Ending in o, e, и, у, ю, or a   33
   Hard Nouns Ending in a Sibilant or ц   33
   Soft Nouns Ending in a Sibilant or ц   34
   The Prepositional Endings -ьё and -ии   34
   Nouns Ending in мя   34
   The Noun дитя   34
DECLENSION OF FEMININE NOUNS, SINGULAR   34
Special Rules Pertaining to Feminine Nouns   34
   The Genitive, Dative, and Prepositional of Nouns Ending in -ия and -ь   34
   The Dative and Prepositional of Nouns Ending in -a or -я   35
   The Accusative of Nouns Ending in -ь   35
   The Instrumental   35
Irregular Feminine Declensions   35
   Declension of мать and дочь   35
   Declension of любо́вь, це́рковь, ложь, and рожь   35
DECLENSION OF NOUNS IN THE PLURAL   36
General Pattern   36
   Masculine   36
   Feminine   36
   Neuter   36
Rules Pertaining to the Declension of Nouns in the Plural   37
   The Dative, Accusative, Instrumental, and Prepositional   37
   The Genitive Plural   37
     Hard Nouns   38
     Soft Nouns   39
     Isolated Cases of Irregularities in the Genitive Plural   41
   Insertion of e and o in the Genitive Plural   41
     Feminine Nouns   41
     Neuter Nouns   42
   Genitive of Nouns Which Occur Only in the Plural   42
Miscellaneous Irregular Declensions in the Singular and Plural   43
   Masculine Nouns   44
   Feminine Nouns   44
   Neuter Nouns   45
DECLENSION OF PROPER NAMES   45
   First Names and Patronymics   45
   Last Names   46

Geographical Names   47
→ THE USAGE OF CASES   48
The Nominative   48
   Basic Function   48
   Special Constructions   48
   Verbs   48
   Prepositions   48
The Genitive   49
   Basic Function   49
   Special Constructions   50
   Verbs Governing the Genitive   53
   Prepositions   54
The Dative   58
   Basic Function   58
   Special Constructions   58
   Verbs Governing the Dative   60
   Prepositions   62
The Accusative   64
   Basic Function   64
      Negated Sentences   64
   Special Constructions   65
   Verbs Governing the Accusative   65
   Prepositions   66
The Instrumental   69
   Basic Function   69
   Special Constructions   69
   Verbs Governing the Instrumental   72
   Prepositions   74
The Prepositional   76
   Basic Function   76
   Verbs and Special Constructions   76
   Prepositions   76

CHAPTER 4 ADJECTIVES

Endings, Singular   80
Stems in н   80
   List of Currently Used Soft Adjectives   80
MIXED ADJECTIVES   81
Plural of Adjectives   82
   Declension of Adjectives in the Singular   82
      Declension of Mixed Adjectives   82
   Declension of Adjectives in the Plural   83
QUALITATIVE, RELATIVE, AND POSSESSIVE ADJECTIVES   83
   Possessive Adjectives Pertaining to Persons   84
Adjectives Ending in -ий, -ья, -ье, -ьи   85
SHORT ADJECTIVES   86
Insertion of o or e in Short Adjectives   87
USAGE OF ADJECTIVES   87
Long and Short Form   87
   Agreement Between Nouns and Qualifiers   89

The Comparative Degree of Adjectives   90
    The Simple Comparative   90
        Formation   90
        Irregular Formation   90
        Comparatives Not Formed   91
    The Compound Comparative   91
Usage of the Comparative Degree   92
    Simple Comparative   92
    Compound Comparative   92
    Constructions Expressing a Comparison   92
The Superlative Degree of Adjectives   93
    The Simple Superlative   93
        Formation   93
    The Compound Superlative   94
        Formation   94
Usage of the Superlative Degree   94
    Simple Form   94
    Compound Form   95
        Constructions Used with the Superlative Degree   95
Adjectives with Variable Meanings   96

CHAPTER 5 PRONOUNS

PERSONAL PRONOUNS   98
    Declension of Personal Pronouns   98
    Usage of Personal Pronouns   99
    The Reflexive Pronoun себя—self   101
POSSESSIVE PRONOUNS   101
    Declension of Possessive Pronouns   101
    Usage of Possessive Pronouns   102
DEMONSTRATIVE PRONOUNS   104
    Declension of Demonstrative Pronouns   105
    Usage of Demonstrative Pronouns   105
DEFINITE PRONOUNS   107
    Declension of Definite Pronouns   107
    Usage of Definite Pronouns   108
INTERROGATIVE RELATIVE PRONOUNS   110
    Declension of Interrogative Relative Pronouns   111
    Usage of Interrogative Relative Pronouns   111
NEGATIVE PRONOUNS   113
    Declension of Negative Pronouns   114
    Usage of Negative Pronouns   115
INDEFINITE PRONOUNS   116
    Declension of Indefinite Pronouns   117
    Usage of Indefinite Pronouns   118
PRONOUN-NUMERALS   121
    Usage of Pronoun-Numerals   122

CHAPTER 6 NUMERALS

CARDINAL NUMERALS   123
Table of Cardinal Numerals   123
Spelling Rule   124
The Numerals тысяча, миллион, and миллиард   124
Declension of Cardinal Numerals   124
Table of Declensions   125
Agreement of Numerals with Nouns   126
Agreement of Numerals, Nouns, and Adjectives   129
ORDINAL NUMERALS   130
Table of Ordinal Numerals   130
Declension of Ordinal Numerals   131
USAGE OF SOME CARDINAL AND ORDINAL NUMERALS   132
Dates   133
Time of Day   134
COLLECTIVE NUMERALS   135
Table of Collective Numerals   135
Declension of Collective Numerals   135
Usage of Collective Numerals   136
FRACTIONAL NUMERALS AND OTHER NUMERICAL EXPRESSIONS   138
    Fractions   138
        Numeral-Nouns   139
Usage of Fractional Numerals and Other Numerical Expressions   139
Remark on Rules *vs.* Usage   141

CHAPTER 7 VERBS

STRUCTURE   142
DERIVATION OF VERBAL FORMS   142
THE INFINITIVE   143
Usage of the Infinitive   144
THE PRESENT TENSE   146
Regular Verbs   146
Irregular Verbs   147
    Irregular Verb Endings   150
Verbs Belonging to Both Conjugations   152
Usage of the Present Tense   152
THE PAST TENSE   154
    Regular Formation   154
    Irregular Formation   155
THE ASPECTS   157
Formation of the Aspects   158
    Prefixes   159
    Internal Changes   161

  Different Roots 162
  Change in Stress 162
Single Verbs 162
  Verbs Occurring in the Imperfective Only 163
  Verbs Occurring in the Perfective Only 163
  Verbs Used in Either Aspect 164
Usage of the Past Tense: Imperfective and Perfective 165
  Perfective Instead of the Expected Imperfective 165
  Imperfective Instead of the Expected Perfective 165
THE FUTURE 168
Formation of the Imperfective Future 168
Formation of the Perfective Future 168
Usage of the Future Tense: Imperfective and Perfective 169
  Imperfective Future 170
  Perfective and Imperfective Future 170
  Perfective Future 171
THE CONDITIONAL MOOD 172
Formation of the Conditional 172
Usage of the Conditional 173
THE IMPERATIVE MOOD 176
  Regular Formation 176
  Special Cases 177
Usage of the Imperative 178
  Imperfective Imperative 178
  Negated Imperfective 179
  Perfective Imperative 179
  Third-Person Imperatives 180
  Joint Imperative 180
  Remarks on the use of да and -ка 182
REFLEXIVE VERBS 182
Preliminary Remark on Transitive and Intransitive Verbs 182
Formation and Conjugation of Reflexive Verbs 183
Classification and Usage of Reflexive Verbs 185
IMPERSONAL VERBS 189
  Verbs with No Subject 189
  Verbs with the Logical Subject in the Dative or in the Accusative 189
Usage of Impersonal Verbs 189
VERBS OF MOTION 190
Basic Verbs of Motion 190
  Motion on Foot and Not on Foot 190
  Definite and Indefinite Verbs 190
  The Perfective of Verbs of Motion 193
Usage of Basic Verbs of Motion 194
  Literal Meaning 194
    Definite Verbs of Motion 194
    Definite and Indefinite Verbs of Motion 195
    Indefinite Verbs of Motion 195
    The Imperative Mood of Verbs of Motion 196
    Verbs of Motion Pertaining to Travel and Transportation 196
  Figurative Meaning 197
  The Verbs идти́ and ходи́ть 198
  The Verbs вида́ть and слыха́ть 200

Prefixed Verbs of Motion   200
    Characteristics   200
    Irregular Formation   201
    List of Prefixes   203
    Variation in the Spelling of Prefixes   203
    Prefixed Verbs with Dual Meaning   204
    Prefixes with Multiple Meaning   204
    Various Combinations of Prefixes and Verbs   206
Usage of Prefixed Verbs of Motion   206
    Literal Meaning   206
    Figurative Meaning   207
PARTICIPLES   208
    Classification   208
Characteristics of Participles   209
Formation of Active Participles   210
    Present Active Participles   210
    Past Active Participles   211
        Regular Formation   211
        Irregular Formation   211
    Participles Formed from Reflexive Verbs   212
Declension of Active Participles   212
Formation of Passive Participles   213
    Present Passive Participles   213
        Regular Formation   213
        Irregular Formation   213
    Past Passive Participles   214
        Regular Formation   214
        Irregular Formation   215
    The Short Form of Passive Participles   215
Nouns and Adjectives Derived from Participles   216
    The Spelling of Past Passive Participles and Related Adjectives   218
The Usage of Participles   219
    Usage of Active Participles   220
    Usage of Passive Participles   221
    Usage of the Short Form of the Passive Participle   222
GERUNDS   223
    Classification of Gerunds   223
Characteristics of Gerunds   223
Formation of Present Gerunds   224
    Irregular Formation   224
Formation of Past Gerunds   225
    Irregular Formation   226
Gerunds Formed from Verbs Ending in -ся   227
Usage of Gerunds   227
    Gerunds versus Subordinate Clauses   227
    Present Gerunds   229
    Past Gerunds   229
    Clauses Containing Past and Present Gerunds   230
AGREEMENT OF VERB PREDICATES WITH SUBJECTS   230
Agreement in Number   231
Agreement in Gender   234
Agreement in Case   235

TABLE OF RUSSIAN VERBS   236
Table Guide   236
   Ending:
      -ать   238
      -ять   241
      -еть   242
      -уть   243
      -оть   244
      -ыть   244
      -ти, -сть, -зть   245
      -чь   246
      -ить   247

CHAPTER 8 ADVERBS

FORMATION OF ADVERBS   249
Adverbs Formed from
   Adjectives   249
   Nouns   251
   Numerals   252
   Verbs   252
   Pronouns   252
   Other Adverbs   252
CLASSIFICATION AND USAGE OF ADVERBS   253
Qualifying Adverbs   253
   Adverbs of Quality   253
      Usage of Adverbs of Quality   253
   Adverbs of Quantity or Measure   255
      Usage of Adverbs of Quantity or Measure   256
   Adverbs of Manner   258
      Usage of Adverbs in -ски   259
Specifying Adverbs   260
   Adverbs of Time   260
      Usage of Adverbs of Time   261
   Adverbs of Place   263
      Usage of Some Adverbs of Place   265
   Adverbs of Cause or Reason   266
   Adverbs of Purpose   266
PRIMARY ADVERBS   266
Table: Examples of Primary Adverbs   267
Formation and Usage of Some Primary Adverbs   268
PREDICATIVE ADVERBS   269
Usage of Some Predicative Adverbs   271

CHAPTER 9 PREPOSITIONS

Table of Prepositions   273
Variations in the Spelling of Prepositions   276
Isolated Rules   277
Classification and Usage of Prepositions   279
   Primary Meaning   279
   Secondary Meaning   281
CURRENT EXPRESSIONS WITH "VERB + PREPOSITION" CONSTRUCTION   285
IDIOMATIC USAGE   288
Current Expressions and Idioms   289

CHAPTER 10 CONJUNCTIONS

Types of Conjunctions   294
CLASSIFICATION AND USAGE OF CONJUNCTIONS   295
Coordinate Conjunctions   295
   Joining Words or Sentences   295
   Expressing Contrast or Opposition   297
   Expressing Choice or Alternation   300
   Having an Explanatory Meaning   301
Subordinate Conjunctions   301
   Used to Express Reason or Cause   301
      Purpose   302
      Consequence   303
      Condition   303
      Concession   304
      Comparison   305
      Temporal Relations   307
      Ideas or Feelings   310
Conjunctive Words   315

CHAPTER 11 PARTICLES

CLASSIFICATION AND USAGE OF PARTICLES   317
   Demonstrative   317
   Limitative   319
   Emphatic   319
   Definite   321
   Affirmative   321
   Negative   322
   Interrogative   323
   Exclamatory   325
   Indecisive   325
   Comparative   326
   Auxiliary   326

CHAPTER 12 INTERJECTIONS

CLASSIFICATION OF INTERJECTIONS 328
    Primary 328
    Secondary 328
    Idiomatic 329
    Foreign-borrowed 329
    Imitative 329
USAGE OF INTERJECTIONS 330
SOUNDS AS INTERJECTIONS 332

1. ALPHABET AND PRONUNCIATION

The Alphabet

There are 33 letters in the Russian alphabet:

Printed Capital	Printed Small	Written Capital	Written Small	Name	Approximate pronunciation in English
А	а	*A*	*a*	ah	*a* in c*a*r
Б	б	*Б*	*б*	beh	*b* in *b*oy
В	в	*В*	*в*	veh	*v* in *v*ery
Г	г	*Г*	*г*	gheh	*g* in *g*o
Д	д	*Д*	*g,д*	deh	*d* in *d*o
Е	е	*Е*	*е*	yeh	*ye* in *ye*s
Ё	ё	*Ё*	*ё*	yoh	*yo* in *Yo*rk
Ж	ж	*Ж*	*ж*	zheh	*s* in mea*s*ure
З	з	*З*	*з,3*	zeh	*z* in *z*ero
И	и	*И*	*и*	ee	*i* in mach*i*ne
Й	й	*Й*	*й*	ee kratkoye	*i* in vo*i*ce
К	к	*К*	*к*	kah	*c* in *c*lean
Л	л	*Л*	*л*	ell	*l* in *l*ift
М	м	*М*	*м*	em	*m* in *m*ake
Н	н	*Н*	*н*	en	*n* in *n*o
О	о	*О*	*о*	aw	*o* in n*o*r
П	п	*П*	*п*	peh	*p* in *p*lease
Р	р	*Р*	*р*	err	*r* in *r*ich
С	с	*С*	*с*	ess	*s* in *s*ay
Т	т	*Т*	*т*	teh	*t* in *t*o
У	у	*У*	*у*	oo	*oo* in b*oo*ty
Ф	ф	*Ф*	*ф*	eff	*f* in *f*at

1

Printed		Written		Name	Approximate pronunciation in English
Capital	Small	Capital	Small		
Х	х	*X*	*x*	hah	*h* in *h*ouse (but strongly aspirated)
Ц	ц	*Ц*	*ц*	tseh	*ts* in ca*ts*
Ч	ч	*Ч*	*ч*	cheh	*ch* in *ch*eck
Ш	ш	*Ш*	*ш*	shah	*sh* in *sh*oe
Щ	щ	*Щ*	*щ*	shchah	*shch* in fre*sh ch*eese
Ъ	ъ		*ъ*	tvyordy znak	no sound
Ы	ы		*ы*	ooee	*y* in s*y*llable
Ь	ь		*ь*	myahky znak	no sound
Э	э	*Э*	*э*	eh	*e* in m*e*t
Ю	ю	*Ю*	*ю*	you	*u* in *u*se
Я	я	*Я*	*я*	ya	*ya* in *ya*rd (but shorter)

Notes:

(*a*) The letters **ъ**, **ы**, and **ь** cannot begin a word; therefore they are never capitalized in handwriting. (They are capitalized in print when the whole word is printed in capitals.)

(*b*) Several letters have closer corresponding sounds in other foreign languages. Thus, the Russian **a** is like the French *a* in *ma* (or the *a* in the colloquial *mama*); the Russian **ж** is like the French *j* in *bonjour*; the Russian **р** and **х** are pronounced like the Spanish *r* and *j* respectively.

Handwriting

1. An individual handwriting may often not follow exactly the specimens of written letters given above. Thus, for example, *Н* is frequently written *Н* or *Н*, *В* – *В*, *Б* – *Б*, *К* – *К*, *Р* – *Р*, *П* – *Т*, *Х* – *Х*, *т* – *т*, *р* – *р*.
However, the written alphabet given here is the one recommended in textbooks.

ALPHABET AND PRONUNCIATION

2. The small "hooks" in *л*, *м*, and *я* should always be written. Without them, a word like *земля* could be easily misread.

3. The connecting of letters is often a matter of habit or individual preference. Generally speaking, it depends on where the first letter ends and the second begins. Thus connect *ал*, *он*, *ар*, etc.; do not connect *ол*, *ом*, etc. when the stroke of the first letter only is completed above the line.

Capitalization

In Russian, capital letters are used:

1. At the beginning of a sentence: Сегодня тепло—Today it is warm.
2. With proper names: Пушкин—Pushkin; Волга—Volga; Москва—Moscow
3. With possessive adjectives: Катина книга—Kate's book
4. With the pronoun вы—you (customarily capitalized in correspondence)

Capital letters are not used for:

1. Days of the week and names of the months: среда—Wednesday; январь—January
2. Adjectives derived from proper nouns: московские улицы—the Moscow streets, except when they enter into a proper noun: Московская улица—Moscow street
3. The pronoun я—I

In compound proper names, as a rule, only the first member is capitalized: Чёрное море—Black Sea; Атлантический океан—Atlantic Ocean

Except when:

1. The second member is also a proper name: Южная Америка—South America
2. Referring to high-ranking agencies: Верховный Совет—Supreme Soviet; Совет Безопасности—Security Council

Pronunciation of Hard and Soft Sounds

Vowels

The hard vowels and the phonetically corresponding soft ones are:

        Hard: А Э О У Ы
        Soft: Я Е Ё Ю И

Morphologically, the characteristic letters in declensions follow the relation:

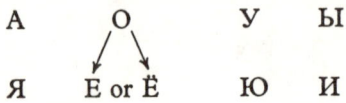

Consonants

The same Russian consonants can be pronounced hard or soft, except ж, ш, ц, which are always hard, and й, ч, щ, which are always soft.*
The hard pronunciation (given in the Alphabet) occurs:

1. Before a hard vowel: бума́га—paper
2. At the end of a word: стол—table
3. Before another hard consonant: два—two

Most consonants can be softened, i.e., pronounced with the middle part of the tongue slightly raised and touching the palate. This is especially marked with д, т, л, and н. Compare the following sounds:

	HARD SOUND	SOFT SOUND
д	as *d* in *do*	as, sometimes, *d* in *duty* (that is with a barely perceptible "Z sound" following the d)†
т	as *t* in *to*	as, sometimes, *t* in *tube* (again with a barely perceptible "Z sound" following the t)†

* See page 10.
† The Russian soft *d* and *t* are closer to the French *d* and *t* in *du, tu*.

ALPHABET AND PRONUNCIATION

	HARD SOUND	SOFT SOUND
л	as *l* in *milk*, or *ll* in *well*	as *ll* in *million*.
н	as *n* in *no*	as *n* in *onion*.

The softening is much less noticeable with **б, в, з, м, п, р, с, ф**: for example, hard **б** as *b* in *barn*; soft **б** as *b* in *bat*.

The softening of a consonant takes place:

1. In front of a soft vowel: дя́дя—uncle; тётя—aunt
2. In front of a **ь**: дать—to give; соль—salt
3. When preceding another softened consonant, especially **д, т, л, н**: вме́сте—together; гво́зди—nails

In Russian words the consonants **г, к,** and **х** are softened only when they precede **е** or **и**: ге́ний—genius; кипе́ть—to boil; хи́трый—sly

Hard and Soft Signs

A hard sign may separate a consonant from the vowels **е, ё, ю,** or **я**. This usually takes place after prefixes, such as **от, с,** or **об**, and sometimes without prefixes: отъе́зд—departure; съёмка—survey; объясне́ние—explanation; адъюта́нт—adjutant.
The vowel which follows the **ъ** becomes jotated. (See Jotation below.) Compare оте́ц (otets—soft т) with отъе́зд (ot-yest—hard т).
A soft sign may separate one consonant from another. In this case, the first consonant is softened: пальто́—topcoat (*l* like *ll* in *million*).
A soft sign may separate a consonant from the vowels **е, ё, и, ю, я,** and **о**.

пье́са—play; льёт—pours; воробьи́—sparrows; вьюга—snow storm; пе́рья—pens, feathers; почтальо́н—postman

The vowel which follows the **ь** becomes jotated. This jotation is clearly noticeable when comparing the pronunciation of пье́са (pyessa) with пе́шка (peshka)—pawn.
Finally, a soft sign may end a word, in which case the preceding consonant is softened: мать—mother; соль—salt.

Pronunciation of Vowels

The basic rules for pronunciation of vowels are given earlier in this chapter. Some additional rules follow:

Jotation

The letters **e, ё, ю,** and **я** are jotated at the beginning of a word, or when they follow a vowel, a hard sign, or a soft sign. They are pronounced then with an initial "y sound," such as *ye* in *yes*, *yo* in *York*, *u* in *use*, *ya* in *yard*.

ест	(he) eats	is pronounced "yest"
каюта	cabin	"kayoota" ("kah-uta")
объявление	advertisement	"obyavlenie"
пьёт	(he) drinks	"pyot"

However, when **e, ё, ю,** and **я** follow a consonant, the jotation is markedly less and often practically inaudible. The same letters may be compared to the following English sounds:

e in лес (wood, forest) is similar to *e* in *less* or *ai* in *lair*.
ё in сёл (gen. pl. of село—village) is similar to *eou* in *Seoul*.
ю in бюро (office) is similar to *u* in *bureau*.
я in пятый (fifth) is similar to *a* in *Patrick*.

The letter **и** has but a slight jotation, and only in the words им, ими, and их, or after a soft sign: лисьи норы—fox holes; судьи—judges.

Stressed and Unstressed Vowels

All Russian words have one vowel stressed, i.e., pronounced louder. This stress is indicated in textbooks by an accent mark: вода́; мо́ре. (A compound noun containing the letter **ё** may carry a secondary stress: трёхэта́жный дом—three-story house.)

When unstressed, all Russian vowels lose their clarity and some undergo changes in pronunciation.

ALPHABET AND PRONUNCIATION

1. **o** and **a**

When **o** is stressed, it is pronounced close to *o* in *nor*.
When **o** is not stressed it is pronounced close to *o* in *connection*.
When **a** is stressed, it is pronounced close to *a* in *car*.
When **a** is not stressed it is pronounced close to *a* in *cigarette*.

> *Note:* In a few foreign words the unstressed **o** is pronounced the same way as a stressed one: оа́зис—oasis; боа́—boa; and to some degree, in ра́дио—radio.

2. **е, э** and **я**

These letters, when unstressed, are all pronounced in much the same way—similarly to the first *e* in *between*. Compare, for example, the marked difference in the pronunciation of **я** and **е** in пять and шесть (stressed) with practically the same sounds in пятна́дцать and шестна́дцать (unstressed).

> *Remark:* The letter **ё** is always stressed.

3. **и, у, ю** and **ы**

Each one of these letters has basically the same sound, regardless of the stress. There may be just a slight difference in the way they are pronounced, i.e. the stressed ones with more effort. For example, the letter **у** in у́же (narrower) is pronounced with the lips further out than the **у** in уже́ (already).

> *Remark:* The letter **и**, stressed or unstressed, is pronounced **ы** after ж, ц and ш.

Open and Closed Vowels

The letters **а, е, о,** and **э** are pronounced with the mouth more open in front of hard consonants and less open in front of the soft ones. Thus:

Open **a** in ма́ло is similar to the *a* in *market*.
Closed **a** in ма́ленький is followed by a barely audible "y-sound," similar to the first part of the sound *i* in *mile*.
Open **е** in ел is similar to *ye* in *yell*.
Closed **е** in е́ли is similar to *ya* in *Yale*.
Open **о** in стол sounds like the *o* in *old*.

Closed **o** in сто́лько is followed by a barely perceptible "y-sound"* similar to the *first* part of the diphthong *oi* in *oil*.

Open **э** in э́то sounds like *e* in *get*.

Closed **э** in э́ти sounds like *a* in *gates*.

One may see from the above how a retroactive effect takes place: In

$$\underset{\smile}{\text{э́т и}} \qquad \underset{\smile}{\text{ст о́}} \underset{\smile}{\text{л ь к о}} \qquad \text{в м } \underset{\smile}{\text{е́ с т}} \text{ е}$$

the consonants **т, л** and **ст** are softened by the succeeding soft letters; as a result, the preceding vowels become closed.

Pronunciation of Consonants

The basic rules for pronunciation of consonants are given earlier in this chapter. Some additional rules follow.

Voiced and Voiceless Consonants

Consonants are divided into voiced and voiceless, according to the use of vocal chords. Some of these undergo a change in their pronunciation:

VOICED PRONOUNCED VOICELESS

The voiced consonants **б в г д ж з** are pronounced like the corresponding voiceless **п ф к т ш с**. This takes place:

In front of **п ф к т ш с х ц ч щ**.

		Phonetic Pronunciation
гу́бка	sponge	goupka
о́бщество	society	opshchestvo

---

* "Лёгкий при́звук"—slight additional sound (Грамма́тика ру́сского языка́, Акаде́мия нау́к СССР).

ALPHABET AND PRONUNCIATION

		Phonetic Pronunciation
а́втор	author	aftor
овца́	sheep	oftsa
левша́	left-handed person	lefsha
бе́гство	flight, hasty retreat	bekstvo
во́дка	vodka	votka
ло́жка	spoon	loshka
мужчи́на	man	mooshcheena
ска́зка	fairy tale	skaska

When they end a word.

		Phonetic Pronunciation
дуб	oak	doop
ров	moat	rof
шаг	step	shahk
сад	garden	saht
нож	knife	nosh
глаз	eye	glahs

VOICELESS PRONOUNCED VOICED

The voiceless consonants **к с т** are pronounced like the corresponding voiced ones in front of **б г д ж з**.

		Phonetic Pronunciation
вокза́л	station, terminal	vogzal
сда́ча	change (money)	zdacha
отда́ть	to return, to give back	oddat'

The Ending го

The ending **го** in declinable parts of speech is pronounced "*vo*": кра́сного "*krasnovo*"; пе́рвого "*pervovo.*" The adverb сего́дня (originally **сего́ дня**) is pronounced "*sevodnia.*"

Unpronounced Consonants

Occasionally, a consonant from a "cluster of consonants" is not pronounced.

In по́здно	(late)	the д is not pronounced.
In счастли́вый	(happy)	the т is not pronounced.
In гру́стный	(sad)	the т is not pronounced.
In чу́вство	(feeling)	the first в is not pronounced.
In здра́вствуйте	(hello, good morning, etc.)	the first в is not pronounced.

Isolated Cases

In the words Бог (God), лёгкий (light), and мя́гкий (easy, soft) the г is pronounced like a х.

The Letter й

The letter й is regarded as a consonant, since it does not form a syllable. Alternatively, it has often been classified as a "semivowel," which seems to be perfectly justifiable because of its closeness to vowels. (Compare, for example, the pronunciation of сара́й [barn] with сара́и [barns].)

Stress

The stress in Russian words is most important. A misplaced stress may alter the meaning of a word (за́мок—castle; замо́к—lock), or render it incomprehensible. A stressed vowel is pronounced louder; it is also slightly lengthened—except when final.
Only a few helpful rules can be given in regard to stress.

Nouns

1. The ending is always stressed in masculine nouns which end in **у** in the prepositional case: в саду́—in the garden; на полу́—on the floor.
2. The ending is always stressed in masculine nouns which end in **а** or **я**

in the nominative plural: дома́—houses; края́—lands, edges; учителя́—teachers (page 19).

3. Feminine nouns, as a rule, are not stressed on the ending in the nominative plural: ру́ки—hands; го́ры—mountains, (with the singular, рука́, гора́).

    Exceptions: статьи́—articles; скамьи́—benches; черты́—traits; and a few others.

4. Most neuter dissyllabic nouns change the stress in going from singular to plural: окно́—о́кна (windows); по́ле—поля́ (fields).

5. The stress remains fixed in all nouns which in the nominative singular are not stressed on the first or on the last syllable: уче́бник—textbook; газе́та—newspaper; внима́ние—attention.

The only exceptions are masculine nouns which in the plural end in stressed **а** or **я**: профессора́, учителя́ (see para. 2 above).

Adjectives

In the same word, the stress never varies. Thus, кра́сный will retain the stress on **а** in all genders, numbers, and cases.

In the comparative degree and with short adjectives, it may or may not vary: кра́сный, красне́е, красна́. But: краси́вый, краси́вее, краси́ва.

Verbs

The stress is fixed throughout a verb when it does not fall on the ending of the infinitive: слу́шать—to listen; пла́вать—to swim.

Spelling Rule

The following important spelling rule should be noted: The letters **г, к, х, ж, ч, ш, щ** are *never* followed by **ы, ю**, or **я** (even if they may sound as if they were—like **и** in жил or **а** in чай).

A few foreign words are exceptions: жюри́—jury; парашю́т—parachute; акы́н—a Kazakh bard; Кя́хта—the city of Kyahta.

The letter **ц** is *never* followed by **ю** or **я**. It may be followed by **и** or **ы**, but in either case the sound is **цы**: цирк—circus; цыплёнок—chicken.

2. NOUNS

Gender

Russian nouns have three genders: masculine, feminine, and neuter.
Masculine nouns end in a consonant, **й** or **ь**: дом—house; чай—tea; день—day.
Feminine nouns end in **a, я**, or **ь**: кни́га—book; земля́—earth; ночь—night.
Neuter nouns end in **о, е,** or **ё**: окно́—window; мо́ре—sea; ружьё—gun.
Nouns ending in a consonant, **a**, or **o** are hard nouns.
Nouns ending in **й, ь, я, е,** and **ё** are soft nouns.

Nouns Ending in ь

A few rules may be helpful in determining the gender of nouns ending in **ь**:

(*a*) Nouns pertaining to male persons are, of course, masculine: писа́тель—writer; дика́рь—savage.
(*b*) All nouns with the suffix **–тель** are masculine: учи́тель—teacher; истреби́тель—fighter plane; числи́тель—numerator.
These nouns should not be confused with others, where **–тель** is not a suffix: мете́ль—snow storm, посте́ль—bed are feminine.
(*c*) All names of months are masculine: янва́рь—January; февра́ль—February.
(*d*) Most abstract nouns are feminine.
  Exceptions: The following abstract nouns are masculine:

вихрь	whirlwind
вопль	yell
день	day
ка́шель	cough
контро́ль	control
паро́ль	password
спекта́кль	show
стиль	style

NOUNS

(*e*) Nouns with the suffix **-ость** are feminine: ра́дость—joy; го́рдость—pride.
These nouns should not be confused with others where –ость is not a suffix. Thus, гость—guest is masculine.
Most nouns ending in **-есть** are feminine: честь—honor; лесть—flattery.
(*f*) Nouns ending in a sibilant and a **ь** are feminine: ночь—night; вещь—thing.

Additional Rules for Determining Gender

Masculine Nouns Ending in A, Я, O, or E

Male persons ending in **а** or **я**.
  1. Nouns denoting male persons are masculine regardless of their ending: мужчи́на—man; дя́дя—uncle; ю́ноша—young man, boy; старшина́—foreman.
  2. Some proper names, especially diminutives, may end in **а** or **я**: Лука́, Ники́та, Серёжа (*diminutive* of Серге́й), Ва́ня (*diminutive* of Ива́н), etc.
Animate masculine diminutives may end in **а**: сыни́шка—son; дя́дюшка—uncle; де́душка—grandfather.
Inanimate diminutives may end in **о**: доми́шко—small house; городи́шко—small town.
Augmentatives may end in **е**: доми́ще—huge house; городи́ще—huge city (a type not frequently used).
The noun подмасте́рье—apprentice is masculine.

Common Gender Nouns: Masculine and Feminine Ending in A

The following nouns ending in **а** are among those which can apply to a male or female person:

за́йка	stutterer	пья́ница	drunkard
кале́ка	cripple	сирота́	orphan

кривля́ка	poser, affected person	тупи́ца	a blunt, stupid person
пла́кса	someone who cries constantly	уби́йца	murderer
неве́жа	rude person	молодчи́на	smart person, "a brick"
неря́ха	untidy person	у́мница	a clever person
обжо́ра	glutton		

(It may be noticed that, curiously enough, most of these nouns imply a negative or cheerless characteristic. The last two examples are among the few which do not.)

Gender of Nouns of Foreign Origin

(a) Inanimate nouns borrowed from foreign languages and ending in **o** or **e** are neuter:

пальто́	overcoat	пиани́но	piano
кино́	movies	э́хо	echo
бюро́	office	шоссе́	highway
метро́	subway	кашне́	scarf
ра́дио	radio	желе́	jelly
кило́	kilogram	кафе́	cafe

Exception: Ко́фе is masculine.

Кре́пкий ко́фе—strong coffee.

Animate nouns of the same type are masculine: маэ́стро—maestro; атташе́—attaché.

(b) A few nouns of foreign origin end in **и, у, ю,** and stressed **á**.
The inanimate are neuter: такси́—taxi; рагу́—ragout; интервью́—interview; боа́—necklet, boa.
The animate are usually masculine: коли́бри—humming-bird (colibri); кенгуру́—kangaroo.

Gender of Nouns Ending in мя

(a) The ten nouns which end in **мя** are neuter:

и́мя	(first) name	бре́мя	burden
вре́мя	time	пле́мя	tribe

NOUNS

зна́мя	banner	пла́мя	flame
се́мя	seed	вы́мя	udder
те́мя	crown of the head	стре́мя	stirrup

(b) The noun дитя́ (child) is neuter.

Substantivized Adjectives

Many adjectives have become nouns, while keeping their characteristic adjectival endings. Their gender is determined by the rule of adjectival endings (see page 80):

    MASC.   портно́й—tailor; ни́щий—beggar
    FEM.   гости́ная—living room; столо́вая—dining room
    NEUT.   прида́ное—dowry; насеко́мое—insect

Some of these may be used as both nouns and adjectives:

    приёмная—reception room; приёмные часы́—reception hours.
    столо́вая—dining room; столо́вая ло́жка—tablespoon.

Note: There are very few neuter animate nouns: чудо́вище (monster); существо́ (creature); живо́тное (animal); насеко́мое (insect); лицо́ (person, man), and the above-mentioned дитя́—child.

Usage of the Gender

Nouns Indicating Professions and Occupations

Many nouns (formerly pertaining to "masculine" professions or occupations) may be applied to either men or women:

    до́ктор—doctor; врач—doctor, physician; инжене́р—engineer;
    профе́ссор—professor; агроно́м—agronomist; касси́р—cashier

Some of them have developed parallel feminine forms, which perhaps are not used in official language, but nevertheless are acceptable:*

    до́кторша, секрета́рша, касси́рша

  * The Слова́рь ру́сского языка́ (Акаде́мия нау́к СССР) classifies them as colloquial.

Others have developed feminine forms universally recognized:

> студе́нт (student) студе́нтка; конду́ктор (conductor) конду́кторша; пиани́ст (pianist) пиани́стка.

Qualifying words agree with the *grammatical* gender of these nouns:

> Она́ хоро́ший до́ктор—She is a good doctor.
> Э́та да́ма наш но́вый секрета́рь—This lady is our new secretary.
> Кто ва́ша секрета́рша?—Who is your secretary?

The verb (in the past tense) usually agrees with the *actual* gender, especially when the name of the person is given:

> До́ктор Ива́нова приняла́ меня́ у́тром—Dr. Ivanova received me this morning.
> Говори́ла профе́ссор Остро́вская—Professor Ostrovskaya spoke.

Common Gender Nouns

The common gender nouns ending in **а** (pages 13–14) are treated according to the actual gender: большо́й неря́ха—a very untidy man; больша́я неря́ха—a very untidy woman.

The Nouns ЧЕЛОВЕ́К, ДРУГ, ТОВА́РИЩ, ВРАГ

These nouns may apply to either men or women: Он хоро́ший челове́к.—He is a good man. Она́ хоро́ший челове́к—She is a good person.

Nouns of Foreign Origin Ending in О, Е, И, У, Ю, А

It has been stated that inanimate nouns of this type are neuter, and animate nouns are masculine. The word ле́ди (lady) is, of course, feminine:

NEUT. но́вое метро́—a new subway; широ́кое шоссе́—a wide highway; интере́сное пари́—an interesting bet; меню́ лежа́ло на столе́—the menu lay on the table.

MASC. вое́нный атташе́—military attaché; маэ́стро прие́хал—the maestro arrived.

FEM. англи́йская ле́ди—English lady (the wife of a nobleman).

NOUNS

Remark: With the names of animals and birds, the rule is less definite. Usually, they are considered masculine: один кенгуру—one kangaroo; наш шимпанзе—our chimpanzee. However, grammarians quote examples of these words being used in the feminine and occasionally in the neuter: кенгуру убежала—the kangaroo fled; наше шимпанзе—our chimpanzee.

Foreign Geographical Nouns

The same endings (о, е, и, у, ю, á) are encountered in a few foreign geographical names. They normally take the gender of the class to which they belong: старый Толедо—the ancient city of Toledo (город—*masc.*); Пятая авеню—Fifth Avenue (улица—*fem.*); бурное Онтарио—the stormy Ontario (озеро—*neut.*).

Number

There are two numbers in Russian: the singular and the plural.

Rules for the Plural of Nouns

1. Basic Plural Endings

Masculine nouns ending in a consonant *add* ы in the plural. Other nouns *replace* their characteristic endings by those indicated in the table.

HARD NOUNS

	Singular	*Example*	*Plural*	*Example*
MASC.	Consonant	стол (table)	ы	столы́
FEM.	a	ка́рта (card, map)	ы	ка́рты
NEUT.	o	окно́ (window)	a	о́кна

SOFT NOUNS

	Singular	Example	Plural	Example
MASC.	ь	словарь (dictionary)	и	словари́
	й	музе́й (museum)	и	музе́и
	й	ге́ний (genius)	и	ге́нии
FEM.	ь	дверь (door)	и	две́ри
	я	дере́вня (village)	и	дере́вни
	я	исто́рия (story)	и	исто́рии
NEUT.	е	по́ле (field)	я	поля́
	ё	ружьё (rifle)	я	ру́жья
	е	зда́ние (building)	я	зда́ния

2. Plural of Nouns with Stems Ending in г, к, х, ж, ч, ш, щ, ц

Hard masculine and feminine nouns with stems ending in г, к, х, ж, ч, ш, щ take и in the plural: враг, (enemy) враги́; каранда́ш, (pencil) карандаши́; соба́ка, (dog) соба́ки; ту́ча, (cloud) ту́чи.

A few neuter nouns ending in е take а in the plural: се́рдце, (heart) сердца́; учи́лище (school) учи́лища (see spelling rule, p. 11).

3. Irregular Plural Endings

NOUNS

MASCULINE NOUNS

(*a*) Some sixty masculine nouns take a stressed **а** or **я** in the plural:

áдрес (address)	адресá	óрден (order, medal)	орденá
бéрег (shore)	берегá	пáспорт (passport)	паспортá
бок (side, flank)	бокá	пáрус (sail)	парусá
век (century)	векá	пóвар (cook)	поварá
вéчер (evening)	вечерá	пóгреб (cave, cellar)	погребá
глаз (eye)	глазá	пóезд (train)	поездá
год (year)	годá	пóяс (belt)	поясá
гóлос (voice)	голосá	прóвод (wire, conductor)	проводá
гóрод (town)	городá	рог (horn)	рогá
дóктор (doctor)	докторá	снег (snow)	снегá
дом (house)	домá	сорт (sort, kind)	сортá
кóлокол (bell)	колоколá	том (volume, book)	томá
край (edge; country)	края́	тон (tone)	тонá
кýпол (dome)	куполá	тóрмоз (brake)	тормозá
лáгерь (camp)	лагеря́	цвет (color)	цветá
кýчер (coachman)	кучерá	я́корь (anchor)	якоря́
лес (wood, forest)	лесá	And the recent ones:	
луг (meadow)	лугá	дизель (Diesel)	дизеля́
мáстер (specialist, skilled worker)	мастерá	штéпсель (plug *electr.*)	штепселя́
мех (fur)	мехá	вéксель (promissory note)	векселя́
нóмер (number)	номерá		
óбраз (icon, holy image)	образá		
óстров (island)	островá		

(*b*) Some nouns have two types of endings in the plural: **а, я,** or the regular **ы, и**. There is a difference of meaning with the following nouns:

мехá	furs
мéхи	bellows

образа́	icons, holy images
о́бразы	images, visions
пояса́	belts
по́ясы	geographical belts
провода́	electrical wires
про́воды	farewell(s)
счета́	bills
счёты	abacus
тона́	shades of color
то́ны	shades of sound
цвета́	colors (sing.: цвет)
цветы́	flowers (sing.: цвето́к)

The difference is slight in the following ones:

PLURAL

учителя́	teachers, instructors
учи́тели	usually, teachers of a doctrine
года́	years
го́ды	"the years," such as "the twenties," etc.

(c) In some instances there is no difference in the meaning, and the type of ending to use is a matter of personal preference:

директора́	or	дире́кторы	directors
профессора́	or	профе́ссоры	professors
тополя́	or	то́поли	poplars
якоря́	or	я́кори	anchors

(d) Masculine nouns ending in **-анин** or **-янин** form their plural as follows:

1. The suffix **-ин** is replaced by **-е**:

SINGULAR		PLURAL
граждани́н	citizen	гра́ждан**е**

NOUNS

	SINGULAR		PLURAL
крестья́нин	peasant		крестья́не
христиани́н	Christian		христиа́не
славяни́н	Slav		славя́не
англича́нин	Englishman		англича́не
армяни́н	Armenian		армя́не
датча́нин	Dane		датча́не
лютера́нин	Lutheran		лютера́не

2. Irregularly:

	SINGULAR		PLURAL
господи́н	gentleman, mister		господа́
болга́рин	Bulgarian		болга́ры
тата́рин	Tartar		тата́ры
хозя́ин	host		хозя́ева

(e) Two hard nouns, **сосе́д** and **чёрт,** have soft endings in the plural: сосе́д (neighbor) сосе́ди; чёрт (devil) че́рти.

The plural of челове́к (man, person) is **лю́ди**; the plural of ребёнок (child) is **де́ти** although the form **ребя́та** exists, usually meaning: kids, fellows.

Nouns pertaining to young animals and ending in **-ёнок** or **-онок** form their plural as follows: котёнок (kitten) котя́та; медвежо́нок (cub bear) медвежа́та.

(f) A few masculine nouns take **-ья** in the plural. The most common are:

	SINGULAR		PLURAL
брат	brother		бра́тья
друг	friend		друзья́
муж	husband		мужья́
кол	stake, stick		ко́лья
ко́лос	ear (of corn, etc.)		коло́сья
ком	lump (of earth)		ко́мья
князь	prince		князья́
прут	rod, twig		пру́тья
стул	chair		сту́лья
сук	branch		су́чья
сын	son		сыновья́

Among these nouns, several have two types of endings in the plural, corresponding to two different meanings:

SINGULAR	PLURAL IN –ья		REGULAR PLURAL
зуб	зу́бья	teeth (of a saw, for example)	зу́бы teeth
лист	ли́стья	leaves	листы́ sheets (of paper, for example)
ко́рень	коре́нья	spices	ко́рни roots

Сыновья́ and **друзья́** are the current plurals of сын (son) and друг (friend). **Сыны́** and **дру́ги** are archaic or poetical.

NEUTER NOUNS

(a) Neuter nouns ending in –мя have the plural ending –ена:

и́мя (name): имена́; вре́мя (time): времена́.
Зна́мя (banner) has знамёна.
Вы́мя (udder), пла́мя (flame), бре́мя (burden), and те́мя (crown of head) have no plural.

(b) Neuter nouns ending in –ко (some of them diminutives) take –и in the plural:

око́шко (small window): око́шки; я́блоко (apple): я́блоки; ве́ко (eyelid): ве́ки; коле́чко (little ring): коле́чки.

Exceptions:
   во́йско (army) войска́; о́блако (cloud) облака́.

(c) A few neuter nouns take –ья in the plural:

SINGULAR	PLURAL	SINGULAR	PLURAL
де́рево (tree)	дере́вья	крыло́ (wing)	кры́лья
звено́ (link)	зве́нья	поле́но (log)	поле́нья
перо́ (feather, pen)	пе́рья		

(d) Isolated cases of irregularities:

SINGULAR	PLURAL	SINGULAR	PLURAL
у́хо (ear)	у́ши	коле́но (knee)	коле́ни
о́ко (eye *obsolete*)	о́чи	не́бо (sky)	небеса́

NOUNS

SINGULAR	PLURAL	SINGULAR	PLURAL
су́дно (boat, vessel)	суда́	чу́до (miracle)	чудеса́
плечо́ (shoulder)	пле́чи		

Note: Коле́но has actually three plurals: коле́ни (knees), коле́нья (knots on a bamboo, etc.) and коле́на (tribes—more specifically, the twelve tribes of Israel).

The plural of дно (bottom) is до́нья or дны. However, neither of these forms is currently used, and the singular is preferred: на дне море́й—at the bottom of the sea(s).

FEMININE NOUNS

The following feminine nouns form their plural irregularly:
мать (mother): ма́тери; дочь (daughter): до́чери; ку́рица (hen): ку́ры (or ку́рицы).

THE FLEETING O OR E

Many masculine and some feminine nouns form their plural irregularly by deleting an **o** or **e**. For example:

кусо́к (piece)	куски́	орёл (eagle)	орлы́
оте́ц (father)	отцы́	це́рковь (church)	це́ркви

Some of them insert a **ь** or an **й** in the plural:

лев (lion) львы   бое́ц (soldier) бойцы́*

Nouns Having Only One Number

1. The following types of nouns are used only in the singular:

   Metals: желе́зо—iron; зо́лото—gold; серебро́—silver, etc.
   Liquids: вода́—water; вино́—wine; молоко́—milk, etc.
   Other substances: рис—rice; са́хар—sugar; соль—salt, etc.
   Collective nouns: бельё—linen; ме́бель—furniture; посу́да—dishes (plates, glasses, etc.); крестья́нство—peasantry; аристокра́тия—aristocracy; артилле́рия—artillery, etc.
   Many abstract nouns: любо́вь—love; не́нависть—hatred; ра́дость—joy; оптими́зм—optimism; вес—weight; длина́—length, etc.

* This is discussed later in the chapter on Declension of Nouns (p. 27).

2. The following nouns are found only in the plural:

(a) "Paired" nouns, or those which normally consist of two similar components:

брю́ки	trousers	око́вы	irons, chains
весы́	scales	очки́	glasses, spectacles
воро́та	gate	панталóны	trousers
гéтры	gaiters	пери́ла	handrail, banister
кавы́чки	quotation marks	подтя́жки	suspenders
кандалы́	handcuffs, irons	са́ни	sleigh
каче́ли	swing	тру́сики	shorts
клещи́	pincers, tongs	штаны́	trousers
но́жницы	scissors	щипцы́	tongs, pliers, tweezers
носи́лки	stretcher		

(b) Others currently used:

бега́	races	обо́и	wallpaper
бры́зги	splash, spray, drops	перегово́ры	negotiations
		потёмки	darkness
бу́дни	weekdays, work days	по́хороны	funeral
		припа́сы	provisions, food supplies
вы́боры	elections		
гра́бли	rake	про́воды	send-off
де́бри	dense thicket	ро́ды	childbirth
де́ньги	money	сла́сти	sweets, candy
джу́нгли	jungle	сли́вки	cream
дрова́	fire logs	су́мерки	twilight
дро́жжи	yeast	субтро́пики	sub-tropics
духи́	perfume	су́тки	day and night (24 hours)
имени́ны	name's day		
кани́кулы	vacation	фина́нсы	finances
крести́ны	christening	хло́пья	flakes
ке́гли	bowling (pins)	хло́поты	cares, troubles, solicitations
консе́рвы	canned goods		
ко́лики	colic, cramps	часы́	watch, clock
макаро́ны	macaroni	черни́ла	ink
мемуа́ры	memoirs	ша́шки	checkers, draughts
напа́дки	fault-finding, unprovoked attacks	ша́хматы	chess
		щи	cabbage soup

NOUNS

(c) Names of many mountain ranges and other geographical names:

Альпы—Alps; Анды—Andes; Карпа́ты—Carpathian Mountains; Пирене́и—Pyrenees; Афи́ны—Athens; Дарданéллы—Dardanelles; Сираку́зы—Syracuse; Соко́льники—Sokolniki.

Usage of the Singular and Plural

1. Nouns used normally in the singular, and occasionally in the plural. To this class belong nouns which express:

(a) Long duration or repetition

| се́верные ве́тры | northern winds |
| креще́нские моро́зы | cold spells expected to occur at the beginning of January |

(b) Large quantities

| ве́чные снега́ | eternal snows |
| территориа́льные во́ды | territorial waters |

(c) Collective nouns or nouns belonging to a whole class

| францу́зские ви́на | French wines |
| минера́льные во́ды | mineral waters |

2. Abstract nouns.
Many abstract nouns expressing feelings or various characteristics are found in the singular only; these include the above-mentioned любо́вь, оптими́зм, вес.
Others occur both in the singular and in the plural: наде́жда—hope; сомне́ние—doubt; тру́дность—difficulty; спосо́бность—capability, aptitude.

    Мои́ наде́жды оправда́лись.   My hopes have come true.
    С лу́чшими пожела́ниями.   With best wishes.

Note: The above is comparable to the English usage.

3. Names of vegetables and berries.

In contrast to English, some of these nouns are found in the singular only, others in both singular and plural.

Singular only: морко́вь (carrot); лук (onion); капу́ста (cabbage); земляни́ка (strawberry); мали́на (raspberry), and a few others.

Singular and plural: огуре́ц (cucumber)—огурцы́; тома́т, помидо́р (tomato)—тома́ты, помидо́ры; баклажа́н (eggplant)—баклажа́ны; я́года (berry)—я́годы, etc.

4. Singular used to imply plurality.

(*a*) Occasionally, the singular is used to imply plurality. It may refer to a group or class:

Швед, ру́сский ко́лет, ру́бит, ре́жет. (Пу́шкин)	Swedes, Russians stab, saber, slash.
Я́блоня цветёт весно́й.	Apple trees blossom in the spring.
Соба́ка—друг челове́ка.	The dog is the friend of man.

(*b*) It may be also used when referring to something common to a whole group:

Все опусти́ли го́лову.	They all lowered their heads.
Повеле́но брить им бо́роду. (Пу́шкин)	They were ordered to shave their beards.
Пра́вое плечо́ вперёд—марш!	Column left . . . march! (a military command)
Подними́те ле́вую ру́ку! Нагни́те ту́ловище!	Raise your left hands! Bend your bodies! (in calisthenics, for example)

3. DECLENSION OF NOUNS

Russian nouns are declined: their endings change according to the case. There are six cases. Their <u>principal</u> meaning is summarized below:

The Nominative expresses the subject or predicate in answer to: who? what?—кто? что?

The Accusative expresses the direct object in answer to: whom? what?—кого? что?

The other four cases are rendered into English with the aid of prepositions:

The Genitive answers the question: of whom? (whose?) of what?—кого? (чей?) чего?

The Dative answers the question: to whom? to what?—кому́? чему́?

The Instrumental answers the question: by whom? with (by) what?—кем? чем?

The Prepositional answers the question: about whom? about what? where?—о ком? о чём? где?

The use of a case may also be determined by a preposition, a verb, or a special construction (such as an expression of time). This will be discussed in detail in "Usage of Cases" (page 48).

Declension of Masculine Nouns, Singular

HARD NOUNS

	Inanimate	Animate
NOM.	стол	брат
GEN.	стола́	бра́та
DAT.	столу́	бра́ту
ACC.	стол	бра́та
INSTR.	столо́м	бра́том
PREP.	столе́	бра́те

	Inanimate	Animate	Inanimate	Animate
		SOFT NOUNS		
NOM.	слова́рь	учи́тель	чай	геро́й
GEN.	словаря́	учи́теля	ча́я	геро́я
DAT.	словарю́	учи́телю	ча́ю	геро́ю
ACC.	слова́рь	учи́теля	чай	геро́я
INSTR.	словарём	учи́телем	ча́ем	геро́ем
PREP.	словаре́	учи́теле	ча́е	геро́е

Special Rules Pertaining to Masculine Nouns

Masculine nouns ending in the nominative in **а** or **я**, such as мужчи́на, дя́дя, are declined like feminine nouns.

Masculine nouns of foreign origin and ending in a vowel, such as атташе́, маэ́стро, ку́ли, are not declined.

Rules for the Genitive Case

Many nouns have, besides the ending **а** or **я**, a parallel form of the genitive ending in **у** or **ю**. This form may be used in the following instances:

(a) When a certain quantity, or a part of a whole, is referred to:

бензи́ну	benzine, gasoline	лу́ку	onion
виногра́ду	grapes	льду	ice
горо́ху	peas	маргари́ну	margarine
жи́ру	grease	мёду	honey
изю́му	raisins	ме́лу	chalk
карто́фелю	potatoes	минда́лю	almonds
кероси́ну	kerosene	одеколо́ну	eau de cologne
кле́ю	glue	пе́рцу	pepper
коньяку́	brandy	песку́	sand
кипятку́	boiling water	по́роху	gunpowder
ле́су	wood	ри́су	rice
лимона́ду	lemonade	са́хару	sugar

DECLENSION OF NOUNS

су́п**у**	soup	у́ксус**у**	vinegar
сы́р**у**	cheese	ча́**ю**	tea
табак**у́**	tobacco	чесно́к**у́**	garlic

Note: The same nouns, however, take the endings **а** or **я** when no part of a whole is implied: цена́ ча́я—the price of tea; э́кспорт табака́—the export of tobacco. Or, usually, when preceded by an adjective: стака́н кре́пкого ча́я—a glass of strong tea.

(*b*) After мно́го, ма́ло, нет:

ве́с**у**	weight	наро́д**у**	people
вздо́р**у**	nonsense	све́т**у**	light
во́здух**у**	air	сне́г**у**	snow
жа́р**у**	heat	со́р**у**	litter, dirt
кри́к**у**	shout(s)		

(*c*) After the prepositions **из** and **до** (expressing motion, distance) with the nouns **дом** and **лес**: вы́йти из ле́су—to go out of the wood; до до́му бы́ло далеко́*—the house was far away.
After the prepositions **до, с, о́коло** with the noun **час**: до ча́су дня—until (before) 1:00 P.M.; с ча́су—from 1 o'clock on; ждал о́коло ча́су—waited for about an hour.
After the preposition **с** when expressing a reason: умере́ть с го́лоду—to die from hunger; со стра́ху—from fear.

(*d*) Finally, in a rather large number of idiomatic or set expressions, such as:

упусти́ть из ви́ду	to let out of sight, to forget about
ни слу́ху, ни ду́ху	no news (whatsoever)
ни ра́зу	not a single time
сбить с то́лку	to confuse
до упа́ду	until exhaustion
ни ша́гу да́льше	not a step further

* Also, и́з лесу; до́ дому.

Rules for the Accusative Case

In the masculine singular, the accusative of inanimate nouns is like the nominative; the accusative of animate nouns is like the genitive: Я вижу дом. (I see a house.); Я вижу бра́та. (I see [my] brother.)

> *Notes:*
> (*a*) This does not apply to collective animate nouns such as полк—regiment; наро́д—people, etc.: Он лю́бит свой полк.—He likes his regiment.
> (*b*) A few *inanimate* nouns take the genitive case ending: туз—ace; ко́зырь—trump; и́дол—idol; числи́тель—numerator; знамена́тель—denominator.
>
> Examples:
> дать туза́ пик—to give the ace of spades; помно́жить на знамена́теля—to multiply by the denominator.

Rules for the Instrumental Case

After **ж, ч, ш, щ, ц** hard masculine nouns have the ending **ом** in the instrumental, when the stress falls on this ending: ножо́м (knife), отцо́м (father).
When the ending is not stressed, it becomes **ем**: това́рищем (friend), америка́нцем (American).
With soft nouns, the ending **ём** is, of course, always stressed. The ending **ем** is not stressed: словарём (dictionary); ручьём (brook); учи́телем (teacher); бо́ем (battle).

Rules for the Prepositional Case

(*a*) Many masculine nouns take the stressed endings **у** or **ю** when they follow the prepositions **в** or **на** (or either), and when they express:
 location: в саду́ (in the garden); на полу́ (on the floor).
 time (occasionally): в про́шлом году́ (last year); в кото́ром часу́? (at what time?).
 a condition (sometimes): в бреду́ (delirious); в долгу́ (in debt).

DECLENSION OF NOUNS

Examples:
With **в**:

аду́	hell	плену́	captivity
боку́	side, flank	полку́	regiment
бою́	battle	порту́	port
бреду́	delirium	пруду́	pond
виду́	sight	раю́	paradise
глазу́	eye	(во) рву́	moat
году́	year	(во) рту́	mouth
долгу́	debt	ряду́	row
дыму́	smoke	саду́	garden
краю́	edge; country	снегу́	snow
кругу́	circle	строю́	formation (milit.)
Крыму́	Crimea	тазу́	basin
лесу́	wood	тылу́	rear
(во) льду́	ice	углу́	corner, angle
носу́	nose	шкапу́ (шкафу́)	closet, cupboard
отпуску́	leave		

With **на**:

балу́	ball (dance)	носу́	nose
берегу́	shore	пиру́	feast, banquet
боку́	side, flank	плоту́	raft
борту́	board, edge	полу́	floor
Дону́	Don River	посту́	post
краю́	edge	пруду́	pond
лбу	forehead	снегу́	snow
лугу́	meadow	суку́	branch, twig
льду	ice	углу́	corner
мосту́	bridge	шкапу́ (шкафу́)	closet, cupboard

Note: With other prepositions governing the same (prepositional) case, the endings are regular: о са́де—about the garden; при ви́де—seeing, at the sight of.

(b) A few masculine nouns with the nominative ending in –**ий** take **ии** in the prepositional: ге́ний—genius; жре́бий—lot (as in "to cast lots"); коммента́рий—comment; пролета́рий—proletarian; санато́рий—sanatorium; алюми́ний—aluminum; ка́льций—calcium, etc.

Example: в санато́р**ии**, об алюми́**нии**.

The Fleeting o and e

1. Many masculine nouns containing **o** or **e** (**ё**) in their final syllable drop these letters throughout the declension. This takes place:

(*a*) Primarily in front of the letters **л** or **н**:

cough	кашель	кашля	boiler	котёл	котла
(billy) goat	козёл	козла	donkey	осёл	осла
eagle	орёл	орла	corner, angle	угол	угла
ambassador	посол	посла	knot	узел	узла
coal	уголь	угля	stone	камень	камня
day	день	дня	fire, flame	огонь	огня
root	корень	корня	belt	ремень	ремня
fellow, "guy"	парень	парня	dream	сон	сна

(*b*) In front of an **й**, in which case **e** is replaced by a **ь**.

sparrow	воробей	воробья	ant	муравей	муравья
brook	ручей	ручья	nightingale	соловей	соловья

(*c*) In a few other instances:

wind	ветер	ветра	carpet	ковёр	ковра
claw	коготь	когтя	campfire	костёр	костра
elbow	локоть	локтя	lump, slice (of bread)	ломоть	ломтя
finger nail	ноготь	ногтя			
mouth	рот	рта	dog	пёс	пса

> *Note:* It should not be assumed that **o** and **e** are always dropped in front of **л, н,** or **й**: shot—выстрел: выстрела; deer—олень: оленя; villain—злодей: злодея, etc.

2. Most masculine nouns with the suffixes **ок, ек,** or **ец** drop **o** or **e** throughout the declension: palace—дворец: дворца; soldier—боец: бойца; piece—кусок: куска; sand—песок: песка; kerchief—платок: платка. Also, father—отец: отца.

Their number is very large, since it includes diminutives: орешек diminutive of орех (nut), городок diminutive of город (city), etc. and derivatives: подарок (gift), американец (American), etc.

> *Note:* With nouns ending in –**лец** a **ь** is inserted when the **e** is dropped: owner—владелец: владельца; finger—палец: пальца.

DECLENSION OF NOUNS

Remark: It should not be assumed that all nouns ending in **-ок** or **-ец** drop **o** or **e**. All *diminutives* do so, but some other nouns do not. lesson—уро́к: уро́ка; player—игро́к: игрока́; east—восто́к: восто́ка; blacksmith—кузне́ц: кузнеца́; rascal, villain—подле́ц: подлеца́; sage—мудре́ц: мудреца́; brave man—храбре́ц: храбреца́, etc.

Declension of the Noun путь

The masculine noun путь (way, road) is declined like a feminine noun, except for the ending of the instrumental:

NOM.	путь
GEN.	пути́
DAT.	пути́
ACC.	путь
INSTR.	путём
PREP.	пути́

Declension of Neuter Nouns, Singular

	Hard Nouns		Soft Nouns	
NOM.	окно́	мо́ре	ружьё	зда́ние
GEN.	окна́	мо́ря	ружья́	зда́ния
DAT.	окну́	мо́рю	ружью́	зда́нию
ACC.	окно́	мо́ре	ружьё	зда́ние
INSTR.	окно́м	мо́рем	ружьём	зда́нием
PREP.	окне́	мо́ре	ружье́	зда́нии

Special Rules Pertaining to Neuter Nouns

1. Neuter nouns of foreign origin ending in **o, e, и, у, ю,** or **a**, such as метро́, шоссе́, такси́, рагу́, меню́, боа́ (page 14), are not declined.

2. Hard neuter nouns ending in a sibilant or **ц** followed by **o** are stressed on the ending: плечо́—shoulder; яйцо́—egg.

3. Soft neuter nouns ending in a sibilant or **ц** followed by **e** are not stressed on the ending: учи́лище—school; се́рдце—heart. In these, the genitive: учи́лищ**а**, се́рдц**а** and the dative: учи́лищ**у**, се́рдц**у** have hard endings because of the spelling rule given in page 11.

4. The prepositional ending of nouns in **-ьё** is **-ье**: о ружье́—about the gun.

5. The prepositional ending of nouns in **-ие** is **-ии**: в зда́нии—in the building.

6. The ten neuter nouns ending in **мя** are declined as follows:

NOM.	и́мя	вре́мя
GEN.	и́мени	вре́мени
DAT.	и́мени	вре́мени
ACC.	и́мя	вре́мя
INSTR.	и́мен**ем**	вре́мен**ем**
PREP.	и́мени	вре́мени

7. In current speech the noun **дитя́** (*nominative and accusative*) is used only in these two cases in the singular. (Otherwise, **ребёнок** is currently used and declined.)

Declension of Feminine Nouns, Singular

	Hard Nouns		Soft Nouns	
NOM.	ко́мнат**а**	дере́вн**я**	ли́ни**я**	ло́шадь
GEN.	ко́мнат**ы**	дере́вн**и**	ли́ни**и**	ло́шад**и**
DAT.	ко́мнат**е**	дере́вн**е**	ли́ни**и**	ло́шад**и**
ACC.	ко́мнат**у**	дере́вн**ю**	ли́ни**ю**	ло́шадь
INSTR.	ко́мнат**ой**	дере́вн**ей**	ли́ни**ей**	ло́шад**ью**
PREP.	ко́мнат**е**	дере́вн**е**	ли́ни**и**	ло́шад**и**

Special Rules Pertaining to Feminine Nouns

1. *The Genitive, Dative, and Prepositional* of nouns ending in **-ия** and **-ь** coincide in form: часть Росси́и, к Росси́и, в Росси́и.

DECLENSION OF NOUNS

2. *The Dative and Prepositional* of nouns ending in –а and –я coincide in form.

3. *The Accusative* of nouns ending in –ь coincides with the nominative.

4. *Instrumental.* Nouns ending in –а or –я in the nominative may have instrumental endings **–ой, –ей** or **–ою, –ею**. The last type, found chiefly in poetry, is otherwise infrequent: wave—волна́: волно́ю; storm—бу́ря: бу́рею.

Hard feminine nouns with the stem ending in **ж, ч, ш, щ,** or **ц** have the ending **–ой** in the instrumental when the case ending is stressed: candle—свеча́: свечо́й; sheep—овца́: овцо́й. They have **–ей** in the instrumental when the ending is not stressed: (wooden) country house—да́ча: да́чей; bird—пти́ца: пти́цей.

Nouns ending in **–я** in the nominative may have the stressed ending **–ёй** or the unstressed **–ей** in the instrumental: earth, land—земля́: землёй; village, country—дере́вня: дере́вней.

Irregular Feminine Declensions

Declension of **мать** (mother) and **дочь** (daughter)

NOM.	мать	дочь
GEN.	ма́тери	до́чери
DAT.	ма́тери	до́чери
ACC.	мать	дочь
INSTR.	ма́терью	до́черью
PREP.	ма́тери	до́чери

Declension of **любо́вь** (love), **це́рковь** (church), **ложь** (lie, falsehood), and **рожь** (rye).

NOM.	любо́вь	це́рковь
GEN.	любви́	це́ркви
DAT.	любви́	це́ркви
ACC.	любо́вь	це́рковь
INSTR.	любо́вью	це́рковью
PREP.	любви́	це́ркви

Ложь and рожь are declined similarly, i.e., the **о** is dropped in the genitive, dative, and prepositional. However, the proper name Любо́вь (Lubov) retains the **о**: Мы идём к Любо́ви Петро́вне.

Declension of Nouns in the Plural

General Pattern

MASCULINE

	Hard Nouns (*in a consonant*)	Soft Nouns (*in* ь)	(*in* й)
NOM.	столы́	словари́	слу́чаи
GEN.	столо́в	словаре́й	слу́чаев
DAT.	стола́м	словаря́м	слу́чаям
ACC.	столы́	словари́	слу́чаи
INSTR.	стола́ми	словаря́ми	слу́чаями
PREP.	стола́х	словаря́х	слу́чаях

FEMININE

	Hard Nouns (*in* а)	(*in* я)	Soft Nouns (*in* ия)	(*in* ь)
NOM.	ко́мнаты	дере́вни	ли́нии	тетра́ди
GEN.	ко́мнат	дереве́нь	ли́ний	тетра́дей
DAT.	ко́мнатам	деревня́м	ли́ниям	тетра́дям
ACC.	ко́мнаты	дере́вни	ли́нии	тетра́ди
INSTR.	ко́мнатами	деревня́ми	ли́ниями	тетра́дями
PREP.	ко́мнатах	деревня́х	ли́ниях	тетра́дях

NEUTER

	Hard Nouns (*in* о)	Soft Nouns (*in* е)	(*in* ие)
NOM.	о́кна	моря́	зда́ния
GEN.	о́кон	море́й	зда́ний
DAT.	о́кнам	моря́м	зда́ниям
ACC.	о́кна	моря́	зда́ния
INSTR.	о́кнами	моря́ми	зда́ниями
PREP.	о́кнах	моря́х	зда́ниях

Rules Pertaining to the Declension of Nouns in the Plural

The Dative, Instrumental and Prepositional take the following endings for all genders:

PLURAL	Dat.	Instr.	Prep.
Hard Nouns	ам	ами	ах
Soft Nouns	ям	ями	ях

The Accusative of all nouns in the plural is like the nominative with inanimate nouns, and like the genitive with animate nouns:

	Inanimate	Animate
MASC.	столы́ (tables)	ученико́в (pupils)
FEM.	ко́мнаты (rooms)	коро́в (cows)
NEUT.	учи́лища (schools)	чудо́вищ (monsters)

The Instrumental plural of the nouns дверь (door), ло́шадь (horse) and дочь (daughter) has two parallel forms:

> дверя́ми, лошадя́ми, дочеря́ми
> дверьми́, лошадьми́, дочерьми́

The instrumental plural of де́ти and лю́ди is **детьми́** and **людьми́**.

THE GENITIVE PLURAL

The genitive plural has a variety of endings and has therefore to be studied in detail.

HARD NOUNS

	Nominative Singular		Genitive Plural	
	ENDING	EXAMPLE	ENDING	EXAMPLE
MASC.	consonant	стол	**ов** (1)†	столо́в
FEM.	**а**	река́	—	рек
NEUT.	**о**	сло́во	— (2)	слов

1. Masculine Nouns Ending in a Consonant

(*a*) Nouns ending in **ж, ч, ш, щ** in the nominative singular take **–ей** in the genitive plural: нож: ноже́й; каранда́ш: карандаше́й.

(*b*) Nouns ending in unaccented **–ец** in the nominative singular take **–ев** in the genitive plural: па́лец: па́льцев.

(*c*) Several nouns have the same ending in their genitive plural as in the nominative singular: воло́с—hairs (this noun changes the stress from the nominative singular во́лос); вольт—volts; глаз—eyes; гренаде́р—grenadiers; грузи́н—Georgians; гуса́р—hussars; драгу́н—dragoons; каде́т—cadets; раз—times; партиза́н—partisans; сапо́г—boots; солда́т—soldiers; ту́рок—Turks; челове́к—people (when used with numerals, such as пять челове́к).

(*d*) Nouns with the irregular ending **–ья** in the nominative plural (see page 21) take **ьев** in the genitive plural: брат (brother) бра́тья: бра́тьев; лист (leaf) ли́стья: ли́стьев.

> *Exceptions:* друг (friend) друзья́: друзе́й
> сын (son) сыновья́: сынове́й
> князь (prince) князья́: князе́й
> муж (husband) мужья́: муже́й

(*e*) Nouns which are "masculine in the singular and neuter in the plural"* form their genitive plural correspondingly:

> ребёнок (child) ребя́та: ребя́т.
> котёнок (kitten) котя́та: котя́т.

† See Remarks under corresponding numbers. See also "Isolated Cases of Irregularities" (page 41) and "Insertion of **о** and **е**" (page 41).

* Nevill Forbes, *Russian Grammar*.

DECLENSION OF NOUNS

2. Neuter Nouns Ending in -o

Nouns with the irregular ending **-ья** in the nominative plural (page 22) take **ьев** in the genitive plural: де́рево (tree) дере́вья: дере́вьев.

SOFT NOUNS—FIRST GROUP

All nouns in this group take the ending **-ей** in the genitive plural.

	Nominative Singular		Genitive Plural	
	ENDING	EXAMPLE	ENDING	EXAMPLE
MASC.	ь	рубль	ей	рубле́й
FEM.	ь	дверь	ей	двере́й
NEUT.	е	мо́ре	ей (3)	море́й

3. Neuter Nouns Ending in ж, ч, ш, and щ

Neuter nouns with the stem ending in **ж, ч, ш, щ** and most neuter nouns with the stem ending in **ц** drop the final **e** in their genitive plural: учи́лище (school) учи́лищ; се́рдце (heart) серде́ц.

SOFT NOUNS—SECOND GROUP

	Nominative Singular		Genitive Plural	
	ENDING	EXAMPLE	ENDING	EXAMPLE
MASC.	й	слу́чай; бой	ев; ёв	слу́чаев; боёв
FEM.	я after a consonant	бу́ря	ь (4)	бурь
FEM.	я following a vowel	ли́ния	й (5)	ли́ний
NEUT.	ие; ье	зда́ние	й (6)	зда́ний

4. Feminine Nouns Ending in -я Following a Consonant or -ь

(a) The following nouns take the ending **-ен** in the genitive plural:

ба́сня (fable)	ба́сен	спле́тня (gossip)	спле́тен
ба́шня (tower)	ба́шен	тамо́жня (customs house)	тамо́жен
ви́шня (cherry)	ви́шен		
пе́сня (song)	пе́сен	чита́льня (reading room)	чита́лен
со́тня (a hundred)	со́тен		
спа́льня (bedroom)	спа́лен		

(b) The following nouns take the endings **-ень** and **-онь** in the genitive plural:

ба́рышня (young girl)	ба́рышень	дере́вня (village)	дереве́нь
		ку́хня (kitchen)	ку́хонь

(c) A few nouns with the feminine ending **-я** take **-ей** in the genitive plural:

до́ля (part)	доле́й	ра́спря (conflict, quarrel)	ра́спрей
дя́дя (uncle)	дя́дей		
западня́ (trap)	западне́й	тётя (aunt)	тётей
ноздря́ (nostril)	ноздре́й		

(d) Feminine nouns ending in stressed **-ья** in the nominative singular take **-ей** in the genitive plural: статья́ (article): стате́й. Feminine nouns ending in unstressed **-ья** in the nominative singular take **-ий** in the genitive plural: колду́нья (witch): колду́ний.

5. Feminine Nouns Ending in -я Following a Vowel

The formation of the genitive plural is the same with *any* vowels preceding **я**: иде́я: иде́й; ста́туя: ста́туй.

6. Neuter Nouns Ending in -ье or -ьё

Most nouns ending in **-ье** or **-ьё** take the ending **-ий** in the genitive plural: воскресе́нье (Sunday): воскресе́ний; копьё (spear, lance): ко́пий.

Exceptions: пла́тье (dress): пла́тьев; ку́шанье (dish, food): ку́шаньев; побере́жье (coastline): побере́жий or побере́жьев; ружьё (gun, rifle): ру́жей.

DECLENSION OF NOUNS

ISOLATED CASES OF IRREGULARITIES IN THE GENITIVE PLURAL

MASCULINE: ю́ноша (young man), a noun with a feminine ending, has ю́нош**ей** in the genitive plural.

FEMININE: вожжа́ (rein): вожж**е́й**; свеча́ (candle): свеч**е́й** or the regular свеч. Мечта́ (dream, longing) has no genitive plural.

NEUTER: о́блако (cloud) has облако́в; се́мя (seed): семя́н; стре́мя (stirrup): стремя́н; су́дно (boat, vessel): судо́в; яйцо́ (egg): яи́ц.

INSERTION OF E AND O IN THE GENITIVE PLURAL

o and **e** are inserted in the genitive plural ending of many feminine and neuter nouns—and in the genitive plural ending of a few masculine diminutives with feminine or neuter endings: мальчи́шка, доми́шко, etc. The number of these nouns is very large, since it includes not only diminutives, but also nouns derived from other nouns or other parts of speech.

Examples:

> но́жка (leg) но́жек; ру́чка (hand) ру́чек; тетра́дка (notebook) тетра́док; око́шко (window) око́шек; коле́чко (ring) коле́чек, etc.
> запи́ска (note) запи́сок; америка́нка (American woman) америка́нок; по́лька (Polish woman) по́лек; etc.

Note: Actually, diminutives are translated by "little + noun." **Но́жка** and **ру́чка** have independent meanings, respectively: leg (of a table, etc.) and penholder, knob, handle.

Feminine Nouns

1. **e** is inserted in front of a **к**

    (*a*) when **к** is preceded by **ж, ч, ш,** or **ц**:

    > де́вочка (girl) де́вочек; кни́жка (book, booklet) кни́жек

    (*b*) when **к** is preceded by **ь** or **й**. The letters **ь** or **й** are then dropped:

    > копе́йка (kopeck) копе́ек; по́лька (Polish woman) по́лек

2. **e** is inserted in front of **л** or **н** preceded by a consonant:

    > земля́ (land) земе́ль; пе́сня (song) пе́сен.

Exceptions: ку́кла (doll): ку́кол; княжна́ (daughter of a prince): княжо́н; волна́ (wave): волн.

3. **e** is inserted in a few other instances:

   овца́ (sheep): ове́ц; сва́дьба (wedding): сва́деб; тюрьма́ (prison): тю́рем.

4. **e** is inserted in the following nouns which occur only in the plural (and where the nominative singular is then no longer a guide):

   де́ньги (money): де́нег; подтя́жки (suspenders): подтя́жек.

5. **o** is inserted in front of **к** which is <u>not</u> preceded by **ж, ч, ш, ц**:

   па́лка (stick): па́лок; доска́ (board): досо́к; ла́вка (store): ла́вок.

6. **o** is also inserted in the following nouns which occur only in the plural:

   носи́лки (stretcher): носи́лок; сли́вки (cream): сли́вок; су́тки (day and night (24 hours): су́ток.

Neuter Nouns

1. **e** is inserted after a consonant or a **ь**

   (*a*) when these letters are followed by **–ко, –цо** or **–це**:

   око́шко (small window): око́шек; се́рдце (heart): серде́ц; кольцо́ (ring): коле́ц.

   (*b*) In most cases, when these letters are followed by **–ло, –мо, –но**, or **–ро**:

   кре́сло (armchair): кре́сел; письмо́ (letter): пи́сем; пятно́ (spot): пя́тен; ведро́ (bucket): вёдер.

2. **o** is inserted when **–ло, –мо, –но, –ро** are preceded by **к**:
   окно́ (window): о́кон; стекло́ (glass, pane): стёкол.

GENITIVE OF NOUNS WHICH OCCUR ONLY IN THE PLURAL

Since the nominative singular cannot serve here as a guide, the following rules will be helpful:

1. The few nouns which in the nominative plural end in **a** drop this

ending in the genitive: воро́та (gate): воро́т; черни́ла (ink): черни́л. These nouns are declined like слова́.

2. The nouns ending in the nominative plural in **-ы** or **-и**—when the letter **и** is preceded by **г, к,** or **х**—have two types of endings, depending on the stress in the nominative plural:

(*a*) When the endings **-ы** or **-и** are stressed, the genitive plural ends in **ов**:

часы́ (watch): часо́в; духи́ (perfume): духо́в; штаны́ (trousers): штано́в; очки́ (glasses): очко́в.

These nouns are declined like столы́.

(*b*) When the endings are not stressed, they are dropped in the genitive plural:

брю́ки (trousers): брюк; кани́кулы (vacation): кани́кул; макаро́ны (macaroni): макаро́н; но́жницы (scissors): но́жниц.

These nouns are declined like кни́ги, ко́мнаты.

Exceptions: The following nouns with unstressed endings have a genitive plural ending in **-ов**: консе́рвы (canned goods): консе́рвов; мемуа́ры (memoirs): мемуа́ров; перегово́ры (negotiations): перегово́ров; про́воды (seeing-off): про́водов; фина́нсы (finances): фина́нсов.

3. The nouns ending in **-и** not preceded by г, к, or х have the ending **-ей** in the genitive plural: бу́дни (week days): бу́дней; гра́бли (rake): гра́блей; де́бри (jungle, thicket): де́брей; дро́жжи (yeast): дрожже́й; лю́ди (people): люде́й; са́ни (sleigh): саней. These nouns are declined like "словари́," "но́чи" (except the above-mentioned instrumental: людьми́).

Miscellaneous Irregular Declensions in the Singular and in the Plural

In the following recapitulation, many nouns are representative of a group. (See pages 21–23.)

Masculine Nouns

	Singular	Plural	Singular	Plural
NOM.	англича́нин	англича́не	брат	бра́тья
GEN.		англича́н		бра́тьев
DAT.	Regular	англича́нам	Regular	бра́тьям
ACC.		англича́н		бра́тьев
INSTR.		англича́нами		бра́тьями
PREP.		англича́нах		бра́тьях

	Singular	Plural	Singular	Plural
NOM.	сын	сыновья́	друг	друзья́
GEN.		сынове́й		друзе́й
DAT.	Regular	сыновья́м	Regular	друзья́м
ACC.		сынове́й		друзе́й
INSTR.		сыновья́ми		друзья́ми
PREP.		сыновья́х		друзья́х

	Singular	Plural	Singular	Plural
NOM.	сосе́д	сосе́ди	телёнок	теля́та
GEN.		сосе́дей		теля́т
DAT.	Regular	сосе́дям	Regular	теля́там
ACC.		сосе́дей	(fleeting o)	теля́т
INSTR.		сосе́дями		теля́тами
PREP.		сосе́дях		теля́тах

	Singular	Plural
NOM.	путь	пути́
GEN.	пути́	путе́й
DAT.	пути́	путя́м
ACC.	путь	пути́
INSTR.	путём	путя́ми
PREP.	пути́	путя́х

Feminine Nouns

	Singular	Plural
NOM.	мать	ма́тери
GEN.	ма́тери	матере́й
DAT.	ма́тери	матеря́м

DECLENSION OF NOUNS

	Singular	Plural
ACC.	мать	матере́й
INSTR.	ма́терью	матеря́ми
PREP.	ма́тери	матеря́х

Neuter Nouns

	Singular	Plural	Singular	Plural
NOM.	перо́	пе́рья	не́бо	небеса́
GEN.		пе́рьев		небе́с
DAT.	Regular	пе́рьям	Regular	небеса́м
ACC.		пе́рья		небеса́
INSTR.		пе́рьями		небеса́ми
PREP.		пе́рьях		небеса́х

	Singular	Plural	Singular	Plural
NOM.	у́хо	у́ши	и́мя	имена́
GEN.		уше́й	и́мени	имён
DAT.	Regular	уша́м	и́мени	имена́м
ACC.		у́ши	и́мя	имена́
INSTR.		уша́ми	и́менем	имена́ми
PREP.		уша́х	и́мени	имена́х

	Singular	Plural
NOM.	се́мя	семена́
GEN.	се́мени	семя́н
DAT.	се́мени	семена́м
ACC.	се́мя	семена́
INSTR.	се́менем	семена́ми
PREP.	се́мени	семена́х

Declension of Proper Names

First Names and Patronymics

Both first names and patronymics are declined like nouns:

	Masculine	Feminine
NOM.	Ива́н Петро́вич	А́нна Петро́вна
GEN.	Ива́на Петро́вича	А́нны Петро́вны

	Masculine	Feminine
DAT.	Ивáну Петрóвичу	Áнне Петрóвне
ACC.	Ивáна Петрóвича	Áнну Петрóвну
INSTR.	Ивáном Петрóвичем	Áнной Петрóвной
PREP.	Ивáне Петрóвиче	Áнне Петрóвне

Last Names

(*a*) Proper names ending in **-ов, -ев** or **-ин** (Чéхов, Тургéнев, Пýшкин) are declined as follows:

	Masculine	Feminine	Plural
NOM.	Чéхов	Чéхова	Чéховы
GEN.	Чéхова	Чéховой	Чéховых
DAT.	Чéхову	Чéховой	Чéховым
ACC.	Чéхова	Чéхову	Чéховых
INSTR.	Чéховым	Чéховой	Чéховыми
PREP.	Чéхове	Чéховой	Чéховых

(*b*) Last names with adjectival endings **-ий** or **-ой** are declined like adjectives in the masculine, feminine, and plural.

(*c*) Last names ending in **-ич** are declined like regular nouns in the masculine and in the plural:

Я написáл Ивáну Милорáдовичу.

Я написáл Милорáдовичам.

Last names ending in **-ич** are not declined in the feminine: Я написáл Елéне Милорáдович.

(*d*) Russian last names with somewhat unusual endings, such as Седы́х or Дурновó, are not declined. Neither, as a rule, are Ukranian names ending in **-ко**: Шевчéнко, Родзя́нко, and the like.

(*e*) Foreign names ending in a consonant, in **ь**, or in **й** are declined like nouns. The declension is limited to the masculine and the plural:

пáмятник Христофóру Колýмбу	a monument to Christopher Columbus
закóн Бóйля—Мариóтта	the law of Boyle—Mariotte
эксперимéнты Фарадéя	the experiments of Faraday
дина́стия Тюдóров	the Tudor dynasty

DECLENSION OF NOUNS

Note the difference in the instrumental case endings between Russian names and foreign ones:

> Это написано Чехов**ым**.
> Это написано Байрон**ом**.

Feminine foreign names and all foreign names ending in a vowel are not declined:

концерт Мариан Андерсон	a concert by Marian Anderson
стихи Эйми Лауэлл	the poems of Amy Lowell
роман Дюма	a novel by Dumas
картины Коро	the paintings of Corot

Exception: Masculine nouns ending in an unstressed **-a**, such as Коста or Капабланка, may be declined.

> играть против Капабланки   to play against Capablanca

Geographical Names

(*a*) Most geographical names, both Russian and foreign, are declined regularly as nouns:

около Киева	near Kiev
на Волге	on the Volga
в Лондоне	in London
между Сеной и Марной	between the Seine and the Marne

(*b*) Some Russian geographical names in **о**—namely, those which do not end in **-ово, -ево, -ино** or **-ыно**—are not declined: в Ровно

(*c*) Foreign geographical names ending in **е, и, о, у** and (as a rule)* in a stressed **á** are not declined:

недалеко от Кале	not far from Calais
в Чили	in Chile
на берегах Арно	on the shores of the Arno
в Перу	in Peru

---

* There is a divergence of opinion regarding geographical names ending in stressed **á**. Добромыслов и Розенталь (Трудные вопросы грамматики и правописания) state that names such as Анкара, Алма-Ата, Фергана may be declined.

The Usage of Cases

The cases will be discussed with reference to:

A. Basic function
B. Special constructions
C. Verbs governing the cases
D. Prepositions governing the cases (including the so-called adverbial and verbal prepositions)

> *Remark:* Many prepositions (в, за, на, по, etc.) have a variety of meanings. Some govern more than one case; this will be discussed in detail later. (Chapter 9, Prepositions.)

The Nominative

BASIC FUNCTION

The nominative case expresses the subject or the predicate of a sentence:

Ма́льчик чита́ет.	The boy reads.
Москва́—го́род.	Moscow is a city.
Он ста́рый.	He is old.

SPECIAL CONSTRUCTIONS

The nominative is used as the logical object in expressions of possession:

У бра́та есть ключ.	(My) brother has a key.
Ва́ша кни́га у меня́.	I have your book.

VERBS

The only verbs which *cannot* be used with the nominative are the impersonal: хоте́ться, зноби́ть, etc. (See page 189.)

PREPOSITIONS

The following prepositions govern the nominative case in rather special constructions:

За in the expression **что за**—what (kind of).

Что э́то за кни́га?	What (kind of a) book is this?
Что за ве́тер!	What a wind!

DECLENSION OF NOUNS

По is followed by the nominative case of the numerals два, три, четы́ре, 200, 300, 400 in "distributive" constructions.

Де́ти получи́ли по два я́блока.	The children received two apples apiece.
В ка́ждой каю́те по три пасса́жира.	There are three passengers in each cabin.
У нас по четы́ре офице́ра на ро́ту.	We have four officers per company.

The same applies to the compound numerals 22, 23, 34, etc.

Note: See distributive usage of **по**, Chapter 9.

In a few instances, the preposition **в** is followed by nouns with nominative case endings (a remnant of an old grammatical form):

пойти́ в го́сти—to visit; произвести́ в офице́ры—to give a commission (officer's)

The Genitive

BASIC FUNCTION

The genitive normally expresses relations between two nouns. These relations are usually rendered into English with the aid of the preposition "of" in answer to: of whom?—кого́?; of what?—чего́?; whose?—чей? These relations include:

1. Possession

>дом учи́теля   the house *of* the teacher (or: the teacher's house)

2. Connection

брат жены́ (the brother of [my] wife); нача́льник отде́ла (the head of the department); у́лицы го́рода (city streets); дом о́тдыха (rest home)

3. Part (of a whole; of a substance)

кры́ша до́ма (the roof of the house); но́жка стола́ (the leg of a table) кусо́к де́рева (a piece of wood); стака́н воды́ (a glass of water)

4. Partitive meaning (translated into English by "some," "any")

Он вы́пил воды́—He drank some water; Да́йте мне хле́ба—Give me some bread; Вы купи́ли пи́ва?—Did you buy any beer?

> *Remarks:* (1) In the plural, the partitive genitive has even wider usage. It suggests then "a few": купи́ть конве́ртов и ма́рок (to buy envelopes and stamps); доста́ть папиро́с (to get cigarettes). (2) The direct object is in the accusative when the action pertains to the entire object: вы́пить во́ду—to drink the water; дать хлеб—to give the bread (to give a loaf of bread).

5. Characteristics (concrete, visible; abstract)

цвет пла́тья (the color of the dress); челове́к высо́кого ро́ста (a tall man); цена́ кни́ги (the price of the book); вес багажа́ (the weight of the luggage); вопро́с большо́й ва́жности (a question of great importance)

6. Action or implied action

прода́жа биле́тов (the sale of tickets); нача́ло уро́ка (the beginning of the lesson); игра́ дете́й (children's play)

7. Feeling and reasoning

чу́вство до́лга (a sense of duty); мне́ние президе́нта (the president's opinion)

> *Remark:* Needless to say, not all constructions with "of" are rendered by the genitive in Russian: He is a friend of mine—Он мой друг; quarter of five—без че́тверти пять; the city of Moscow—(го́род) Москва́.

SPECIAL CONSTRUCTIONS

The genitive is used in the following constructions:

1. In negated sentences—after нет, не́ было, не бу́дет—regardless of gender or number:

У нас нет хле́ба.	We have no bread.
Там не́ было ме́бели.	There was no furniture there.
За́втра не бу́дет уро́ков.	Tomorrow there will be no lessons.

DECLENSION OF NOUNS

The same type of sentence is encountered with animate logical subjects:

Его́ нет.	He is not (here).
Меня́ не́ было до́ма.	I wasn't at home.
Вас не бу́дет на ле́кции?	You won't be at the lecture?

Sometimes the meaning of such sentences is just about identical with the personal ones: Меня́ не́ было до́ма may be reworded Я не́ был до́ма. However, the first construction often suggests that something expected did not happen (at a specific place or time).

Sentences such as: Я никогда́ не́ был в Евро́пе (I have never been to Europe) should not be replaced with the impersonal ones.

In addition to нет, не́ было, and не бу́дет, the genitive is used in other *impersonal* constructions: after не followed by быва́ть (to be, to happen); проходи́ть, пройти́ (to pass); происходи́ть, произойти́ (to happen, to take place); остава́ться, оста́ться (to remain, to be left); выходи́ть, вы́йти (to turn out to be) and существова́ть (to exist).

Давно́ не быва́ло тако́й жары́.	There hasn't been such heat for a long time.
Ничего́ не вы́шло.	Nothing came out (of it).
Не прошло́ и дня.	A day didn't pass.
К сча́стью, сканда́ла не произошло́.	Fortunately there was no scandal.
Ничего́ не оста́лось.	Nothing remained.

2. In negated sentences—after transitive verbs

| Я не пью вина́. | I don't drink (any) wine. |
| Он не получи́л отве́та. | He didn't get an answer. |

Remarks:

(a) The accusative case may also be used in negated constructions. This important (and often debated) point is discussed with the Accusative Case. (See page 64.)

(b) The genitive is seldom used in negated sentences after intransitive verbs. This only takes place with some constructions referring to time, distance, etc.

Examples:

| Он и го́да не рабо́тает здесь, а уже́ хо́чет уходи́ть. | He hasn't worked here a year and already wants to leave. |

Не проехали мы километра, как лопнула шина.	We had hardly driven a kilometer, when we got a flat tire.

3. With the comparative degree

    Брат ста́рше сестры́. The brother is older than the sister.
    Сестра́ моло́же бра́та. The sister is younger than the brother.

4. With numerals (except 1, 21, 31, etc.) and other expressions of quantity:
   (*a*) Genitive singular is used after два (две), три, четы́ре; the compound numerals ending in 2, 3, 4, such as 22, 43, 74, etc., and after о́ба (о́бе).

    два до́ллара, со́рок три рубля́, о́ба бра́та.

   (*b*) Genitive plural after all other numerals, from 5 up.

    шесть столо́в, два́дцать семь книг.

Also, after the collective numerals дво́е, тро́е, че́тверо, etc.

    дво́е ученико́в, тро́е дете́й.

   (*c*) Genitive singular or genitive plural—with fractions: че́тверть—1/4, треть—1/3, полови́на—1/2, три пя́тых—3/5, etc.

    полови́на кни́ги; де́вять деся́тых ученико́в.

   (*d*) Genitive singular or genitive plural after мно́го, ма́ло, ско́лько, кило́, фунт, etc.

    мно́го воды́—a lot of water; мно́го книг—many books.

   (*e*) Genitive plural after не́сколько (several); большинство́ (majority); меньшинство́ (minority), etc.

    не́сколько книг; большинство́ ученико́в.

5. In expressions of time—when something takes place on a certain date:

Я прие́хал пе́рвого ма́рта.	I arrived on March 1st.
Мы вернёмся шесто́го ию́ля.	We will return on July 6th.

6. With the short or long adjectives, по́лный (full), and досто́йный (worth, deserving).

дом по́лон наро́ду	the house is full of people
челове́к, досто́йный уваже́ния	a man deserving respect

DECLENSION OF NOUNS

VERBS GOVERNING THE GENITIVE

The genitive is used after the following verbs:

боя́ться, по-	to be afraid of, to fear
добива́ться, доби́ться	to seek, to aim, to (try to) get, obtain
достига́ть, дости́гнуть	to reach, to attain, to obtain
заслу́живать, заслужи́ть	to deserve
избега́ть, избежа́ть	to avoid
каса́ться, косну́ться	to touch (imp. only: to concern)
лиша́ть, лиши́ть	to deprive
лиша́ться, лиши́ться	to be deprived of
пуга́ться, испуга́ться	to be frightened
слу́шаться, послу́шаться	to obey
опаса́ться	to fear
сто́ить	to cost (an effort, etc.)
стесня́ться, постесня́ться	to feel shy, embarrassed
стыди́ться, постыди́ться	to be ashamed of

Examples:

Она́ бои́тся грозы́.	She is afraid of the storm.
Вас э́то на каса́ется.	This does not concern you.
Э́то сто́ило большо́го уси́лия.	It cost a lot of effort.

The genitive is used with expressions formed from недостава́ть and нехвата́ть (both meaning: to miss, to be short of).

Ему́ недостаёт о́пыта.	He lacks experience.
Мне нехвата́ло вас.	I missed you.

The following verbs are followed by the genitive, when something rather indefinite or something abstract is referred to: жела́ть, пожела́ть (to wish); ждать, подожда́ть (to wait); иска́ть, поиска́ть (to look for); проси́ть, попроси́ть (to ask for); ожида́ть (to await); тре́бовать, потре́бовать (to demand); хоте́ть, захоте́ть (to wish, to want).

Мы жда́ли авто́буса.	We were waiting for a bus.
Он иска́л слу́чая.	He was looking (waiting) for an occasion.
Она́ попроси́ла сло́ва.	She asked for the right to speak.
Страна́ хо́чет (жела́ет) ми́ра.	The country wishes peace.

When something more specific or concrete is referred to the accusative is used:

Я жду сестру́.	I am waiting for (my) sister.
Он и́щет каранда́ш.	He is looking for (his) pencil.
Он попроси́л счёт.	He asked for the bill (check).
Что вы хоти́те?	What do you want (wish)?

PREPOSITIONS

The following prepositions govern the genitive:

без	*without*: Я пришёл без шля́пы. I came without a hat.
близ	*near*: Близ го́рода есть река́. Near the town is a river.
в ви́де	*in the way of*, *as*: в ви́де нача́льного жа́лования as a starting salary
ввиду́	*on account of*: ввиду́ его́ отсу́тствия on account of his absence
вдоль	*along*: Мы е́хали вдоль бе́рега. We drove along the shore.
вме́сто	*instead of*: Он пришёл вме́сто бра́та. He came instead of his brother.
вне	*out of*, *outside*: вне го́рода outside of the city *beyond*: вне сомне́ния beyond doubt
внутри́	*inside*: внутри́ зда́ния inside the building
во́зле	*near*: Мы живём во́зле ле́са. We live near the wood.
вокру́г	*around*: Они́ сиде́ли вокру́г стола́. They were sitting around the table.
впереди́	*in front of*: Он шёл впереди́ нас. He was walking in front of us.
в продолже́ние	*during, throughout*: В продолже́ние всего́ уро́ка он молча́л. He was silent throughout the whole lesson.
вро́де	*like* (which looks like): Он наде́л что-то вро́де шля́пы. He put on something (which looked) like a hat.

DECLENSION OF NOUNS

вследствие	*as a consequence, as a result:* вследствие этого разговора as a result of this conversation
в течение	*during:* в течение всего года during the whole year
для	*for:* Вот деньги для него. Here is the money for him. *for* (implied—with expressions of purpose): шкап для белья linen closet; щётка для ногтей nail brush
до	*before:* прийти до завтрака to come before lunch *until:* остаться до конца to remain until the end *to:* До станции очень далеко. It is very far to the station. *as far as:* дойти до угла to go as far as the corner
за исключением	*except, excepting:* Все пришли, за исключением Ивана. Everybody came except John.
из	*from:* Она написала из Бостона. She wrote from Boston. *out of:* Он вынул деньги из кармана. He took the money out of his pocket. Это сделано из стекла. This is made out of glass.
из-за	*from behind:* Человек вышел из-за дома. A man came from behind the house. *because of, on account of:* опоздать из-за погоды to be late on account of the weather
из-под	*from under:* Кошка выбежала из-под стола. The cat ran out from under the table.
кроме	*besides:* Кто там был, кроме доктора? Who was there besides the doctor? *except:* Кроме доктора, никого не было. Nobody was there except the doctor.
кругом	*around:* Кругом нас вода. Water is all around us.
мимо	*past, by:* ехать мимо школы to drive past the school
накануне	*the day before, on the eve:* накануне праздника on the eve of the holiday
напротив	*across from:* Мы живём напротив почты. We live across from the post office.

насчёт	*about, regarding:* Он пи́шет насчёт сы́на. He is writing about (his) son.
не счита́я	*excluding, not counting:* В до́ме два этажа́, не счита́я подва́ла. There are two storeys in the house not counting the basement (cellar).
о́коло	*near:* Она́ стоя́ла о́коло де́рева. She stood near a tree. *about* (usually implying "less than"): Мы жи́ли там о́коло го́да. We lived there for about a year. *around:* Он прие́хал о́коло двух часо́в. He came around two o'clock.
от	*from:* письмо́ от бра́та a letter from (my) brother; Дом недалеко́ от реки́. The house is not far from the river. *from, because of:* Он не мог говори́ть от волне́ния. He couldn't speak from excitement. *from* (implied): лека́рство от ка́шля cough medicine.
относи́тельно	*regarding, concerning:* относи́тельно его́ письма́ regarding his letter
позади́	*behind:* Он стоя́л позади́ авто́буса. He stood behind the bus.
поми́мо	*apart from:* Поми́мо э́того, я ничего́ не зна́ю. Apart from this, I don't know anything.
поперёк	*across:* Поперёк доро́ги лежа́ло де́рево. A tree lay across the road.
по по́воду	*in connection with, regarding:* Я с ним говори́л по по́воду письма́. I spoke with him in connection with the letter.
по́сле	*after:* по́сле обеда after dinner
по слу́чаю	*because of, on account of, in connection with:* Мы не рабо́таем по слу́чаю пра́здника. We are not working because of the holiday.
посреди́	*in the middle of:* посреди́ са́да in the middle of the garden
посре́дством	*by means of, with:* посре́дством э́той маши́ны with this machine

DECLENSION OF NOUNS

про́тив	*opposite:* Он живёт про́тив шко́лы. He lives opposite the school. *against:* Э́то про́тив зако́на. This is against the law.
ра́ди	*for the sake of:* Она́ всё сде́лает ра́ди сы́на. She will do everything for the sake of (her) son.
с	*off:* сойти́ с трамва́я to get off the streetcar *from:* перево́д с ру́сского a translation from Russian *since:* с де́тства since childhood
сверх	*over, above:* сверх но́рмы above the norm
сза́ди	*behind:* Кто е́дет сза́ди на́шего автомоби́ля? Who is driving behind our car?
снару́жи	*outside of:* Он стоя́л снару́жи до́ма. He stood outside (of) the house.
среди́	*in the middle of:* среди́ но́чи in the middle of the night *among:* Среди́ пи́сем я нашёл счёт. Among the letters I found a bill.
у	*near, by* (with objects): Она́ стоя́ла у окна́. She was standing near the window. *at* (with persons): Мы бы́ли у до́ктора. We were at the doctor's. *from:* Я взял кни́гу у сестры́. I took a book from (my) sister. *to express possession:* У меня́ (есть) ключ. I have the key.

Notes:

(*a*) Есть is added in case of a more or less permanent possession: У меня́ есть слова́рь.—I have (possess) a dictionary.

(*b*) Есть is omitted in case of a temporary possession: У меня́ перо́ (*or:* Перо́ у меня́)—I have the pen (not necessarily mine); У кого́ ключ?—Who has the key?

(*c*) Есть is not used with parts of body: У неё краси́вые глаза́ (She has beautiful eyes) or with many abstract notions: У него́ на́сморк (He has a cold).

Remarks:

(*a*) Вблизи́, внутри́, вокру́г, впереди́, круго́м, напро́тив, позади́, поперёк, про́тив, сза́ди and снару́жи are used independently as adverbs: Они́ живу́т напро́тив. (They live across.) Он сиде́л где́-то сза́ди. (He was sitting somewhere behind.) И ти́хо, ти́хо всё круго́м. (And it's quiet and quiet all around.)

(*b*) For prepositions calling for more than one case consult table, page 273.

The Dative

BASIC FUNCTION

The dative expresses an action directed towards a person or an object. Usually—but not always—it is expressed in English with the aid of the preposition "to" in answer to кому́? (to whom?) чему́? (to what?). In a few instances, the dative expresses a feeling, or a state, rather than an action.

Я пишу́ учи́телю.	I am writing *to* the teacher.
Он подари́л сы́ну часы́.	He gave a watch *to* his son (or: He gave his son a watch).
Мы вам ве́рим.	We believe you.

SPECIAL CONSTRUCTIONS

1. The logical subject of a sentence is in the dative case:

(*a*) With predicate adverbs followed by the infinitive: мо́жно (one may); на́до (one must); ну́жно (one must); необходи́мо (it is absolutely necessary); нельзя́ (one can't, one shouldn't); не́когда (there is no time to); пора́ (it is time to), etc.

До́ктор сказа́л, что мне мо́жно встава́ть.	The doctor said that I may get up.
Вам на́до идти́.	You must go.
Больно́му нельзя́ кури́ть.	The patient shouldn't smoke.
Де́тям пора́ идти́ спать.	It is time for the children to go to bed.

DECLENSION OF NOUNS

(*b*) With жаль (жа́лко).

Мне жа́лко уезжа́ть отсю́да.	I am sorry to go away from here.
Учи́телю жаль ученика́.	The teacher feels sorry for the pupil.

(*c*) Sometimes, with interrogative pronouns and adverbs; the logical subject in these constructions is then followed by the infinitive:

Что нам де́лать?	What shall we do?
Где мне сесть?	Where shall I sit?

(*d*) With adverbs in **o** formed from short adjectives: ве́село (gay), гру́стно (sad), жа́рко (hot), неприя́тно (disagreeable), ску́чно (boring), сты́дно (shameful), тру́дно (difficult), хо́лодно (cold), хорошо́ (good), etc.

Мне жа́рко.	I am hot.
Вам бы́ло ску́чно?	Were you bored?
Бою́сь, что де́тям здесь бу́дет хо́лодно.	I am afraid the children will be cold here.

(*e*) With impersonal verbal forms, such as хо́чется—(I) feel like; ка́жется—it seems (to me); нра́вится—(I) like; прихо́дится—(I) have to; нездоро́вится—(I) don't feel well; не спи́тся—(I) can't sleep.

Мне хо́чется пить.	I am thirsty.
Ему́ не понра́вилась э́та карти́на.	He didn't like this picture.

(*f*) In expressions pertaining to age

Ско́лько ва́шему сы́ну лет? Ему́ де́сять лет.	How old is your son? He is ten years old.

(*g*) With the long or short form of the following adjectives: благода́рный (grateful); ве́рный (true); подо́бный (similar); сво́йственный (characteristic); ну́жный (needed); необходи́мый (indispensable).

Я вам о́чень благода́рен.	I am very grateful to you.
Вы мне не нужны́.	I don't need you.
ве́рный своему́ сло́ву	true to his word

2. A noun may govern the dative case:

> подража́ние Пу́шкину   an imitation of Pushkin
> по́мощь бе́дным   assistance to poor people
> па́мятник Ломоно́сову   a monument to Lomonosov

3. The dative is used in addressing letters: Ольге Петро́вне Смирно́вой. До́ктору А. П. Ива́нову.

VERBS GOVERNING THE DATIVE

аплоди́ровать	to applaud
ве́рить, пове́рить	to believe
возвраща́ть, возврати́ть, верну́ть	to return (trans.), to give back
вреди́ть, повреди́ть	to damage
дава́ть, дать*	to give
дари́ть, подари́ть	to give (a present)
говори́ть, сказа́ть	to tell, to say
грози́ть, погрози́ть	to threaten
жа́ловаться, пожа́ловаться	to complain
завеща́ть	to bequeath
зави́довать, позави́довать	to envy
запреща́ть, запрети́ть	to forbid
звони́ть, позвони́ть	to ring, to telephone
изменя́ть, измени́ть	to betray, to be unfaithful
кла́няться, поклони́ться	to greet, to bow
льстить, польсти́ть	to flatter
меша́ть, помеша́ть	to hinder, to prevent, to disturb
моли́ться, помоли́ться	to pray
мстить, отомсти́ть	to revenge oneself on
надоеда́ть, надое́сть	to bother, to annoy
напомина́ть, напо́мнить	to remind
обеща́ть	to promise
отвеча́ть, отве́тить	to answer
передава́ть, переда́ть	to give, to pass, to transmit
писа́ть, написа́ть	to write
плати́ть, заплати́ть	to pay
подража́ть	to imitate
подходи́ть, подойти́	to suit

* And prefixed verbs formed from it.

DECLENSION OF NOUNS

пока́зывать, показа́ть	to show
покупа́ть, купи́ть	to buy
помога́ть, помо́чь	to help
поруча́ть, поручи́ть	to entrust
предлага́ть, предложи́ть	to offer, to suggest
приводи́ть, привести́	to bring, to lead to
привози́ть, привезти́	to bring (*by conveyance*)
признава́ться, призна́ться	to admit, to confess
принадлежа́ть	to belong
приноси́ть, принести́	to bring
продава́ть, прода́ть	to sell
противоре́чить	to contradict
равня́ться	to equal
ра́доваться, пора́доваться	to rejoice
служи́ть, послужи́ть	to serve
сове́товать	to advise
соотве́тствовать	to correspond
сочу́вствовать	to sympathize
телеграфи́ровать	to telegraph
телефони́ровать	to telephone
удивля́ться, удиви́ться	to be surprised
улыба́ться, улыбну́ться	to smile
учи́ть, вы́учить	to teach (*something*)
учи́ться, вы́учиться	to learn (*something*)
чита́ть, прочита́ть	to read

and a few others. For example:

Он помога́ет сы́ну.	He is helping his son.
Она́ чита́ет де́тям.	She is reading to the children.
Все ему́ зави́довали.	Everybody envied him.
Напо́мните мне.	Remind me.

Note that ве́рить, зави́довать, ра́доваться, сочу́вствовать, удивля́ться express a feeling.

Remark: The verbs given in the list are, of course, followed by the dative only when the context calls for it and not otherwise, as in the following:

Он чита́ет кни́гу.	He is reading a book.

Она́ улыбну́лась.	She smiled.
Мы пи́шем по-ру́сски.	We are writing in Russian.
Что вы принесли́?	What did you bring?

Nouns related to the verbs given in the list may also govern the dative:

отве́т учи́телю	an answer to the teacher
пода́рок жене́	a present for (my) wife
письмо́ бра́ту	a letter to (my) brother

PREPOSITIONS

The following prepositions govern the dative:

благодаря́   *thanks to, because of:* благодаря́ ва́шей по́мощи   thanks to your help

вопреки́   *in spite of, against:* вопреки́ жела́нию отца́   against his father's wish

к*   *to:* Я иду́ к до́ктору.   I am going to the doctor.
     Мы е́дем к друзья́м.   We are going to our friends.
     Он подошёл к две́ри.   He came up to the door.
     пое́здка к мо́рю   a trip to the sea
   towards: Де́ти побежа́ли к реке́.   The children ran towards the river.
   by, towards: К ве́черу ста́ло холодне́е.   Towards the evening it became colder.
   for: Всё гото́во к отъе́зду.   Everything is ready for the departure.

навстре́чу   *towards* (direction)*:* Кто-то шёл нам навстре́чу.   Somebody was coming towards us.

назло́   *for spite, to displease:* Назло́ всем   to displease everybody

напереко́р   *in defiance, in opposition, against:* Напереко́р инстру́кциям   in defiance of instructions

по   *along, on, in, according to.* (See below.)

согла́сно   *according to:* согла́сно э́той резолю́ции   according to this resolution

---

* The preposition к is very often found with verbs of motion. For other verbs see page 286.

DECLENSION OF NOUNS

Note:

The prepositions навстре́чу, назло́, and напереко́р may be used independently as adverbs: Кто́-то идёт навстре́чу.—Somebody is coming towards (us). Как назло́, пошёл дождь.—Unfortunately it started to rain.

The preposition **по**, when used with the dative case, enters into a variety of constructions to express:

(*a*) Motion (along; within; following something)

е́хать по у́лице	to drive along the street
гуля́ть по са́ду	to walk in the garden
идти́ по следа́м	to follow a trail

(*b*) A distributive idea, often corresponding to the English "each."

получи́ть по я́блоку	to get an apple each
дать по до́ллару	to give a dollar apiece

(*c*) A succession (of different places; of different times)

ходи́ть по магази́нам	to go around shops (one after another)
чита́ть по вечера́м	to read in the evenings

(*d*) Manner, way, accordance

говори́ть по телефо́ну	to talk over the telephone
узна́ть по газе́там	to find out through the newspapers
посла́ть по по́чте	to send by mail
рабо́тать по пла́ну	to work according to a plan
суди́ть по фа́ктам	to judge by the facts
прийти́ по расписа́нию	to come on schedule
называ́ть по и́мени	to call by the first name

(*e*) Reason, occasion

по боле́зни	on account of sickness
по дру́жбе	on account of, because of (our) friendship
по э́тому слу́чаю	because of this, on account of this

(*f*) Occupation, profession

специали́ст по меха́нике	a specialist in mechanics
учи́тель по профе́ссии	a teacher by profession

(g) Closeness, connection

  товарищ по школе   a school friend
  родственник по жене   a relative through (my) wife

(h) Form or type of activity

  экзамен по математике   an examination in mathematics
  исследование по физике   research in physics

The Accusative

BASIC FUNCTION

In its basic meaning, the accusative denotes the direct object. It is used only with verbs, and answers the questions: кого?—whom? что?—what?

NEGATED SENTENCES

It has been stated (page 51) that transitive negated verbs call for the genitive. However, the accusative case is also quite frequently used:

(Gen.)	Я не пью вина.	I don't drink wine.
(Acc.)	Я не люблю это вино.	I don't like this wine.
(Gen.)	Мы давно не получали писем.	We haven't received any letters for a long time.
(Acc.)	Я не получил вашу телеграмму.	I did not get your telegram.

(a) The accusative is rather frequently used with feminine nouns, both in conversational and literary Russian.

Я не читал эту книгу.   I did not read this book.
Не стану описывать оренбургскую осаду. (Пушкин)   I will not start to describe the siege of Orenburg.

(b) The accusative is used with proper names and with other words pertaining to one particular notion.

Вы не видели Анну Ивановну?   You didn't see Anna Ivanovna?
Он не любит балет.   He doesn't like ballet.
Вы, пожалуйста, не думайте, что я не умею ценить серьёзную музыку. (Тургенев)   Please don't think that I cannot appreciate serious music.*

---

* Example from Грамматика русского языка, АН СССР [Том 2, Синтаксис].

DECLENSION OF NOUNS

(c) The accusative is preferred when reference is made to something definite, known to the persons concerned.

| Не забудь чемодан. | Don't forget the suitcase.* |
| Почему ты не выпил молоко? | Why didn't you drink the milk?* |

(d) The accusative is used to avoid a close succession of nouns in the genitive.

| Он не помнит номер телефона. | He doesn't remember the telephone number. |
| Я не знаю сестру жены. | I don't know my wife's sister. |

Notes:

(a) In the last example, the combined reasons—feminine noun, one definite person, succession of genitives—would simply preclude "сестры жены."

(b) Some English verbs which are followed by a preposition take in Russian a direct object without prepositions.

Я жду учительницу.	I am waiting for the teacher.
Он ищет ключ.	He is looking for the key.
Мы попросили счёт.	We asked for the bill.

SPECIAL CONSTRUCTIONS

(a) The accusative may follow some intransitive verbs when expressing a length of time, a distance, the price, or the weight.

Я работал неделю.	I worked for a week.
Мы проехали одну милю.	We drove one mile.
Перо стоит рубль.	The pen costs a ruble.
Это весит тонну.	This weighs one ton.

(b) The accusative is used after **жаль**.

| Мне жаль его жену. | I am sorry for his wife. |

VERBS GOVERNING THE ACCUSATIVE

As a rule, all transitive verbs are followed by the accusative. The exceptions are the constructions discussed with the genitive case, such as дайте мне хлеба (partitive meaning) and он не пьёт молока (negated predicate).

* Examples from Грамматика русского языка, АН СССР [Том 2, Синтаксис].

PREPOSITIONS

A list of prepositions governing the accusative case is given below. It should be noted that **в, за, на,** and **под** govern the accusative when they express motion, and not location. However, the three prepositions **в, за,** and **на** have quite a variety of additional meanings.

в
    in, into (direction):

Я иду́ в сад.	I am going into the garden.
Он положи́л де́ньги в карма́н.	He put the money in his pocket.

    to (implying "into"):

пойти́ в банк	to go to the bank
посла́ть телегра́мму в Вашингто́н	to send a telegram to Washington

    on (expressing time—with days of the week): в сре́ду, в четве́рг on Wednesday, on Thursday

    at (expressing time with hours): в час, в два часа́, в че́тверть второ́го* at one o'clock, at two o'clock, at quarter past one.

    not translated:

В э́ту ночь я не спал.	That night I did not sleep.
В оди́н прекра́сный день он появи́лся в го́роде.	One fine day he appeared in town.

    in (often pertaining to weather):

В дождли́вую пого́ду лу́чше сиде́ть до́ма.	In rainy weather it is better to stay home.
В таку́ю бу́рю я никуда́ не пое́ду.	In such a storm I won't go anywhere.

    in (expressing the result of an action which has lasted a certain time): В оди́н ме́сяц всё бы́ло гото́во. In one month everything was ready.

    not translated: expressing comparison:

в два ра́за доро́же	twice as expensive
в три ра́за длинне́е	three times longer

включа́я
    including: Три до́ллара, включа́я по́шлину three dollars including the tax.

---

* With the half hour, **в** is followed by the prepositional: в полови́не второ́го—at half past one.

DECLENSION OF NOUNS 67

за   *behind, beyond:*
    Он пошёл за дом.   He went behind the house.
    Мы поéхали за рéку.   We drove beyond the river.
  for (implying exchange, reciprocation):
    рабóтать за товáрища   to work for a friend (in his place)
    купить за рубль   to buy for a ruble
    заплатить за книгу   to pay for the book
    отплатить за чтó-нибудь   to pay back for something
    спасибо за письмó   thanks for the letter
  during: За э́тот год я ви́дел егó тóлько оди́н раз. During this year I saw him only once.
  before (in combination with до): Онá приéхала за недéлю до нас. She came a week before us.

исключáя   *excluding:* исключáя прису́тствующих present company excepted (excluded)

на   *on, onto* (direction):
    пойти́ на у́лицу   to go onto the street
    положи́ть на стол   to put on the table
  to:
    поéхать на лéкцию   to go to a lecture
    пойти́ на базáр   to go to the market
  На is also used with a few public buildings: на пóчту (to the post office); на телегрáф (to the telegraph office); на вокзáл (to the terminal); на стáнцию (to the station); на фáбрику (to the factory); на завóд (to the plant)
  for (future plans): уéхать на всё лéто (to leave for the whole summer); приéхать на недéлю (to come for a week)
  for (purpose, use): Скóлько вы истрáтили на почи́нку? How much did you spend for repairs?
  not translated (expressing a difference in comparing): на год стáрше (a year older); на два мéтра вы́ше (two meters higher)
  На is used with many verbs: серди́ться на (to be angry with); надéяться на (to count on), etc. (see page 287)

несмотря́ на   *in spite of:* Несмотря́ на мою́ прóсьбу, он ничегó не сдéлал. In spite of my request, he did not do anything.

о	*against* (implying shock, or contact with an object)*:* Ло́дка уда́рилась о ка́мни. The boat struck against the rocks.
	Note: **Об** is used with non-jotated vowels: Я уда́рился об э́то. (I hit myself against it.) Very seldom with consonants: Рука́ о́б руку (hand in hand)
по	*up to;* sometimes: *until* (in both cases implying a limit): Он стоя́л по грудь в воде́. He stood in the water up to his chest. У меня́ о́тпуск по двадца́тое сентября́. I am on leave until September 20th.
под	*under:* Положи́те чемода́н под крова́ть. Put the suitcase under the bed.
про	*about:* Он про э́то не писа́л. He didn't write about this.
с (со)	*about; the size of:* Мы жи́ли там с неде́лю. We lived there for about a week. Сли́ва величино́й с я́блоко. A plum the size of an apple. "Ма́льчик с па́льчик" "Tom Thumb"
сквозь	*through* (frequently implying an obstacle)*:* Мы прошли́ сквозь толпу́. We passed (we made our way) through the crowd. Сквозь тума́н ничего́ не́ было ви́дно. Through the fog one couldn't see anything.
спустя́	*thereafter, after that:* Неде́лю спустя́ он уе́хал. A week after that, he left.
че́рез	*over; through:* Мост че́рез ре́ку a bridge over the river Мо́жно пройти́ че́рез парк. One may go through the park. *in* (with expressions of time): Она́ напи́шет че́рез неде́лю. She will write in a week.

DECLENSION OF NOUNS

through, with the help of:

| Он получи́л ме́сто че́рез объявле́ние в газе́те. | He got a job through an ad in the paper. |
| Мы разгова́ривали че́рез перево́дчика. | We talked through an interpreter. |

The Instrumental

BASIC FUNCTION

1. The instrumental expresses the instrument or agent with which or by which something is done. The instrumental answers the questions кем?—by whom? чем?—with (by) what? The instrumental is found in active or passive constructions:

Я пишу́ перо́м.	I am writing with a pen.
Он был ра́нен пу́лей.	He was wounded by a bullet.
Дом постро́ен бра́том.	The house was built by my brother.
Письмо́ начина́лось слова́ми.	The letter began with the words.

Note: Often, for stylistic reasons, a close succession of nouns in the instrumental case has to be avoided. Sentences such as: Письмо́ бы́ло напи́сано ученико́м перо́м (The letter was written *by* the pupil *with* a pen), should be reworded: Учени́к написа́л письмо́ перо́м (The pupil wrote the letter with a pen).

2. The instrumental may express the manner in which something is done.

| Мы говори́ли шёпотом. | We spoke in a whisper. |
| Они́ е́хали по́лным хо́дом. | They drove full speed. |

SPECIAL CONSTRUCTIONS

1. The instrumental may be found in numerous expressions pertaining to manner, time, place, motion (travel), occupation, comparison and size. These expressions, however, have various parallel forms (*without* the instrumental), which are frequently preferred and which are of a wider usage:

(*a*) MANNER:

| петь соловьём | to sing like a nightingale |
| лете́ть стрело́й | to fly like an arrow, i.e. very fast |

Or:

петь как соловей
лететь как стрела.

Note: Here, the manner is merely a suggestion, a rather remote comparison, in contrast to paragraph 2 above, which does not have a parallel form.

(*b*) PLACE:
Они шли берегом. Мы ехали лесом.

Or:

Они шли вдоль берега. Мы ехали через лес.

} They were walking along the shore. We were driving through the wood.

(*c*) MOTION (travel):
ехать пароходом; приехать поездом

Or:

ехать на пароходе; приехать на поезде

} to travel by boat; to come by train

Note: The parallel forms with **на** are preferred in literary Russian. Moreover, with some nouns, they are the only ones which can be used:

ездить на велосипеде	to ride a bicycle
ехать на лодке	to go by (in a) boat
приехать на телеге	to arrive by cart

The same applies, of course, to the non-declined метро and такси.

ехать на метро — to go by subway

(*d*) OCCUPATION:
работать секретарём — to work as a secretary

Or:

работать как секретарь;
работать в качестве секретаря
} (of the same meaning as the above).

DECLENSION OF NOUNS

(*e*) COMPARISON:
го́дом ста́рше   a year older
ча́сом по́зже   one hour later

Or:

на́ год ста́рше
на час по́зже

(*f*) SIZE, MEASURE:
The instrumental is currently used in expressions such as:

длино́й в два ме́тра   two meters long
ве́сом в три килогра́мма   weighing three kilograms
в па́лец толщино́й   one finger thick

2. The instrumental is used with the adjectives **бога́тый, го́рдый, сла́бый, дово́льный, изве́стный**—frequently with their short form.

На́ша страна́ бога́та углём и желе́зом.	Our country is rich in coal and iron.
Мы горды́ э́тими результа́тами.	We are proud of these results.
Он всем дово́лен.	He is pleased with everything.
изве́стный свои́ми труда́ми	known by his works
сла́бый здоро́вьем	of delicate (weak) health

3. Many nouns in the instrumental are adverbialized: у́тром, днём, ве́чером, но́чью, весно́й, ле́том, о́сенью, зимо́й.

4. The instrumental is used in the following expressions:

каки́м о́бразом	how, in what way
таки́м о́бразом	thus, this way
гла́вным о́бразом	chiefly
каки́м-то чу́дом	by some miracle
бо́льшей ча́стью	mostly
одни́м сло́вом	in a word; to sum up
други́ми слова́ми	in other words
ины́ми слова́ми	in other words
тем лу́чше	all the better
тем ху́же	so much the worse
тем бо́лее	all the more
тем не ме́нее	nevertheless
пе́рвым де́лом	first of all

VERBS GOVERNING THE INSTRUMENTAL

(a) Compound predicates

The instrumental is used as part of a compound predicate with the following verbs:

бы́ть	to be
зва́ть, назва́ть	to call, to name
станови́ться, ста́ть	to become
каза́ться, показа́ться	to seem, to appear to be
называ́ться, назва́ться	to be called
назна́чить, назнача́ть	to appoint
ока́зываться, оказа́ться	to turn out to be
остава́ться, оста́ться	to remain
счита́ться	to be considered
явля́ться, яви́ться	to be, to appear

Examples:

Он счита́лся у́мным, но мне он каза́лся глу́пым.	He was considered clever, but to me he seemed stupid.
Э́то явля́ется я́рким приме́ром.	This is a clear (striking) example.

(b) Predicates with the verb бы́ть

In the present tense the implied verb is always followed by the nominative: Он до́ктор. He is a doctor.

In the past tense, the predicate is usually in the instrumental:

Его́ оте́ц был изве́стным инжене́ром.	His father was a well-known engineer.

The instrumental may often indicate a temporary condition—hence its frequent usage with **тогда́, в то вре́мя,** etc.

Я был тогда́ офице́ром.	I was an officer then.
В то вре́мя Москва́ была́ ма́леньким го́родом.	At that time Moscow was a small town.

With a statement expressing something permanent, independent of time, the nominative predicate is used:

Он был брат мое́й ба́бушки.	He was the brother of my grandmother.

DECLENSION OF NOUNS

Его жена́ была́ ру́сская.   His wife was a Russian.

Note: There are many instances when either the instrumental or the nominative may be used (the latter more often in spoken Russian):

Он был о́чень ми́лым челове́ком.   He was a very nice man.

Or:

Он был о́чень ми́лый челове́к.

In the future, the predicate is normally in the instrumental:

Он бу́дет инжене́ром.   He will be an engineer.

The instrumental predicate must be used with **быть** in the infinitive:

Он хо́чет быть до́ктором.   He wants to be a doctor.

The verbs **звать** and **называ́ться** govern either the instrumental, or the nominative:

Его́ зову́т Ива́ном.   His name is John (He is called John).

Or:

Его́ зову́т Ива́н.

(c) The following verbs govern the instrumental:

боле́ть, заболе́ть	to be sick (with)
владе́ть,	to own
завладе́ть	(perf. meaning): to take by force
восхища́ться, восхити́ться	to admire, to appreciate
горди́ться	to be proud of
грози́ть, погрози́ть	to threaten (with)
дорожи́ть	to value
же́ртвовать, поже́ртвовать	to sacrifice
заве́довать	to be in charge of
занима́ться, заня́ться	to work, to be busy with, to devote time to
злоупотребля́ть, злоупотреби́ть	to take unfair advantage
интересова́ться, за-	to be interested in
кома́ндовать	to command
награжда́ть, награди́ть	to award; to reward

любова́ться, на-	to admire
наслажда́ться, наслади́ться	to enjoy thoroughly
облада́ть	to be in possession
ограни́чиваться, ограни́читься	to limit, to confine (oneself) to
по́льзоваться, вос-	to use
пра́вить	to rule; to drive
пренебрега́ть, пренебре́чь	to discount, to disregard
располага́ть	to have at one's disposal
распоряжа́ться, распоряди́ться	to dispose of, to run (something), to give orders
рискова́ть, рискну́ть	to risk
руководи́ть	to lead, to direct
торгова́ть	to trade (in)
увлека́ться, увле́чься	to be absorbed in, to be very much interested in
управля́ть	to rule, to govern; to drive

Examples:

Он кома́ндовал полко́м.	He commanded a regiment.
Она́ горди́ться свои́м сы́ном.	She is proud of her son.
Он дорожи́л свое́й репута́цией.	He valued his reputation.
Вы уме́ете пра́вить автомоби́лем?	Can you drive a car?

PREPOSITIONS

за   *behind, beyond:*

Они́ за до́мом.	They are behind the house.
За реко́й есть лес.	Beyond the river is a wood.
Мы шли за толпо́й.	We were walking behind the crowd.

Note: За столо́м—at the table; at (behind) the desk.

for (meaning to get, to fetch): пойти́ за газе́той—to go for a newspaper

at, during: разгова́ривать за обе́дом—to talk at dinner

Note: Он сиди́т за рабо́той—he is working

конча́я*   *ending* (with, on): начина́я с понеде́льника и конча́я

* Usually a gerund; here considered a verbal preposition.

DECLENSION OF NOUNS

ме́жду
субботой—starting with Monday and ending on Saturday
between:
Я сиде́л ме́жду бра́том и сестро́й.	I sat between the brother and the sister.
Приходи́те ме́жду двумя́ и тремя́.	Come between two and three.

among: Ме́жду ни́ми мно́го иностра́нцев—There are many foreigners among them (same as: среди́ них).

Note: The use of the *genitive* with ме́жду is becoming obsolete. It is still found in a few set expressions, or when referring to similar objects: ме́жду двух огне́й—between two fires. Доро́га шла ме́жду скал.—The road was going between cliffs.

над
(на́до)
above, over:
Самолёт лети́т над го́родом.	The airplane is flying over the city.
Кто живёт над ва́ми?	Who lives above you?

Note: **Над** may follow other verbs in special constructions: смея́ться над ке́м-нибудь—to laugh at somebody; ду́мать над че́м-нибудь—to think something over. (See page 288.)

пе́ред
(пе́редо)
in front of; ahead:
Де́ти игра́ли пе́ред до́мом.	The children were playing in front of the house.
Пе́ред ва́ми больши́е возмо́жности.	There are great opportunities ahead of you.

before:
Он пришёл пе́ред за́втраком.	He came before lunch.

под
(по́до)
under:
Ту́фли под крова́тью.	The slippers are under the bed.
стоя́ть под де́ревом	to stand under a tree
под кома́ндой генера́ла Н	under the command of general N
Он подписа́лся под проше́нием.	He signed his name under the petition.

	под надзо́ром поли́ции	under police surveillance
	под наблюде́нием врача́	under doctor's care
с (со)	*with*:	
	говори́ть с учи́телем	to speak with the teacher
	слу́шать с интере́сом	to listen with interest
	уйти́ с кни́гами	to leave with the books
	дом с са́дом	a house with a garden
	встать с трудо́м	to get up with difficulty
	(*together*) *with*:	
	е́хать с това́рищем	to drive with a friend
	игра́ть с детьми́	to play with the children
	with (against):	
	сража́ться с враго́м	to fight with (against) the enemy

The Prepositional

BASIC FUNCTION

The prepositional case usually expresses location. It is used only with prepositions and answers о ком?—about whom? о чём?—about what? где?—where? etc.

VERBS AND SPECIAL CONSTRUCTIONS

The prepositional case, after **на** or **в**, is used with a few constructions not pertaining to location. (See pages 286, 287.)

говори́ть на трёх языка́х	to speak three languages
игра́ть на скри́пке	to play the violin
ошиби́ться в счёте	to make a mistake in the bill
обвиня́ть в кра́же	to accuse of theft

Note: Similar constructions are found with nouns related to these verbs, for instance: разгово́р на иностра́нном языке́; обвине́ние в кра́же.

PREPOSITIONS

The following prepositions govern the prepositional case:
в (во) *in, at.*

DECLENSION OF NOUNS

This preposition may refer to any of the following:

1. Location:

Мы бы́ли в теа́тре.	We were at the theater.
в его́ конто́ре	in his office

2. Time:

   (*a*) a certain moment; a period of life

в нача́ле уро́ка	at the beginning of the lesson
в конце́ го́да	at the end of the year
в де́тстве	in childhood

   (*b*) a month, a year, or a century

Он прие́хал в ма́рте.	He arrived in March.
Она́ родила́сь в 1932-м году́.	She was born in 1932.
Го́род был осно́ван в семна́дцатом ве́ке.	The city was founded in the 17th century.

3. Emotion:

быть в хоро́шем настрое́нии	to be in a good mood.
в восто́рге от конце́рта	delighted (in ecstasy) with the concert

4. Dress, garment:

Она́ была́ в бе́лом пла́тье.	She was wearing a white dress. (She was in a white dress.)
Он хо́дит в сапога́х.	He wears (walks in) boots.

5. Distance (in which case **в** is not translated):

в одно́м киломе́тре от го́рода	one kilometer from the city
в двух ми́лях отсю́да	two miles from here

на   *on:* стоя́ть на па́лубе   to stand on the deck
at (referring to occasions, events—rather than location):

чита́ть на уро́ке	to read at the lesson
говори́ть на собра́нии	to speak at the meeting

at (with a few public buildings): на вокза́ле, на ста́нции, на заво́де, на фа́брике, на по́чте, на телегра́фе.

Also, with the following: на база́ре (на ры́нке) at the market.

in (with a few proper names and with points of the compass):

    на Кавка́зе   in the Caucasus
    на Украйне   in the Ukraine
    на Ура́ле   in the Ural (Mountains)

на се́вере, на ю́ге, на за́паде, на восто́ке.

by (in, on): на по́езде; на трамва́е; на парохо́де; на велосипе́де; на автомоби́ле; на авто́бусе; на самолёте; на метро́.

> *Note:* **В** may be also used with по́езд, трамва́й, автомоби́ль, авто́бус, метро́; but then it pertains rather to location than to destination. Compare Я прие́хал на авто́бусе. (I came by bus.) with В авто́бусе е́хало мно́го наро́ду. (There were many people riding in the bus.)

not translated (in expressions of time pertaining to weeks):

    Я прие́хал на про́шлой неде́ле.   I arrived last week.

о
(**об, обо**)
    about, concerning:

    Мы говори́ли о му́зыке.   We spoke about music.
    Я написа́л о его́ боле́зни.   I wrote about his illness.
    Вы слы́шали об э́том?   Did you hear about that?
    Она́ не ду́мала обо мне.   She didn't think about me.

> *Note:* **о** is used in front of consonants or jotated vowels; **об** in front of non-jotated vowels; **обо** in front of мне, всём, всех.

по
    after, upon:

    по прие́зде   after the arrival
    по оконча́нии шко́лы   upon completion of the school

> *Note:* In current speech **по́сле** + genitive is of a wider usage: По́сле (его́) прие́зда.

при
    at, by, near:

    Биле́ты продаю́тся при вхо́де.   The tickets are sold at the entrance.

DECLENSION OF NOUNS

при до́ме есть гара́ж	by (near) the house is a garage
при пе́рвом слу́чае	at the first opportunity
при звёздах и при луне́	by the star light and by the light of the moon

with:

Кто при больно́м?	Who is with the patient?
При мне нет де́нег.	I have no money with me.
при уча́стии певи́цы	with the participation of the singer
при всём его́ уме́нии	with all his skill

in the days of, in the presence of, during:

при Петре́ Пе́рвом	in the days (during the reign) of Peter I
при мне	in my presence
при осмо́тре	during the inspection

4. ADJECTIVES

Adjectives have three genders and two numbers. The endings in the plural are the same for all genders. Adjectives are declined; they agree in number, gender, and case with the noun which they modify.

Endings, Singular

	MASCULINE		FEMININE		NEUTER	
HARD	**ый** or **ой**	кра́сный большо́й	**ая**	кра́сная	**ое**	кра́сное
SOFT	**ий**	си́ний	**яя**	си́няя	**ее**	си́нее

Stress: The masculine ending **-ый** is *never* stressed: кра́сный, но́вый. The ending **-ой** is *always* stressed: большо́й, дорого́й. Soft adjectives are never stressed on the ending: ле́тний, сре́дний.

Stems in н

In soft adjectives, the stem ends in **н**. Most of these adjectives refer to time or place.

LIST OF CURRENTLY USED SOFT ADJECTIVES

GROUP I

| у́тренний | morning | весе́нний | spring |
| вече́рний | evening | ле́тний | summer |

ADJECTIVES

осе́нний	autumn, fall	да́вний	ancient, of long standing, old
зи́мний	winter		
ра́нний	early	пре́жний	previous, former
по́здний	late	дре́вний	ancient, antique, old
сего́дняшний	today's		
за́втрашний	tomorrow's	прошлого́дний	last year's
тепе́решний	present, current	трёхле́тний	three-year
тогда́шний	of that time	(четырёхле́тний, etc.)	

GROUP 2

зде́шний	local	да́льний	distant
ве́рхний	upper	вну́тренний	inner, internal
ни́жний	lower	вне́шний	outer, external
пере́дний	front	кра́йний	extreme
сре́дний	middle; average	сосе́дний	neighboring
за́дний	rear	после́дний	last

GROUP 3 Various meanings

си́ний	blue
дома́шний	home; domestic
ли́шний	extra, superfluous
и́скренний	sincere
посторо́нний	alien, strange, unfamiliar

Examples:

вече́рняя газе́та	evening paper
да́льний ро́дственник	distant relative
ли́шнее сло́во	extra word
дома́шние живо́тные	domestic animals

Mixed Adjectives

The so-called "mixed adjectives" have both hard and soft endings. Actually, adjectives ending in **ж, ч, ш, щ,** such as све́жий (fresh), горя́чий (hot), хоро́ший (good), о́бщий (general, common), are soft. Adjectives ending in **г, к, х,** such as стро́гий (strict), ру́сский (Russian), тихий (quiet), are hard. The endings in хорошая, русский, etc., simply follow the spelling rule (page 11).

Plural of Adjectives

As mentioned above, there is no distinction in the plural of adjectives as regards gender. Hard adjectives end in **–ые**; soft in **–ие**.

Hard: новые заводы, фабрики, здания.
Soft: здешние магазины, дороги, поля.

Declension of Adjectives

DECLENSION OF ADJECTIVES IN THE SINGULAR

	Hard			Soft		
	Masc.	Neut.	Fem.	Masc.	Neut.	Fem.
NOM.	бел**ый**	бел**ое**	бел**ая**	син**ий**	син**ее**	син**яя**
GEN.	бел**ого**		бел**ой**	син**его**		син**ей**
DAT.	бел**ому**		бел**ой**	син**ему**		син**ей**
ACC.	бел**ый**	бел**ое**	бел**ую**	син**ий**	син**ее**	син**юю**
(*anim.*)	бел**ого**			син**его**		
INSTR.	бел**ым**		бел**ой**	син**им**		син**ей**
PREP.	бел**ом**		бел**ой**	син**ем**		син**ей**

DECLENSION OF MIXED ADJECTIVES

	Masc.	Neut.	Fem.	Masc.	Neut.	Fem.
NOM.	русск**ий**	русск**ое**	русск**ая**	хорош**ий**	хорош**ее**	хорош**ая**
GEN.	русск**ого**		русск**ой**	хорош**его**		хорош**ей**
DAT.	русск**ому**		русск**ой**	хорош**ему**		хорош**ей**
ACC.	русск**ий**	русск**ое**	русск**ую**	хорош**ий**	хорош**ее**	хорош**ую**
(*anim.*)	русск**ого**			хорош**его**		
INSTR.	русск**им**		русск**ой**	хорош**им**		хорош**ей**
PREP.	русск**ом**		русск**ой**	хорош**ем**		хорош**ей**

ADJECTIVES

	Masc.	Neut.	Fem.
NOM.	больш**о́й**	больш**о́е**	больш**а́я**
GEN.	больш**о́го**		больш**о́й**
DAT.	больш**о́му**		больш**о́й**
ACC.	больш**о́й**	больш**о́е**	больш**у́ю**
(*anim.*)	больш**о́го**		
INSTR.	больш**и́м**		больш**о́й**
PREP.	больш**о́м**		больш**о́й**

DECLENSION OF ADJECTIVES IN THE PLURAL

	Hard	Soft
NOM.	бе́л**ые**	си́н**ие**
GEN.	бе́л**ых**	си́н**их**
DAT.	бе́л**ым**	си́н**им**
ACC.	бе́л**ые**	си́н**ие**
(*anim.*)	бе́л**ых**	си́н**их**
INSTR.	бе́л**ыми**	си́н**ими**
PREP.	бе́л**ых**	си́н**их**

With animate nouns, the accusative of adjectives is like the genitive
(*a*) with *all* nouns in the plural: ста́р**ых** офице́ров, ру́сск**их** дам, больш**и́х** живо́тных.
(*b*) with masculine nouns only—in the singular: ста́р**ого** офице́ра, ру́сскую да́му, большо́е живо́тное.

In the plural, adjectives with stems ending in г, к, х, ж, ч, ш, or щ are declined like **си́ние**.

Qualitative, Relative, and Possessive Adjectives

QUALITATIVE ADJECTIVES express a characteristic which may be possessed in variable degrees: ма́ленький дом (small house); холо́дная вода́ (cold water); большо́е зда́ние (large building).

RELATIVE ADJECTIVES express a characteristic which cannot vary in degree and which is related to a noun: деревя́нный дом (wooden house); вече́рняя газе́та (evening paper); у́личное движе́ние (street traffic).

Note: The characteristic difference between nouns and related adjectives is apparent here in all three Russian expressions, but only in the first English example.

POSSESSIVE ADJECTIVES PERTAINING TO PERSONS

1. Possessive adjectives ending in –ов or –ев are formed from masculine nouns.

Examples:

отцо́в дом   father's house   кня́зева жена́   prince's wife

Their usage is quite obsolete; in present-day speech they are replaced by constructions with the genitive: дом отца́, жена́ кня́зя.
A few set expressions remain:

Дамо́клов меч	The Sword of Damocles
Го́рдиев узел	Gordian knot
Ада́мово я́блоко	Adam's apple
Ахилле́сова пята́	Achilles' heel
А́вгиевы коню́шни	The Stables of Augias
Крокоди́ловы слёзы	Crocodile tears

2. Possessive adjectives ending in –ин are formed from feminine nouns, or masculine nouns ending in the nominative in –а or –я. They are used in current speech, frequently with diminutives.

Ко́лин брат	Nick's brother	Ка́тина сестра́	Kate's sister
Па́пины часы́	Father's (Daddy's) watch	Дя́дин дом	Uncle's house

In their declension, the masculine and neuter adjectives have alternate forms in the genitive and in the dative. The second variant given in the table below is used more frequently than the first.

Declension:

	Masculine	Feminine	Neuter
NOM.	Ко́лин	Ко́лин**а**	Ко́лин**о**

ADJECTIVES

GEN.	Ко́лин**а**	Ко́лин**ой**	Ко́лин**а**
	or: Ко́лин**ого**		or: Ко́лин**ого**
DAT.	Ко́лин**у**	Ко́лин**ой**	Ко́лин**у**
	or: Ко́лин**ому**		or: Ко́лин**ому**
ACC.	Nom. or Gen.	Ко́лин**у**	Ко́лин**о**
INSTR.	Ко́лин**ым**	Ко́лин**ой**	Ко́лин**ым**
PREP.	Ко́лин**ом**	Ко́лин**ой**	Ко́лин**ом**

	Plural
NOM.	Ко́лин**ы**
GEN.	Ко́лин**ых**
DAT.	Ко́лин**ым**
ACC.	Nom. or Gen.
INSTR.	Ко́лин**ыми**
PREP.	Ко́лин**ых**

Adjectives Ending in -ий, -ья, -ье, -ьи

A small number of adjectives, ending in –ий, –ья, –ье, or –ьи, are formed from names of animals, fish, birds and sometimes from persons.

Examples:

во́лчий хвост	wolf's tail (from волк).
медве́жья охо́та	bear hunting (from медве́дь).
воро́нье гнездо́	crow's nest (from воро́на).
рыба́чьи ло́дки	fishermen's boats (from рыба́к).

They are declined as follows:

	Masculine	Neuter	Feminine	Plural
NOM.	во́лч**ий**	во́лч**ье**	во́лч**ья**	во́лч**ьи**
GEN.	во́лч**ьего**	во́лч**ьего**	во́лч**ьей**	во́лч**ьих**
DAT.	во́лч**ьему**	во́лч**ьему**	во́лч**ьей**	во́лч**ьим**
ACC.	Nom. or Gen.	во́лч**ье**	во́лч**ью**	Nom. or Gen.
INSTR.	во́лч**ьим**	во́лч**ьим**	во́лч**ьей**	во́лч**ьими**
PREP.	во́лч**ьем**	во́лч**ьем**	во́лч**ьей**	во́лч**ьих**

Short Adjectives

Short adjectives are formed from most qualitative ones. Masculine short adjectives drop the characteristic endings ый, ой or ий. Feminine short adjectives add –а, neuter –о or –е, plural –ы or –и to the short masculine form:

LONG FORM		SHORT FORM		
Masculine	Masculine	Feminine	Neuter	Plural
краси́вый	краси́в	краси́ва	краси́во	краси́вы
похо́жий	похо́ж	похо́жа	похо́же	похо́жи

1. The following qualitative adjectives have no short form:

   (*a*) Those with the suffixes –ск or –ов which were originally relative adjectives: дру́жеский—friendly; практи́ческий—practical; делово́й—business-like; передово́й—leading, progressive.

   (*b*) A few others: це́льный—whole, entire; родно́й—native, own; отде́льный—separate; про́шлый—past, last. Also, some adjectives pertaining to colors (see p. 89).

2. Short adjectives are practically never formed from soft adjectives in –ний, such as у́тренний, сре́дний.
3. Remnants of the short form of relative adjectives are found in some geographical names: Арха́нгельск, По́лоцк, Смоле́нск, Магнитого́рск.
4. Two important adjectives have a special short form:

   ма́ленький: мал, мала́, мало́, малы́.
   большо́й: вели́к, велика́, велико́, велики́.

5. The following short adjectives do not have a corresponding long form of the same meaning: (я) до́лжен—(I) must, and (я) согла́сен—(I) agree. A long form of рад (glad) does not exist.
6. Short adjectives are not declined. They are used only as predicates: Он бога́т. Она́ была́ краси́ва. Expressions such as: за си́не мо́ре (beyond the blue sea); среди́ бе́ла дня (in the middle of the day, in broad daylight); по бе́лу све́ту (the wide world over), etc. are remnants of old declinable forms. Likewise, a few nouns, originally short adjectives, are regularly declined: спа́льня—bedroom; колоко́льня—belfry; вече́рня—vespers, etc.

Insertion of o or e in Short Adjectives

Short masculine adjectives frequently insert **o** or **e** in front of **н** and **к** when the ending of the adjective has a "cluster of consonants" in the long form.

(*a*) **o** is inserted in front of the suffix **-к**—unless this suffix is preceded by ь, й or ж: краткий: краток—short, brief; низкий: низок—low. Also in: полный: полон—full; смешной: смешон—funny; долгий: долог—long.

(*b*) **e** (**ё**) are inserted in front of **-к** preceded by ь, й or ж: горький: горек—bitter; бойкий: боек—smart, dashing; тяжкий: тяжек—heavy, serious, grave.

e (**ё**) are inserted in front of the suffix **-н**: бедный: беден—poor; больной: болен—sick; нужный: нужен—necessary; умный: умён—clever; сильный: силён—strong.

Also in кислый: кисел—sour; острый: остёр—sharp; хитрый: хитёр—sly, cunning.

> *Notes:*
> (*a*) When the long form ends in **-енный**, the short adjective—with few exceptions ends in **-ен** (**-ный** is simply dropped from the ending): уверенный: уверен—sure.
> (*b*) Feminine, neuter, and plural short adjectives do not insert **o** or **e**: полна, горько, бедны.

Usage of Adjectives

Long and Short Form

1. Both the long and short form may be used as predicates: Она очень **красивая** and она очень **красива**. The long form is found in expressions equivalent to the English "an old one," "a new one," "a good one," etc.

    Эта дорога очень хорошая.   This road is a very good one.

In conversational Russian, the preference often goes to the long form, except in a few instances:

бога́т	rich	непра́в	wrong
бо́лен	sick	похо́ж	like
винова́т	at fault; "sorry"	прав	right
дово́лен	pleased	свобо́ден	free
го́лоден	hungry	согла́сен	agree(s)
гото́в	ready	сча́стлив	happy
жена́т	married (said of a man)	сыт	not hungry
жив	alive	за́нят	busy
наме́рен	intend(s)	здоро́в	well (in good health)

Also, to a certain degree, with:

краси́в	pretty, handsome	стар	old
мо́лод	young	у́зок	narrow
слаб	weak	широ́к	wide

2. The short form sometimes—when logically possible—indicates a temporary condition, in contrast to a more permanent one conveyed by the long form:

Он бо́лен.	He is sick.
Он больно́й.	He is a sick man.

3. Frequently, the short form has a relative value:

Кварти́ра не ма́ленькая, но для нас она́ мала́.	The apartment is not small, but for us it is.

4. The short form is used with the subjects всё and э́то:

Всё я́сно.	Everything is clear.
Э́то о́чень интере́сно.	It is very interesting.

5. The short form is used in certain set expressions: бу́дьте добры́—be so kind; бу́дьте здоро́вы (meaning, occasionally: "good-bye" or "bless you"—when sneezing) (lit.: "be well," "be healthy"), etc.

6. The long form only is used in other set expressions—often in those with a figurative meaning:

кру́глый год	the year round
на чёрный день	for a rainy ("black") day

ADJECTIVES

больно́й вопро́с	a thorny (painful) question
глубо́кая ста́рость	very advanced age
свобо́дное вре́мя	free time
прямо́й у́гол	right angle
ско́рый по́езд	express, fast train
проливно́й дождь	shower, drenching rain

7. The usage of the long form prevails with colors. In fact, many adjectives pertaining to colors do not have any short form at all. Thus: голубо́й—azure, sky-blue; кори́чневый—brown; сире́невый—lilac, etc. Originally, related to nouns (го́лубь—pigeon; кори́ца—cinnamon; сире́нь—lilac)—they still possess the characteristics of relative adjectives, i.e. no short form, for instance.

8. The short and long forms are not used together as two attributives of the same noun. One may say: Она́ умна́ и краси́ва or Она́ у́мная и краси́вая, but not "Она́ умна́ и краси́вая."

Agreement Between Nouns and Qualifiers

1. When nouns are qualified by more than one word (adjective, numeral), they may stand in the singular or in the plural: Большо́й и ма́ленький нож—a big and a small knife, or, Большо́й и ма́ленький ножи́
The usage of the singular apparently prevails. It is used:

(*a*) When the logical connection between the attributes is in evidence:

програ́мма для нача́льной и сре́дней шко́лы (not: школ)—program for the grade school and the high school

глаго́лы соверше́нного и несоверше́нного ви́да—perfective and imperfective verbs*

(*b*) When the idea of singularity is clearly present: не но́вый, а ста́рый костю́м—not a new, but an old suit; ру́сский и́ли англи́йский язы́к—the Russian or the English language.

(*c*) Also, with ordinal numerals and possessive pronouns: ме́жду пе́рвым и вторы́м до́мом—between the first and the second house; Он написа́л мое́й и ва́шей сестре́.—He wrote to my and to your sister.

* Examples from Доброми́слов и Розента́ль: Тру́дные вопро́сы грамма́тики и правописа́ния.

2. In the reverse case (i.e., *one* adjective qualifying *two* nouns) the adjective may also be in the singular or in the plural. It has been claimed that, for example, "вку́сный за́втрак и обе́д" may imply that only the lunch was nice. Yet, "вку́сные за́втрак и обе́д" sounds uneasy. (Stylistically, the best may well be "вку́сный за́втрак и о́чень вку́сный обе́д.")

The Comparative Degree of Adjectives

Only qualitative adjectives have a comparative degree. There are, however, a few qualitative adjectives which, because of their meaning, preclude the idea of a comparison: жена́тый—married; живо́й—alive; мёртвый—dead; холосто́й—bachelor; слепо́й—blind, etc.
There are two forms of the comparative degree: the *Simple* and the *Compound*.

THE SIMPLE COMPARATIVE

1. In the simple form, the suffix **-ee** is added to the stem: long—дли́нный: длинне́е; poor—бе́дный: бедне́е
Sometimes, in poetry for instance, the suffix **-ей** is added: nice—ми́лый: миле́й; white—бе́лый: беле́й
The STRESS in the simple comparative usually falls on the first **e** of the ending: длинне́е, миле́е. When the adjective has three syllables or more, the stress remains fixed: pleasant—прия́тный: прия́тнее; interesting—интере́сный: интере́снее.
2. Sometimes the simple comparative takes the prefix **по**. This prefix implies "somewhat," "a little bit":

Я хочу́ ко́мнату побо́льше.	I want a room somewhat larger.
У вас есть что́-нибудь полу́чше?	Do you have anything a little bit better?

3. Many adjectives have an irregular simple form:

    (a) Those with stems ending in г, к, х, д, т, and ст add **e** and undergo a mutation of consonants:

    dear, expensive—дорого́й: доро́же
    easy, light—лёгкий: ле́гче
    quiet—ти́хий: ти́ше

    young—молодо́й: моло́же
    rich—бога́тый: бога́че
    clean—чи́стый: чи́ще

ADJECTIVES

(*b*) Others have various irregularities in their formation:

near, close—бли́зкий: бли́же [a]
big, large—большо́й: бо́льше [b]
high, tall—высо́кий: вы́ше
deep—глубо́кий: глу́бже
distant—далёкий: да́льше
cheap—дешёвый: деше́вле
yellow—жёлтый: желте́е [c]
liquid—жи́дкий: жи́же
short—коро́ткий: коро́че
small, little—ма́ленький: ме́ньше
low—ни́зкий: ни́же

bad—плохо́й: ху́же
late—по́здний: по́зже, поздне́е
rare—ре́дкий: ре́же
sweet—сла́дкий: сла́ще
old—ста́рый: старе́е, ста́рше [d]
thin—то́нкий: то́ньше
narrow—у́зкий: у́же
good—хоро́ший: лу́чше
thin—худо́й: худе́е
bad—худо́й: ху́же
wide—широ́кий: ши́ре

Notes:

(*a*) In some comparatives, the suffix -к is dropped: бли́зкий: бли́же; ре́дкий: ре́же.

(*b*) In current speech the forms бо́лее and ме́нее function as adverbs

(*c*) There is no mutation of consonants in жёлтый: желте́е.

(*d*) Старе́е is regular. Ста́рше is also formed from ста́рый but it refers to a difference in age, comparable to "elder," "senior."

4. The simple comparative is not formed from:

(*a*) Adjectives with the suffix **-ск**: дру́жеский—friendly; крити́ческий—critical.

(*b*) Adjectives with the suffixes **-ов** or **-ев**: делово́й—businesslike; боево́й—battle, fighting, warlike.

(*c*) Certain other adjectives:

больно́й	sick	пло́ский	flat
гнило́й	rotten	отста́лый	retarded
го́рдый	proud	ро́бкий	timid
го́рький	bitter	ско́льзкий	slippery
де́рзкий	impertinent	уста́лый	tired
ли́пкий	sticky	устаре́лый	outdated, antiquated
ли́шний	superfluous	стра́нный	strange

THE COMPOUND COMPARATIVE

In the compound form, **бо́лее** (or **ме́нее**) are added to the positive degree. Adjectives in this form have three genders and two numbers:

Singular: бо́лее тру́дный уро́к (a more difficult lesson); бо́лее интере́сная кни́га (a more interesting book); бо́лее удо́бное кре́сло (a more comfortable armchair)

Plural: бо́лее дешёвые проду́кты (cheaper products, food stuffs)

Usage of the Comparative Degree

SIMPLE COMPARATIVE

(*a*) The simple form is not declined. It is normally used as a predicate following the subject:

| Эта кни́га интере́снее. | This book is more interesting. |
| Экза́мен был трудне́е. | The examination was harder. |

(*b*) Occasionally, the simple form may be a qualifying word:

| Он написа́л письмо́ длинне́е моего́. | He wrote a letter longer than mine. |

COMPOUND COMPARATIVE

(*a*) The adjective in the compound form is declined. This form has to be used with oblique cases:

| говори́ть о бо́лее интере́сной кни́ге | to speak about a more interesting book |
| гото́виться к бо́лее тру́дному экза́мену | to study for a more difficult examination |

(*b*) The compound comparative can be used with short adjectives:

Э́то бо́лее интере́сно. This is more interesting.

(*c*) The compound form may be used with practically any qualitative adjective. However, with хоро́ший, плохо́й, ма́ленький, and большо́й the simple form should be used: лу́чше, ху́же, ме́ньше, and бо́льше (not "бо́лее большо́й," etc.).

CONSTRUCTIONS EXPRESSING A COMPARISON

A comparison may be expressed with the aid of the genitive case, or with the conjunction **чем** (sometimes with **не́жели**, also meaning "than"):

Сестра́ краси́вее бра́та.

Сестра́ краси́вее, чем брат.

ADJECTIVES

With the compound form, the construction with **чем** has to be used:

> Сестра более красива, чем брат.

The construction with чем must be used, of course, with parts of speech which are not declined:

> Сегодня теплее, чем вчера.

The Superlative Degree of Adjectives

Only qualitative adjectives have a superlative degree. There are two forms of the superlative: the simple and the compound.

THE SIMPLE SUPERLATIVE

1. The simple superlative is formed by adding to the stem of the positive degree

   (*a*) the suffix **–ейший (–ейшая, –ейшее, –ейшие)**:

бедный: беднейший (человек)	the poorest (man).
богатая: богатейшая (страна)	the richest (country).

   (*b*) the suffix **–айший (–айшая, –айшее, –айшие)** to the stems ending in г, к or х; a mutation of consonants then takes place:

строгий: строжайший (выговор)	the sternest (reprimand).
высокие: высочайшие (горы)	the highest (mountains).

2. A few superlatives are formed irregularly: хороший: лучший; плохой: худший; маленький: меньший.

3. A superlative may be formed by using the prefix **наи–**. In current speech this prefix is added only to the following adjectives: больший, меньший, высший, лучший and худший (See page 96.)

наилучший способ	the (very) best way
наименьшие потери	the smallest losses

4. Sometimes, in conversational Russian, the superlative is formed by adding the prefix **пре–** to the positive degree:

премилый человек	an awfully nice man
пренеприятное известие	very pleasant news

The simple superlative is declined:

решить труднейшую задачу	to solve a most difficult problem
оказаться в пренеприятном положении	to find oneself in a most unpleasant situation
с наилучшими пожеланиями	with (very) best wishes

THE COMPOUND SUPERLATIVE

The compound superlative is formed by adding the pronoun самый (the most) to the positive degree. The compound form has three genders and two numbers:

Masculine: самый интересный урок
Feminine: самая интересная лекция } SINGULAR
Neuter: самое интересное письмо

самые интересные книги } PLURAL

Both parts of this form are declined:

перед самым интересным уроком	before the most interesting lesson
после самой интересной лекции	after the most interesting lecture

The compound superlative may also be formed with наиболее (the most), or наименее (the least), added to the positive degree of any gender or number.

In this construction, only the adjective is declined:

перед наиболее интересным уроком	before the most interesting lesson
после наименее интересных лекций	after the least interesting lectures

Usage of the Superlative Degree

SIMPLE FORM

(a) The simple form is used infrequently. It does enter, however, into a number of expressions where actually no comparison is being made. In these, the superlative merely notes that a particular characteristic is possessed to a great degree:

милейшие люди	very nice people
глупейшее письмо	an awfully stupid letter

ADJECTIVES

в кратча́йший срок	in an extremely short time (as soon as possible)
всё к лу́чшему	everything is for the best
он измени́лся к ху́дшему	he has changed for the worst
чисте́йший предрассу́док	pure prejudice
вы́сшее образова́ние	highest (college) education
до мельча́йших подро́бностей	with minute details
с лу́чшими пожела́ниями	with best wishes
с велича́йшим удово́льствием	with greatest pleasure

(b) The simple superlative is not formed from adjectives which do not have a simple comparative (page 91, para. 4), nor from certain others: гро́мкий—loud; молодо́й—young; сухо́й—dry; у́зкий—narrow.

COMPOUND FORM

(a) The compound superlative with са́мый is the one most widely used.

(b) The compound superlative with наибо́лее or наиме́нее is sometimes encountered in conversational Russian, but more often in written or official language.

CONSTRUCTIONS USED WITH THE SUPERLATIVE DEGREE

The superlative degree may be expressed:

(a) With the aid of qualifiers in the genitive case:

са́мая тру́дная часть грамма́тики   the hardest part of the grammar

(b) With the simple comparative followed by the genitive case of всё or все.

Это доро́же всего́.   This is more valuable than anything else.
Он ста́рше всех.   He is the oldest (of all).

(c) With the aid of prepositions—most frequently with из.

велича́йшее из его́ произведе́ний   the greatest of his works

Note also:

са́мый высо́кий дом в го́роде   the highest house in the city
са́мый тала́нтливый среди́ начи-   the most talented among the
на́ющих писа́телей   beginning writers

(d) Frequently, with the combinations оди́н из, одна́ из, одно́ из, одни́ из.

оди́н из са́мых ва́жных вопро́сов	one of the most important questions
одна́ из са́мых тру́дных зада́ч	one of the hardest problems

Adjectives with Variable Meanings

The adjectives бо́льший (greater); ме́ньший (lesser); лу́чший (better, best); ху́дший (worst); вы́сший (highest); ни́зший (lowest); ста́рший (elder, senior), and мла́дший (younger, junior) are in a class by themselves.

They have lost to a great extent the characteristics of the simple comparative degree to which they originally belonged:

1. They have three genders, two numbers, and they are declined:

в лу́чшем слу́чае	in the best case
получи́ть вы́сшую награ́ду	to get the highest award

2. Their *usage* as a comparative degree is quite limited:

(a) Actually, only лу́чший is frequently used—both as a comparative and as a superlative:

Я не зна́ю лу́чшей доро́ги.	I don't know a better road. (*comp.*)
Он лу́чший учени́к в кла́ссе.	He is the best pupil in class (*superl.*)
Э́то лу́чший вы́ход.	This is the best way out. (*superl.*)

(b) Бо́льший and ме́ньший are used only as comparatives, and are found as a rule, in a limited number of expressions pertaining to abstract notions.*

бо́льшая часть вре́мени	the greater part of the time
из двух зол ме́ньшее	the lesser of two evils

(c) Ху́дший is used only as a superlative:

в ху́дшем слу́чае	in the worst case

* Совреме́нный ру́сский язы́к. Морфоло́гия. Под реда́кцией акад. В. В. Виногра́дова.

ADJECTIVES

(*d*) Высший and низший are used in a number of set expressions, such as:

высшее образование	college (*lit.:* highest) education
низшая школа	elementary (*lit.:* lowest) school

and also as superlatives:

высшая похвала	highest praise
низший уровень	lowest level

(*e*) Старший and младший are used in a number of set expressions only:

старший брат	eldest brother
студенты старших курсов	upper class students
младший лейтенант	second lieutenant

(*f*) Finally, лучший and худший may combine with самый to form the *compound* superlative:

самый лучший	the (very) best
самое худшее	the worst (of all)

(The normal compound superlative **самый** followed by the positive degree can also be used here: самый хороший, самое плохое.)

5. PRONOUNS

Pronouns are divided into the following classes:

Personal:	я; они́.
Possessive:	мой; ваш.
Demonstrative:	э́тот; тот.
Definite:	ка́ждый; весь.
Interrogative—Relative:	кто; что.
Negative:	никто́; ничто́.
Indefinite:	кто́-то; что́-нибудь.

Personal Pronouns

Declension of Personal Pronouns

The personal pronouns: я, ты, он, она́, оно́, мы, вы, они́ are declined as follows:

	I	you (thou)	he	it	she
NOM.	я	ты	он	оно́	она́
GEN.	меня́	тебя́	его́		её
DAT.	мне	тебе́	ему́		ей
ACC.	меня́	тебя́	его́		её
INSTR.	мной	тобо́й	им		ей
PREP.	мне	тебе́	нём		ней

	we	you	they
NOM.	мы	вы	они́
GEN.	нас	вас	их
DAT.	нам	вам	им
ACC.	нас	вас	их
INSTR.	на́ми	ва́ми	и́ми
PREP.	нас	вас	них

Notes:

(*a*) The instrumental of я, ты, она́ has a variant form: мно́ю, тобо́ю, е́ю.

(*b*) To express possession, the possessive pronouns мой, твой, etc., are used (and not the genitive case меня́, тебя́, etc.).

(*c*) After most prepositions, third person *personal* pronouns take an initial **н**. Examples: у него́, к ней, с ни́ми.

(*d*) After the prepositions (or prepositional expressions) благодаря́, вне, вопреки́, всле́дствие, за исключе́нием, навстре́чу, напереко́р, по по́воду, согла́сно the letter н is *not* added: благодаря́ ему́—thanks to him; навстре́чу ей—toward her.

(*e*) The prepositions в, к, над, пе́ред, под, and с become **во, ко**, in front of **мне**, and **надо, передо, подо, со** in front of **мной**.

Он пришёл ко мне.	He came to (see) me.
Она́ разочарова́лась во мне.	She became disappointed in me.
Кто идёт со мной?	Who is coming with me?

But:

Он прице́лился в меня́.	He aimed at me.
Начни́те с меня́.	Begin with me.

(*f*) "About me" is обо мне.

Usage of Personal Pronouns

1. Note the characteristic use of мы in constructions such as:

мы с ва́ми	we, you, and I
мы с бра́том	we (two), my brother, and myself

2. Personal pronouns may pertain to objects, when referring to something previously mentioned:

Это но́вая кни́га. Она́ о́чень интере́сная.	That's a new book. It is very interesting.
Где моё перо́? Я не могу́ его́ найти́.	Where is my pen? I can't find it.

3. Omission of personal pronouns

(*a*) Personal pronouns are sometimes omitted in a sentence, often in answer to a question. This may or may not render the sentence somewhat casual:

—Что вы делали днём?	—What did you do this afternoon?
—Играл в теннис.	—Played tennis.
—Что он ответил?	—What did he answer?
—Сказал, что придёт завтра.	—Said he'd come tomorrow.

A great deal depends, however, on the situation and on the tone. Omitting **я** in the following sentences has really nothing casual about it; on the contrary, it modestly draws away the attention from the first person:

| Где он живёт?—Не знаю, правда. | Where does he live?—I don't know, really. |
| Она уже уехала?—Нет, не думаю. | Has she already left?—No, I don't think so. |

Other examples (not in answer to a question):

Пишу Вам с просьбой.	I am writing you with the request.
Простите, что не ответил раньше.	Forgive me for not answering earlier.
Благодарю вас.	Thank you.

(*b*) The pronouns **ты** and **вы** are frequently omitted with the verb знать—when the speaker hardly expects an affirmative answer:

| Знаешь, кого я сейчас встретил? | Do you know whom I just met? |
| Знаете, что я видел во сне? | Do you know what I dreamed about? |

(Compare this to Вы знаете его адрес?—which is definitely a question.)

(*c*) In particular, the omission of the pronoun **они** makes the sentence impersonal:

Здесь не дают на чай.	One doesn't tip here.
Здесь говорят по-английски.	English spoken (a sign on a shop window, for example).
Там чинят дорогу.	They are repairing the road over there. (The road is being repaired.)

The Reflexive Pronoun себя—Self

This pronoun is declined like the personal pronoun ты (page 98). It cannot be the subject of a sentence and has no nominative case.

Gen.	Dat.	Acc.	Instr.	Prep.
себя	себе	себя	собой	себе

It can be used with any noun or personal pronoun, singular or plural.

Я купи́л э́то для себя́.	I bought it for myself.
Она́ себе́ ни в чём не отка́зывает.	She does not deny herself anything.
Э́тот челове́к счита́ет себя́ о́чень у́мным.	This man considers himself very clever.
Почему́ вы недово́льны собо́й?	Why are you displeased with yourself?
Вы написа́ли о себе́?	Did you write about yourself?

Possessive Pronouns

Declension of Possessive Pronouns

(a) Masculine and Neuter

	my, mine	your(s), fam.	our(s)	your(s)	"one's own"
NOM.	мой моё	твой твоё	наш на́ше	ваш ва́ше	свой своё
GEN.	моего́	твоего́	на́шего	ва́шего	своего́
DAT.	моему́	твоему́	на́шему	ва́шему	своему́
ACC.	мой моё	твой твоё	наш на́ше	ваш ва́ше	свой своё
(anim.)	моего́	твоего́	на́шего	ва́шего	своего́
INSTR.	мои́м	твои́м	на́шим	ва́шим	свои́м
PREP.	моём	твоём	на́шем	ва́шем	своём

(b) Feminine

	my, mine	your(s), fam.	our(s)	your(s)	"one's own"
NOM.	моя́	твоя́	на́ша	ва́ша	своя́
GEN.	мое́й	твое́й	на́шей	ва́шей	свое́й
DAT.	мое́й	твое́й	на́шей	ва́шей	свое́й
ACC.	мою́	твою́	на́шу	ва́шу	свою́
INSTR.	мое́й	твое́й	на́шей	ва́шей	свое́й
PREP.	мое́й	твое́й	на́шей	ва́шей	свое́й

(c) Plural—all genders

NOM.	мои́	твои́	на́ши	ва́ши	свои́
GEN.	мои́х	твои́х	на́ших	ва́ших	свои́х
DAT.	мои́м	твои́м	на́шим	ва́шим	свои́х
ACC.	мои́	твои́	на́ши	ва́ши	свои́
(anim.)	мои́х	твои́х	на́ших	ва́ших	свои́х
INSTR.	мои́ми	твои́ми	на́шими	ва́шими	свои́ми
PREP.	мои́х	твои́х	на́ших	ва́ших	свои́х

Agreement: Possessive pronouns pertaining to the first and second persons *agree* with their nouns in gender, number, and case:

Вы нашли́ мою́ кни́гу? (*fem. sing. acc.*)
Напиши́те ва́шим друзья́м. (*plural dat.*)

Possessive pronouns third person—его́—his, её—her, их—their—*never change*; they are not declined, nor do they add an н after a preposition:

GEN.	Я сиде́л о́коло его́ бра́та.
DAT.	Я пришёл к его́ бра́ту.
ACC.	Я написа́л про его́ бра́та.
INSTR.	Я рабо́тал с его́ бра́том.
PREP.	Я говори́л о его́ бра́те.

Usage of Possessive Pronouns

1. Possessive pronouns are sometimes omitted in speech, when the implication is obvious.

Я спрошу́ жену́.	I will ask (my) wife.
Он по́днял ру́ку.	He raised (his) hand.
Сними́те шля́пу.	Take off (your) hat.

PRONOUNS

2. The pronouns свой своя, своё, свои refer to "one's own":

    Я нашёл своё перо.   I found my (own) pen.

Note: This, of course, may not necessarily imply actual ownership, but simply a close personal relation or connection:

Он пошёл в свою контору.	He went to his office.
Я лучше пойду к своему доктору.	I had better go to my own doctor.

(*a*) These pronouns are practically never used in the nominative case:

Я видел своего (*acc.*) учителя.   I saw my teacher.
But:
Мой (*nom.*) учитель видел меня.   My teacher saw me.

A few set expressions are exceptions to this rule:

свой человек—close friend, "a member of the crowd"

Своя рубашка ближе к телу—Charity begins at home (*lit.:* One's own shirt is nearer to the body)—a proverb.

Свой may be used in the nominative with the verb есть, given or implied:

У него, очевидно, есть (были) свои причины.	He apparently has (had) his own reasons.
У каждого барона своя фантазия.	Every baron has his own whim (a proverb, or rather a facetious saying).

(*b*) With the first and second persons, singular or plural, the use of свой is optional:

Я потерял свою книгу.	I lost my book.
or: Я потерял мою книгу.	
Напишите свой адрес.	Write your address.
or: Напишите ваш адрес.	

(*c*) Свой should be used with the third person, singular or plural:

	Он потерял свою книгу.	He lost his book.
Compare to:	Он потерял его книгу.	He lost his (someone else's) book.

(d) Свой is not used with no "acting person" present. Examples:

Банк недалеко́ от мое́й конто́ры.	The bank is not far from my office.
В его́ до́ме пять ко́мнат.	There are five rooms in his house.

The following examples will further illustrate the usage of свой vs. его́:

Я сказа́л, что я продаю́ свой (or: мой) дом.	I said that I am selling my house.
Он сказа́л, что он продаёт свой дом. (*third person*)	He said that he is selling his house.
Он сказа́л, что его́ дом продаётся. (*nom.*)	He said that his house is for sale.
Он сказа́л, что в его́ до́ме нет отопле́ния.	He said that there is no heating in his house.

(no "acting person" in the subordinate clause)

Demonstrative Pronouns

The demonstrative pronouns are:

	Masculine	*Feminine*	*Neuter*	
SINGULAR	э́тот	э́та	э́то	this, that
	тот	та	то	that
	тако́й	така́я	тако́е	such
PLURAL, all genders:	э́ти		these, those	
	те		those	
	таки́е		such	

The pronoun сей (сия́, сие́, сий) "this," "that"—now obsolete—enters into a few set expressions:

сию́ мину́ту	just a minute, right away
до сих пор	up to here, up to now, so far
на сей раз	for this time
ни с того́, ни с сего́	suddenly and for no reason
при сём	"enclosed," herewith

PRONOUNS

It also enters into:

сегóдня	today
сейчáс	now, at present; immediately

Declension of Demonstrative Pronouns

	Singular						Plural	
	Masc.	*Fem.*	*Neut.*	*Masc.*	*Fem.*	*Neut.*		
NOM.	э́тот	э́та	э́то	тот	та	то	э́ти	те
GEN.	э́того	э́той	э́того	тогó	той	тогó	э́тих	тех
DAT.	э́тому	э́той	э́тому	томý	той	томý	э́тим	тем
ACC.	э́тот	э́ту	э́то	тот	ту	то	э́ти	те
(anim.)	э́того			тогó			э́тих	тех
INSTR.	э́тим	э́той	э́тим	тем	той	тем	э́тими	тéми
PREP.	э́том	э́той	э́том	том	той	том	э́тих	тех

Такóй (–ая, –ое, –ие) is declined like an adjective (of the type морскóй, большóй etc.). Thus:

NOM.	такóй большóй дом
GEN.	такóго большóго дóма
DAT.	такóму большóму дóму
ACC.	такóй большóй дом
INSTR.	таки́м больши́м дóмом
PREP.	такóм большóм дóме

Usage of Demonstrative Pronouns

1. Demonstrative pronouns agree in gender, number, and case with their nouns:

| Я написáл э́той дáме | (*fem., sing., dat.*) |
| Я знáю э́того господи́на | (*masc. sing. anim. acc.*) |

2. The pronoun э́то may be a qualifying word: Э́то крéсло нóвое. Or, it may be the subject of a sentence, in which case it remains unchanged regardless of the gender or number of the nouns: Э́то наш дом. Э́то моя́ кóмната. Э́то крéсло. Э́то нóвые кни́ги. Э́то нáши ученики́ и учени́цы.

3. The translation of "it."

(a) As stated on page 99, "it" is translated by **он, она́,** or **оно́** when referring to something previously mentioned.

| Вы чита́ли э́ту кни́гу? **Она́** о́чень интере́сная. | Did you read this book? It is very interesting. |

(b) However, when the predicate of the second sentence is a noun, "it" should be translated "**э́то**."

| Вы чита́ли э́ту кни́гу? **Э́то** но́вый рома́н Шо́лохова. | Did you read this book? It is a new novel by Sholokhov. |

In impersonal sentences, "it" is omitted in translation.

| Сего́дня о́чень хо́лодно. | It is very cold today. |
| Бы́ло по́здно. | It was late. |

4. (a) **Тот, та, то, те** may refer to something rather remote in space or in time:

Ви́дите ту ло́дку?	Do you see that boat?
В то вре́мя я жил недалеко́ от Москвы́.	At that time (in those days) I lived not far from Moscow.
В той стране́ был обы́чай.	In that country there was a custom.

(b) **Тот** may emphasize contrast:

| Э́ту кни́гу я чита́л, а ту нет. | This book I read, that one no. |

(c) Sometimes, **тот** means "the one," and **то** means "(that) what." In this case they carry additional emphasis:

Тот, кто хо́чет пойти́, пусть идёт.	The one who wants to go, may go.
То, что вы сказа́ли, я уже́ зна́ю.	What you said, I already know.
Да́йте мне то, что я прошу́.	Give me what I'm asking for.

Note: In paragraph (c) above, тот and то may not be replaced with э́тот or э́то.

Definite Pronouns

The definite pronouns (masc., fem., neut., and plural) are:

сам, сама́, само́, са́ми	self
са́мый, са́мая, са́мое, са́мые	the very; the most; the same (in combination with тот, э́тот, or тот же)
весь, вся, всё, все	all, the whole
вся́кий, вся́кая, вся́кое, вся́кие	any (kind)
ка́ждый, ка́ждая, ка́ждое, ка́ждые	each, every (one by one)
любо́й, люба́я, любо́е, любы́е	any (one you may wish)

Declension of Definite Pronouns

1. Сам

	Masc.	Fem.	Neut.	Plural
NOM.	сам	сама́	само́	са́ми
GEN.	самого́	само́й	самого́	сами́х
DAT.	самому́	само́й	самому́	сами́м
ACC.	сам	саму́	само́	са́ми
(anim.)	самого́			сами́х
INSTR.	сами́м	само́й	сами́м	сами́ми
PREP.	само́м	само́й	само́м	сами́х

Notes: The feminine accusative may be самоё; however, the form **саму́** given in the table above is preferred in current speech.

The feminine instrumental may be само́ю.

2. Са́мый, вся́кий, ка́ждый, and любо́й.

These pronouns are declined like adjectives (with the stress fixed on the stem). For example:

NOM.	са́мый
GEN.	са́мого
DAT.	са́мому

ACC.	са́мый
(anim.)	са́мого
INSTR.	са́мым
PREP.	са́мом

3. **Весь.**

	Singular			Plural
	Masc.	*Fem.*	*Neut.*	
NOM.	весь	вся	всё	все
GEN.	всего́	всей	всего́	всех
DAT.	всему́	всей	всему́	всем
ACC.	весь	всю	всё	все
(anim.)	всего́			всех
INSTR.	всем	всей	всем	все́ми
PREP.	всём	всей	всём	всех

Usage of Definite Pronouns

1. Сам

The pronoun **сам** refers to something done without any help, or implies *personally*, *in person*:

Я сам написа́л э́то.	I wrote it myself (personally).
Я сам говори́л с дире́ктором.	I personally spoke with the director.
Я говори́л с сами́м дире́ктором.	I spoke with the director himself (in person).

Сам may be used with the reflexive pronoun **себя́**:

Вы са́ми себе́ противоре́чите.	You (yourself) contradict yourself.

Note: A comparison between the usage of сам, себе́, and сам себе́ may be illustrated by the following examples:

Он сам постро́ил дом.	He built the house himself.
Он постро́ил себе́ дом.	He built a house for himself.
Он сам себе́ постро́ил дом.	He (personally) built a house for himself.

PRONOUNS

2. **Са́мый** has the following meanings:

(a) *the very*—when used with nouns:

Мы сиде́ли там до са́мого конца́. We sat there till the very end.

(b) *the most* (or else corresponds to the ending "-est")—when used with the superlative degree of adjectives:

Он живёт в са́мой дорого́й гости́нице. He lives in the most expensive hotel.
Это са́мая коро́ткая доро́га. This is the shortest road.

(c) *the* (emphatic), *the same*, *this very*—when used with тот (тот же) or э́тот:

Это тот са́мый челове́к, о кото́ром я говори́л. This is *the man* about whom I spoke.
Мы мо́жем встре́титься в том же са́мом рестора́не. We can meet at the same restaurant.
на э́том са́мом ме́сте at this very spot

3. **Весь**

(a) Весь means *all*, sometimes *the whole*.

Всё э́то я зна́ю. All this I know.
Я рабо́тал весь день. I worked all day (the whole day).

Note: A *whole* is translated by **це́лый**.

Я ждал це́лый час. I waited for a whole hour.
Мы жи́ли там це́лый год. We lived there for a whole year.

(b) The neuter **всё** also means *everything*. The plural **все** also means *everybody*:

Он всё зна́ет. He knows everything.
Все рабо́тали. Everybody was working.

4. **Вся́кий** means *any; all kinds of*.

во вся́ком слу́чае in any case
Он расска́зывал вся́кие исто́рии. He was telling all kinds of stories.

5. **Ка́ждый** means *each, every*.

Ка́ждый день шёл дождь.	Each day it rained.
В ка́ждой апте́ке продаётся аспири́н.	In every (single) drugstore they sell aspirin.

Note: Ка́ждый usually occurs in the singular. It is found in the plural with nouns which have no singular:

ка́ждые су́тки	every 24 hours

Also, in constructions with numerals:

Ка́ждые пять мину́т звони́л телефо́н.	Every five minutes the telephone rang.

6. **Любо́й**, in contrast to ка́ждый, implies *any one* (you may wish).

Вы мо́жете купи́ть аспири́н в любо́й апте́ке.	You may buy aspirin in any drugstore (you may wish).

Remark: Sometimes the same *idea* may be expressed with ка́ждый; вся́кий, or любо́й:

Ка́ждый (вся́кий, любо́й) челове́к вам ска́жет э́то.	Any man will tell you this.

But frequently these pronouns are not interchangeable, as, for instance, in the following example:

Вся́кие лю́ди приходи́ли к нему́ ка́ждый день, в любо́е вре́мя.	All kinds of people used to visit him every day, at any time (they wished).

Interrogative Relative Pronouns

The interrogative relative pronouns are:

кто	who
что	what
чей, чья, чьё, чьи	whose
како́й, кака́я, како́е, каки́е	which, what (kind of)
кото́рый, кото́рая, кото́рое, кото́рые	which

PRONOUNS

Two set combinations of pronouns function as an interrogative expression: Что такóе? and Кто такóй?

    Что такóе деепричáстие?   What is a gerund?
    Кто он такóй?   What is he? Who is he (really)?

Declension of Interrogative Relative Pronouns

1. **Кто** and **что**.

NOM.	кто	что
GEN.	когó	чегó
DAT.	комý	чемý
ACC.	когó	что
INSTR.	кем	чем
PREP.	ком	чём

2. **Какóй** and **котóрый** are declined like adjectives.

3. **Чей**

	Masc.	Fem.	Neut.	Plural
NOM.	чей	чья	чьё	чьи
GEN.	чьегó	чьей	чьегó	чьих
DAT.	чьемý	чьей	чьемý	чьим
ACC.	чей	чью	чьё	чьи
(anim.)	чьегó			чьих
INSTR.	чьим	чьей	чьим	чьими
PREP.	чьём	чьей	чьём	чьих

Usage of Interrogative Relative Pronouns

1. The pronouns **кто** and **что** have no gender or number. As a rule, with кто the predicate is in the masculine singular, regardless of the gender and number of persons:

    Кто пришёл?—Моя́ сестрá (мой брат).   Who came?—My sister (my brother).
    Кто приéхал?—Мой друзья́.   Who arrived?—My friends.

However, in a conjunctive construction, кто may be followed by the plural predicate when called for:

| Те, кто опоздали, ничего не получили. | Those who were late did not get anything. |

The pronoun-subject что is always followed by a neuter predicate (in the past tense):

| Что случилось? | What happened? |

Note: These constructions should not be confused with others, where кто or что are no longer subjects.

| Кто была эта дама? | Who was that lady? |
| Что вы делали? | What were you doing? |

2. Какой essentially means *what, what kind of, which*. It may refer to various characteristics: color, size, quality, etc.

Какое платье ты наденешь?	Which dress are you going to put on?
Красное.	The red one.
Какой он человек?	What kind of a man is he?
Очень милый.	Very nice.
Какое упражнение самое трудное?	Which is the hardest exercise?
Перевод с английского.	The translation from English.

3. Который means *which*. As such, it may refer to a certain order, to a rank, to one object out of several:

Которое упражнение самое трудное?	Which exercise is the hardest?
Второе.	The second.
Которая дочь выходит замуж?	Which daughter is getting married?
Старшая.	The eldest.

Какой is sometimes used instead of который, or as a variant:

| На каком этаже вы живёте? | On what floor do you live? |
| Какое сегодня число? | What date is it today? |

PRONOUNS

В како́м году́ он роди́лся? What year was he born?
(or: В кото́ром году́ он роди́лся?)

The expressions кото́рый час? and в кото́ром часу́? admit no variant form with како́й.

4. In complex sentences, the use of кото́рый, кто, and что depends on the antecedent part of speech. As a general rule:

(*a*) Кото́рый follows a noun:

челове́к, кото́рый сказа́л э́то   the man who said this
письмо́, кото́рое вы написа́ли   the letter which you wrote

(*b*) Кто and что follow pronouns:

тот, кто сказа́л э́то   the one who said this
то, что вы написа́ли   what you have written
всё, что он чита́ет   all that he reads

However, кото́рый may follow a pronoun when the subject is clearly singled out and when a noun is strongly implied:

Э́ти офице́ры америка́нцы. Тот, кото́рый сиди́т нале́во, о́чень хорошо́ говори́т по-ру́сски.   These officers are Americans. The one who sits on the left speaks Russian very well.
Моя́ ста́ршая сестра́ здесь, а та, кото́рая неда́вно вы́шла за́муж живёт в дере́вне.   My eldest sister is here, and the one who recently got married lives in the country.
Он получи́л ва́ши пи́сьма. То, кото́рое вы посла́ли в сре́ду пришло́ сего́дня.   He received your letters. The one you sent on Wednesday arrived today.

In these sentences, the nouns офице́р, сестра́, and письмо́ are strongly implied in the second sentence of each pair.

Negative Pronouns

The Negative Pronouns are:

никто́   nobody
ничто́   nothing

никако́й, никака́я, никако́е,   no, none at all, not any
    никаки́е
ниче́й, ничья́, ничьё, ничьи́   nobody's
не́кого   nobody (to . . .)
не́чего   nothing (to . . .)

Declension of Negative Pronouns

1. **Никто́, ничто́, ниче́й,** and **никако́й.**

These pronouns are declined like the corresponding interrogative ones. However, when a preposition is present, it is placed after **ни** (as in the prepositional case below).

NOM.	никто́	ничто́
GEN.	никого́	ничего́
DAT.	никому́	ничему́
ACC.	никого́	ничто́
INSTR.	нике́м	ниче́м
PREP.	ни о ком	ни о чём

	Masc.	Fem.	Neut.	Plural
NOM.	ниче́й	ничья́	ничьё	ничьи́
GEN.	ничьего́	ничье́й	ничьего́	ничьи́х
DAT.	ничьему́	ничье́й	ничьему́	ничьи́м
ACC.	ниче́й	ничью́	ничьё	ничьи́
(anim.)	ничьего́			ничьи́х
INSTR.	ничьи́м	ничье́й	ничьи́м	ничьи́ми
PREP.	ни о чьём	ни о чьей	ни о чьём	ни о чьих

	Masc.	Fem.	Neut.	Plural
NOM.	никако́й	никака́я	никако́е	никаки́е
GEN.	никако́го	никако́й	никако́го	никаки́х
DAT.	никако́му	никако́й	никако́му	никаки́м
ACC.	никако́й	никаку́ю	никако́е	никаки́е
(anim.)	никако́го			никаки́х
INSTR.	никаки́м	никако́й	никаки́м	никаки́ми
PREP.	ни о како́м	ни о како́й	ни о како́м	ни о каки́х

PRONOUNS

2. Не́кого and не́чего

NOM.	(*None*)	(*None*)
GEN.	не́кого	не́чего
DAT.	не́кому	не́чему
ACC.	не́кого	не́чего
INSTR.	не́кем	не́чем
PREP.	не́ о ком	не́ о чем

Usage of Negative Pronouns

1. In sentences with никто́, ничто́, никако́й, and ниче́й the predicate is preceded by the particle **не**. The pronouns ниче́й and никако́й agree with their nouns in gender, number, and case.

Я никого́ не ви́дел.	I did not see anybody.
Э́то ничему́ не помеша́ет.	That won't hurt (hinder) anything.
Он никаки́м слу́хам не ве́рит.	He does not believe any rumors.
Я ничьи́х де́нег не брал.	I did not take anybody's money.

Or, with prepositions:

Вы ни о ком не поду́мали.	You didn't think about anybody.
Я ни с чем не согла́сен.	I don't agree with anything.
Он ни на чью по́мощь не рассчи́тывает.	He is not counting on help from anybody.
Мы ни в како́й рестора́н не заезжа́ли.	We did not stop at any restaurant.

2. Both **никто́** and **ничто́** are used in the nominative (the latter is encountered less frequently than the familiar genitive ничего́):

Никто́ не пришёл.	Nobody came.
Ничто́ его́ бо́льше не интересу́ет.	Nothing interests him any longer.

3. **Не́кого** and **не́чего** have no nominative case. (They should not be confused with the indefinite pronouns не́кто, used only in the nominative,

and нечто, used only in the nominative and in the accusative.) Некого and нечего are always followed by the infinitive:

        Некого спросить.   There is no one to ask.
        Здесь нечего есть.   There is nothing to eat here.

Sentences with некого and нечего have no "double negative." Compare:

        Здесь нечего есть.   There is nothing to eat here.
with: Я ничего **не** ел.   I didn't eat anything.

Indefinite Pronouns

The indefinite pronouns are listed below with their current translation into English. (For different shades of meaning, or translation, see "Usage.")

1. кто́-то   somebody
    что́-то   something
    како́й (а́я, о́е, и́е) -то   some (kind of)
    чей (чья́, чьё, чьи) -то   somebody's, someone's

2. кто́-нибудь   anybody
    что́-нибудь   anything
    како́й (а́я, о́е, и́е) -нибудь   any (kind of)
    че́й (чья́, чьё, чьи́) -нибудь   anybody's, anyone's

3. Of the same, or practically the same, meaning as the last four, are:
    кто́-либо
    что́-либо
    како́й (а́я, о́е, и́е) -либо
    че́й (чья́, чьё, чьи́) -либо

Their usage is more characteristic of written than of spoken language.

4. ко́е-кто́   somebody; some, a few
    ко́е-что́   something; a little
    ко́е-како́й (а́я, о́е, и́е)   some
                                  plural: a few, various

5. не́кто   someone, a certain (man)
    не́что   something

PRONOUNS

не́кий (ая, ое, ие) a certain
не́который (ая, ое, ые) a certain; certain
  plural: several, a few

Declension of Indefinite Pronouns

1. The indefinite pronouns with particles **–то, –нибудь,** and **ко́е–** are declined like the corresponding interrogative pronouns. Examples:

NOM.	кто́-то	что́-то
GEN.	кого́-то	чего́-то
DAT.	кому́-то	чему́-то
ACC.	кого́-то	что́-то
INSTR.	ке́м-то	че́м-то
PREP.	ко́м-то	чём-то

Remark: When a preposition is present, it precedes indefinite pronouns (except those with ко́е-): у кого́-то; с чём-нибудь; о како́м-то. In the case of pronouns with the particle ко́е- there are often two variants:

у ко́е-кого́ or: ко́е у кого́.
от ко́е-кого́ or: ко́е от кого́.

Ко́е с кем and ко́е о чём have no variant form.

2. Не́кто and не́что are not declined.

3. Declension of **не́кий**.

	Masc.	Fem.	Neut.	Plural
NOM.	не́кий	не́кая	не́кое	не́кие
GEN.	не́коего	не́кой	не́коего	не́ких
DAT.	не́коему	не́кой	не́коему	не́ким
ACC.	не́кий	не́кую	не́кое	не́кие
(anim.)	не́коего			не́ких
INSTR.	не́ким	не́кой	не́ким	не́кими
PREP.	не́коем	не́кой	не́коем	не́ких

4. **Не́который (ая, ое, ые)** are declined like adjectives.

Usage of Indefinite Pronouns

1. The particle **-то** is usually rendered into English as *some*; the particle **-нибудь** as *any*.

> Кто́-то прие́хал.   Somebody has arrived.
> Вы кого́-нибудь ви́дели?   Did you see anybody?

However, this translation may not always be correct: Thus, the following two sentences are both translated with the aid of *some*.

> Он кому́-то написа́л.   He wrote to somebody.
> На́до кому́-нибудь написа́ть.   We should write to somebody.

Conversely, "Do you need *some*thing?" or "Do you need *any*thing?" could both be translated "Вам что́-нибудь ну́жно?"
It is preferable, then, to think of the **-то** expressions as having one unknown —X; and of the **-нибудь** expressions as admitting a choice between several unknowns—$Y_1, Y_2 \ldots 0$.

> Кто́-нибу́дь звони́л?   Did anybody (somebody) call? (John? Paul? Nobody?)
>
> Да, кто́-то звони́л и сказа́л, что позвони́т по́зже.   Yes, somebody called and said he'll call back later.
>
> Он, наве́рно, че́м-нибудь недово́лен.   He is probably displeased with something. (There is a doubt about the fact itself and the various possibilities.)
>
> Он че́м-то недово́лен.   He is displeased with something. (Very likely, with one thing.)

2. The distinction between the –нибудь and the –либо expressions is delicate. In fact, most authorities consider these expressions synonymous. This is a debatable opinion.*

---

* The Слова́рь ру́сского языка́, АН СССР, for example, states that кто́-либо is the same as кто́-нибудь, and что́-либо is the same as что́-нибудь.
On the other hand, Ушако́в gives somewhat different explanations of кто́-нибудь and кто́-либо in his Толко́вый слова́рь ру́сского языка́. The translations into French of кто́-нибудь and кто́-либо, что́-нибудь and что́-либо by M. André Mazon (*Grammaire de la Langue Russe*) are close but not identical.

PRONOUNS

The examples given below may illustrate the marked difference between (1) the –то and the –нибудь expressions, and (2) the subtle difference between the –нибудь and the –либо expressions—at least as far as their usage in certain instances and their proper translation into English are concerned.

(a) **Кто́-то** к вам прие́хал.
Someone has come to (see) you.

(b) Я ви́жу маши́ну пе́ред до́мом. Наве́рно, **кто́-нибудь** прие́хал.
I see a car in front of the house. Probably, *somebody* has arrived.

(c) Е́сли **кто́-нибудь** придёт, скажи́те что меня́ нет до́ма.
If *anybody* (*somebody*) comes, say that I'm not at home.

(d) Е́сли **кто́-либо** придёт, скажи́те, что меня́ нет до́ма.
Should *anyone* come, say that I'm not at home.

Other examples:

(a) Мой брат ему́ **что́-то** посла́л.
My brother sent him *something*.

(b) Он про́сит де́нег. На́до ему́ **что́-нибудь** посла́ть.
He is asking for money. We have to send him *something*.

(c) Е́сли вы ему́ **что́-нибудь** пошлёте, он бу́дет о́чень рад.
If you send him *something* (*anything*), he will be very happy.

(d) Е́сли вы ему́ **что́-либо** пошлёте, он то́лько оби́дится.
Should you send him *anything* (whatsoever), he will only get offended.

Thus, the particles in the above examples are translated as illustrated in the diagram below:

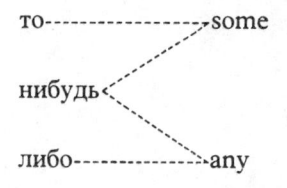

```
то----------------→some
                ╱
нибудь ‹
                ╲
либо--------------→any
```

3. **Ко́е-кто́**, more often than not, refers to several people. It is followed by the masculine singular:

На собра́нии ко́е-кто́ голосова́л про́тив.
At the meeting, a few people voted against (it).

Occasionally, it may imply *one* person, even if not clearly.

Мне ну́жно ко́е с кем поговори́ть.	I have to talk to somebody. (The speaker is not anxious to mention the name of the person, or persons.)

Ко́е-что́ means *something, a thing or two*:

Мне на́до вам ко́е-что́ сказа́ть.	I have to tell you something.

Ко́е-что́ is followed by the neuter singular in the past tense:

Ко́е-что́ в э́той статье́ мне не понра́вилось.	I didn't like a thing or two in this article.

Ко́е-како́й is seldom used in the singular. When used, it often suggests something insignificant, unimportant:

Ко́е-како́й о́пыт у него́ есть.	(Well), he does have some experience.
В чемода́не была́ ко́е-кака́я оде́жда, но бо́льше ничего́.	In the suitcase there were some (kind of) clothes, but that's about all.

In the plural, **ко́е-каки́е** means *certain, some, a few*. It is used currently:

Мне на́до купи́ть ко́е-каки́е ве́щи.	I have to buy a few (some) things.

4. The pronouns **не́кто, не́что,** and **не́кий** are encountered more often in written than in spoken language.

Не́кто is used only in the nominative. It implies *a certain man*:

Пе́ред до́мом стоя́л не́кто в чёрном пальто́.	In front of the house stood a (certain) man in a black overcoat.

Не́кто is used with proper names when referring to someone little known, or not known at all:

Вам звони́л не́кто Ка́рпов.	A certain (person by the name of) Karpov telephoned you.

Не́что is used only in the nominative and in the accusative:

Случи́лось не́что удиви́тельное.	Something amazing happened.

PRONOUNS

Он сказа́л мне не́что о́чень стра́нное.	He told me something very strange.

Не́кий (ая, ое, ие) is declined and has gender and number:

В своём письме́ он пи́шет о не́коем до́кторе Ми́ллере.	In his letter, he writes about a certain Dr. Miller.
Не́кая да́ма, назва́ть кото́рую я не хочу́, сказа́ла мне э́то.	A certain lady, whom I do not wish to name, told me this.

Не́который (ая, ое, ые) is frequently used, both in written and spoken Russian. It is declined like an adjective:

Я прие́хал сюда́ на не́которое вре́мя.	I have come here for some (a certain) time.
У не́которых люде́й бы́ли обра́тные биле́ты.	Some (certain) people had round-trip tickets.

Pronoun—Numerals

The pronoun—numerals are:

сто́лько	so much, so many
ско́лько	how much, how many
не́сколько	several, a few

These pronouns are declined only in the plural.

	Singular	Plural
NOM.	сто́лько воды́	сто́лько ученико́в
GEN.		сто́льких ученико́в
DAT.		сто́льким ученика́м
ACC.	сто́лько воды́	сто́лько ученико́в
		(or: сто́льких ученико́в)
INSTR.		сто́лькими ученика́ми
PREP.		сто́льких ученика́х

Ско́лько and не́сколько are declined similarly.

Note: Сто́лько is sometimes classified as a definite pronoun, ско́лько—as an interrogative, не́сколько—as an indefinite.

Usage of Pronoun—Numerals

1. In the nominative and in the inanimate accusative **столько** and **сколько** are followed by the genitive case of the noun (singular or plural):

    Здесь столько снега!   There is so much snow here!
    Там было столько людей.   There were so many people there.
    Сколько книг вы купили?   How many books did you buy?

Несколько is followed by the genitive plural:

    Он написал несколько писем.   He wrote several letters.

2. In the oblique cases, these pronouns agree with their nouns, which are always in the plural.

    для нескольких учеников   for several pupils
    скольким людям   to how many people
    о стольких вещах   about so many things

3. The animate accusative of these pronouns may either coincide with the genitive:

    Я встретил нескольких учеников.   I met several pupils.

or, with the nominative:

    Я встретил несколько учеников   I met several pupils.
    Мы видели столько туристов!   We saw so many tourists!

The latter form (несколько, столько) is currently preferred.

6. NUMERALS

Numerals are classified as follows:

I. Cardinal: два—two; три́дцать пять—thirty five
II. Ordinal: второ́й—second; три́дцать пя́тый—thirty-fifth
III. Collective: дво́е—two, a couple of; тро́е—three
IV. Fractions and other numerical expressions: одна́ треть—one-third; со́тня—a hundred

Cardinal Numerals

Table of Cardinal Numerals, Including the Cipher Zero

0—ноль
1—оди́н (*masc.*)
  одна́ (*fem.*)
  одно́ (*neut.*)
2—два (*masc.* and neut.*)
  две (*fem.*)
3—три
4—четы́ре
5—пять
6—шесть
7—семь
8—во́семь
9—де́вять
10—де́сять
11—оди́ннадцать
12—двена́дцать
13—трина́дцать

14—четы́рнадцать
15—пятна́дцать
16—шестна́дцать
17—семна́дцать
18—восемна́дцать
19—девятна́дцать
20—два́дцать
30—три́дцать
40—со́рок
50—пятьдеся́т
60—шестьдеся́т
70—се́мьдесят
80—во́семьдесят
90—девяно́сто
100—сто
200—две́сти
300—три́ста
400—четы́реста

500—пятьсо́т
600—шестьсо́т
700—семьсо́т
800—восемьсо́т

900—девятьсо́т
1000—ты́сяча
1,000,000—миллио́н
1,000,000,000—миллиа́рд

Spelling Rule

All numerals from 5 to 20, and also 30, end in **ь**. The ь is dropped in the middle of numerals 15 to 19. The ь is written in the middle of and not at the end of, 50, 60, 70, 80, 500, 600, 700, 800 and 900.

THE NUMERALS ТЫ́СЯЧА, МИЛЛИО́Н, AND МИЛЛИА́РД

Ты́сяча is considered a feminine noun.

Миллио́н and миллиа́рд are masculine nouns.

One may say: пе́рвая ты́сяча, не́сколько миллио́нов.

Declension of Cardinal Numerals

Cardinal numerals are listed here according to the type of their declension.

1—Оди́н (*masc.*), одна́ (*fem.*), and одно́ (*neut.*) have the same case endings as adjectives such as большо́й, except for the nominative—accusative. The same applies to compound numbers ending in 1 (21, 31, etc.).

2—The case endings of два (*masc.* and *neut.*) and две (*fem.*) coincide, except for the nominative—accusative. The same applies to compound numbers ending in 2 (22, 32, etc.).

3 and 4—три and четы́ре are declined alike—except for the endings in the instrumental.

5—пять. Numerals from 5 to 20, and the numeral 30 are declined alike. But: 8—во́семь has two forms in the instrumental: восьмью́ or восемью́.

40—со́рок, 90—девяно́сто, and 100—сто, end in **а** in all oblique cases.

50—пятьдеся́т, 60—шестьдеся́т, 70—се́мьдесят, 80—во́семьдесят have both component parts declined.

200—две́сти, 300—три́ста, and 400—четы́реста have both component parts declined.

NUMERALS

500—пятьсо́т, 600—шестьсо́т, 700—семьсо́т, 800—восемьсо́т and 900—девятьсо́т are declined alike (both component parts).

1000—ты́сяча is declined like a feminine noun. However, the instrumental has two forms: ты́сячей or ты́сячью.

1.000.000—миллио́н and 1.000.000.000—миллиа́рд are declined like masculine nouns.

Remark: In compound numerals (25, 153, etc.) all component parts are declined:

| без двадцати́ пяти́ три | twenty-five minutes to three |
| о ста пяти́десяти трёх рубля́х. | about one hundred and fifty-three rubles |

Table of Declensions

NOM.	оди́н	одно́	одна́	два	две
GEN.	одного́	одного́	одно́й	двух	двух
DAT.	одному́	одному́	одно́й	двум	двум
ACC.	оди́н	одно́	одну́	два	две
(anim.)	одного́			двух	двух
INSTR.	одни́м	одни́м	одно́й	двумя́	двумя́
PREP.	одно́м	одно́м	одно́й	двух	двух

NOM.	три	четы́ре
GEN.	трёх	четырёх
DAT.	трём	четырём
ACC.	три	четы́ре
(anim.)	трёх	четырёх
INSTR.	тремя́	четырьмя́
PREP.	трёх	четырёх

NOM.	пять	со́рок	пятьдеся́т	две́сти	три́ста
GEN.	пяти́	сорока́	пяти́десяти	двухсо́т	трёхсо́т
DAT.	пяти́	сорока́	пяти́десяти	двумста́м	трёмста́м
ACC.	пять	со́рок	пятьдеся́т	две́сти	три́ста
(anim.)				двухсо́т	трёхсо́т
INSTR.	пятью́	сорока́	пятью́десятью	двумяста́ми	тремяста́ми
PREP.	пяти́	сорока́	пяти́десяти	двухста́х	трёхста́х

NOM.	пятьсо́т	ты́сяча	миллио́н	два́дцать пять
GEN.	пятисо́т	ты́сячи	миллио́на	двадцати́ пяти́
DAT.	пятиста́м	ты́сяче	миллио́ну	двадцати́ пяти́
ACC.	пятьсо́т	ты́сячу	миллио́н	два́дцать пять
INSTR.	пятьюста́ми	ты́сячей (or: ты́сячью)	миллио́ном	двадцатью́ пятью́
PREP.	пятиста́х	ты́сяче	миллио́не	двадцати́ пяти́

Agreement of Numerals with Nouns

1. Оди́н, одна́ одно́, and their compounds agree with the noun in the singular throughout the declension:

NOM.	оди́н дом	ACC.	оди́н дом
GEN.	одного́ до́ма	INSTR.	одни́м до́мом
DAT.	одному́ до́му	PREP.	одно́м до́ме

2. Одни́, which functions as an adjective or as an indefinite pronoun, meaning *certain, some; alone, only* agrees with the noun in the plural throughout the declension:

NOM.	одни́ ма́льчики	ACC.	одни́х ма́льчиков
GEN.	одни́х ма́льчиков	INSTR.	одни́ми ма́льчиками
DAT.	одни́м ма́льчикам	PREP.	одни́х ма́льчиках

3. *The nominative case* of два (две), три, четы́ре and of the compound numbers ending in 2, 3, 4 (23, 134, etc.) is followed by the genitive singular of nouns: два стола́—two tables; две кни́ги—two books; два́дцать три окна́—twenty-three windows

> *Note:* The stress in some masculine nouns may change when these nouns are preceded by два, три, четы́ре and their compounds. (They retain the pronunciation of the old "dual number.")
>
> Compare: три часа́   three hours, three o'clock, and
> два шага́   two steps
>
> with: о́коло ча́са   about one hour, and
> по́сле пе́рвого ша́га   after the first step

NUMERALS

4. *The nominative case* of other numerals (from 5 up) is followed by genitive plural of nouns: пять столо́в—five tables; де́сять книг—ten books

5. *The accusative case* with inanimate nouns is like the nominative. A distinction between inanimate and animate nouns is observed only with оди́н, одни́, два, две, три, четы́ре, две́сти, три́ста, четы́реста.

With these numerals the accusative of animate nouns is like the genitive:

купи́ть две кни́ги и три карандаша́	to buy two books and three pencils
знать двух де́вочек и трёх ма́льчиков	to know two girls and three boys

No distinction is made between animate and inanimate nouns with the compounds of these numerals:

купи́ть два́дцать три карандаша́	to buy twenty-three pencils
знать два́дцать три ма́льчика	to know twenty-three boys

6. *In the oblique cases* the numeral and the noun always agree. The noun is declined in the plural:

GEN.	двух столо́в	пяти́ книг
DAT.	двум стола́м	пяти́ кни́гам
INSTR.	двумя́ стола́ми	пятью́ кни́гами
PREP.	двух стола́х	пяти́ кни́гах

7. Ты́сяча, миллио́н and миллиа́рд. These numerals—considered grammatically as nouns—are followed by the genitive plural of nouns in all six cases:

с ты́сячью рубле́й   о миллио́не до́лларов
(*instr.*) (*gen. pl.*)   (*prep.*) (*gen. pl.*)

These constructions are similar to other constructions with *nouns*:

с дю́жиной карандаше́й   with a dozen pencils
(*instr.*) (*gen. pl.*)

and differ from constructions with numerals:

с двена́дцатью карандаша́ми   with twelve pencils.
(*instr.*) (*instr.*)

Note: Тысяча, however, has "a tendency of becoming a numeral."*
Therefore, "к тысяче рублям," "с тысячью рублями," is not unusual.

Remarks:
(*a*) The plural of **год** is **года** (seldom **годы**); the plural of **человек** is **люди**. After a numeral the *genitive plural* is **лет** and **человек**:

	Nom.	Gen. Plural
	пять	лет
	шесть	человек

	Gen.	Gen. Plural
около	двух	лет
у	трёх	человек

With cases other than the genitive plural **года** and **люди** are used:

	Dat.	Dat. Plural	Instr.	Instr. Plural
	к двум	годам	с тремя	людьми

Людей (gen. plural) is used with collective numerals двое, трое, etc. The oblique cases of these numerals, more often than not, coincide with those of два, три, etc. Hence: двое людей, у двух людей, у трёх людей, together with: двое людей, у двоих людей, у троих людей. (See Collective Numerals, page 137, para. 8).

(*b*) Approximation may be expressed by placing the noun before the numeral.

| минут десять | about ten minutes |
| километров двадцать | about twenty kilometers |

These constructions are used with more or less "round figures": часов восемь, минут двадцать пять, миль двести, etc. They would not be used with 347 and the like. Neither are they ever used with один, тысяча, миллион:

| около одного года | about one year |
| около тысячи долларов | about a thousand dollars |

* Аванесов и Сидоров. Очерк грамматики русского литературного языка.

Agreement of Numerals, Nouns, and Adjectives

1. Nominative—Accusative

(a) Adjectives and nouns agree after the numerals оди́н, одна́, одно́ and their compounds; also, after одни́:

оди́н большо́й стол	one big table
одна́ ма́ленькая ко́мната	one small room
одно́ но́вое перо́	one new pen
одни́ ста́рые ве́щи	only (some) old things

Adjectives and nouns agree after numerals from 5 up. The adjective as well as the noun stands in the genitive plural:

пять больши́х столо́в	five big tables
шесть ма́леньких ко́мнат	six small rooms

(b) Adjectives *do not* agree with the nouns after 2, 3, 4 (22, 53, etc.).

MASC.	Два больши́х (*gen. pl.*) стола́ (*gen. sing.*)
NEUT.	Три но́вых (*gen. pl.*) зда́ния (*gen. sing.*)
FEM.	Две больши́е (*nom. pl.*) ко́мнаты (*gen. sing.*)

With feminine nouns, the nominative plural of adjectives is preferred. However, the genitive plural is also used:

две больши́х ко́мнаты	two large rooms
три ру́сских да́мы	three Russian ladies

Remark: When **пе́рвые, после́дние, други́е, еди́нственные,** and **остальны́е** precede a numeral, they remain in the nominative case:

Пе́рвые три уро́ка.	The first three lessons.
Други́е два ма́льчика.	The other two boys.
После́дние два письма́.	The last two letters.
Остальны́е четы́ре рубля́.	The remaining four rubles.

The same applies to **ка́ждые** (which always precedes a numeral in similar constructions):

ка́ждые два го́да	every two years

2. Oblique cases

In the oblique cases, the numerals, adjectives, and nouns agree.

GEN.	двух	больши́х	домо́в
DAT.	двум	больши́м	дома́м
INSTR.	двумя́	больши́ми	дома́ми
PREP.	двух	больши́х	дома́х

Ordinal Numerals

Ordinal numerals have three genders, characterized by adjectival endings.

Examples:

пе́рвый уро́к	the first lesson
втора́я ле́кция	the second lecture
тре́тье упражне́ние	the third exercise

Table of Ordinal Numerals

1st—пе́рвый
2nd—второ́й
3rd—тре́тий
4th—четвёртый
5th—пя́тый
6th—шесто́й
7th—седьмо́й
8th—восьмо́й
9th—девя́тый
10th—деся́тый

11th—оди́ннадцатый
12th—двена́дцатый
13th—трина́дцатый
14th—четы́рнадцатый
15th—пятна́дцатый
16th—шестна́дцатый
17th—семна́дцатый
18th—восемна́дцатый
19th—девятна́дцатый

20th—двадца́тый
30th—тридца́тый
40th—сороково́й
50th—пятидеся́тый
60th—шестидеся́тый
70th—семидеся́тый

80th—восьмидеся́тый
90th—девяно́стый
100th—со́тый
200th—двухсо́тый
300th—трёхсо́тый
400th—четырёхсо́тый

NUMERALS

500th—пятисо́тый 800th—восьмисо́тый
600th—шестисо́тый 900th—девятисо́тый
700th—семисо́тый 1000th—ты́сячный

Remarks:

(*a*) The numerals ending in **-ой** (второ́й, шесто́й, седьмо́й, восьмо́й, сороково́й and their compounds), are stressed on the ending.
(*b*) **Тре́тий** (**со́рок тре́тий,** etc.) has the soft ending **-ий**.
(*c*) In compound numerals, only the last numeral is an ordinal.

два́дцать пе́рвый уро́к the twenty-first lesson
ты́сяча девятьсо́т шестидеся́тый год the year 1960

(*d*) Ordinal numerals may occur in the plural.

Пе́рвые уро́ки са́мые тру́дные.	The first lessons are the hardest.
Вторы́е су́тки идёт дождь.	It has been raining for two days (and nights).
Я хорошо́ по́мню двадца́тые го́ды.	I remember well the twenties (1920s).

Declension of Ordinal Numerals

Ordinal numerals (except тре́тий) are declined like hard adjectives.

	Masc.	Neut.	Fem.
NOM.	пе́рв**ый**	пе́рв**ое**	пе́рв**ая**
GEN.	пе́рв**ого**	пе́рв**ого**	пе́рв**ой**
DAT.	пе́рв**ому**	пе́рв**ому**	пе́рв**ой**
ACC.	пе́рв**ый**	пе́рв**ое**	пе́рв**ую**
(anim.)	пе́рв**ого**		
INSTR.	пе́рв**ым**	пе́рв**ым**	пе́рв**ой**
PREP.	пе́рв**ом**	пе́рв**ом**	пе́рв**ой**

Тре́тий is declined like an adjective of the type во́лчий (page 85):

	Masc.	Neut.	Fem.
NOM.	тре́т**ий**	тре́т**ье**	тре́т**ья**
GEN.	тре́т**ьего**	тре́т**ьего**	тре́т**ьей**

	Masc.	Neut.	Fem.
DAT.	тре́тьему	тре́тьему	тре́тьей
ACC.	тре́тий	тре́тье	тре́тью
(anim.)	тре́тьего		
INSTR.	тре́тьим	тре́тьим	тре́тьей
PREP.	тре́тьем	тре́тьем	тре́тьей

In compound numerals, only the ordinal (the last member) is declined.

Я живу́ на сто два́дцать тре́тьей у́лице.	I live on 123d street.
в ты́сяча девятьсо́т тридца́том году́	in 1930

Usage of Some Cardinal and Ordinal Numerals

(See also *Remark*, page 141.)

1. Ноль (нуль) is used in technical language, as well as in daily life, for instance with temperatures:

Де́сять гра́дусов ни́же нуля́.	Ten degrees below zero.
По́езд отхо́дит в ноль пятна́дцать.	The train leaves at 12:15 a.m.

Ноль is followed by the genitive:

ноль це́лых и две деся́тых	two tenths; *lit.:* zero whole (parts) and two tenths
"ноль внима́ния"	no attention (whatsoever)

2. Оди́н, одна́, одно́, одни́ may function as indefinite pronouns or adjectives—meaning (a) certain, some; alone, only, nothing but:

Я ви́дел одного́ челове́ка.	I saw a certain man.
Она́ живёт одна́.	She lives alone.
Все де́ти бы́ли здесь. Одна́ Ве́ра не смогла́ прийти́.	All the children were here. Only Vera couldn't come.
Прие́хали одни́ мои́ знако́мые.	Some of my friends have arrived.

NUMERALS

Note: In the plural, sometimes the intonation alone gives the clue to the meaning.

    С нами éхали одни американцы.   Some Americans were traveling with us.

But, with одни slightly stressed:

    С нами éхали <u>одни</u> американцы.   Only Americans were traveling with us.

Remark: Одни is used with nouns which have no singular.

    одни часы   one watch
    одни сутки   one day (and night)

3. In counting, the word **раз** is used instead of "один": раз, два, три. . . . Раз means *once* (and also *times*).

    один раз   once
    несколько раз   several times.

4. The usage of ordinal numerals in Russian does not differ essentially from the English usage, except with some expressions pertaining to dates and to the time of the day.

Dates

The case of a date is determined by the structure of the sentence:

    Сегодня пéрвое марта.   Today is March 1st (the first of March).
    (*nominative*)
    Он родился в тысяча девятьсот десятом   He was born in 1910.
    году. (*prepositional*)

One particular instance should be noted: When something *happens* on a certain *date of the month*, this date is in the genitive case (likewise, the month and the year which follow).

    Он приéхал пéрвого марта.   He arrived on March 1st.
    Она родилась пятого апрéля тысяча девятьсот десятого года.   She was born on April 5, 1910.

Time of Day

Both cardinal and ordinal numbers are used to express the time of the day. This can be best explained by examples:

(a) Кото́рый час?—Два часа́.　What time is it?—Two o'clock.
　　В кото́ром часу́?—В час.　At what time?—At one.

(b)　2:01—одна́ мину́та тре́тьего　(*lit.:* one minute of the third)
　　4:10—де́сять мину́т пя́того　(*lit.:* ten minutes of the fifth)
　　5:15—че́тверть шесто́го　(*lit.:* quarter of the sixth)
　　8:20—два́дцать мину́т девя́того　(*lit.:* twenty minutes of the ninth)
　　9:30—полови́на деся́того　(*lit.:* half of the tenth)

Note: Compare the English constructions:

　　Year *1904*—beginning of the *20*th century
　　Year *825*—first part of the *9*th century, etc.

(c) As in English, after the half hour, a different expression is used:

　　3:35—без двадцати́ пяти́ (мину́т) четы́ре (*lit.:* four without 25 min.)
　　6:40—без двадцати́ (мину́т) семь (*lit.:* seven without 20 min.)
　　7:45—без че́тверти во́семь (*lit.:* eight without a quarter)
　　10:56—без четырёх мину́т оди́ннадцать (*lit.:* eleven without 4 min.)
　　12:59—без одно́й мину́ты час (*lit.:* one without one minute)

Remark: Expressions like де́сять пятна́дцать, два со́рок . . . (ten fifteen, two forty, etc.) are quite frequently used to indicate time.

Notes:
(a) Colloquially, пол is used instead of полови́на:

　　　　полвторо́го　half-past one

(b) Very frequently, in the second half-hour, "round figures" are used without the word мину́т: без пяти́ три; без десяти́ четы́ре; без двадцати́ пяти́ де́сять.
On the other hand, мину́ты and мину́т are used with figures below five: без одно́й мину́ты час; без двух мину́т шесть.

(c) "At what time" is expressed:
With **в** + accusative:

NUMERALS

Я прие́хал в де́сять мину́т пе́рвого.	I arrived at ten minutes past twelve.
Я уе́хал в че́тверть второ́го.	I left at quarter past one.

With **в** + prepositional—used only with **полови́на**.

Мы прие́хали в полови́не пя́того.	We arrived at half-past four.

Without **в**:

Вы прие́хали без десяти́ час.	You arrived at ten minutes to one.
Они́ уе́хали без двадцати́ семь.	They left at twenty minutes to seven.

Collective Numerals

The collective numerals are similar in meaning to the cardinals, but their usage is limited.

Table of Collective Numerals

(a)
дво́е	two, "a couple of"
тро́е	three
че́тверо	four
пя́теро	five
ше́стеро	six
се́меро	seven
во́сьмеро	eight ⎫
де́вятеро	nine ⎬ Seldom used.
де́сятеро	ten ⎭

(b)
о́ба	both (*masc.* and *neut.*)
о́бе	both (*fem.*)

Declension of Collective Numerals

Declension of **дво́е, тро́е, че́тверо**

NOM.	дво́е	тро́е	че́тверо
GEN.	двои́х	трои́х	четверы́х

DAT.	двои́м	трои́м	четверы́м
ACC.	дво́е	тро́е	че́тверо
(anim.)	двои́х	трои́х	четверы́х
INSTR.	двои́ми	трои́ми	четверы́ми
PREP.	двои́х	трои́х	четверы́х

Пя́теро, ше́стеро, се́меро, etc. are declined like че́тверо.

Declension of **о́ба** and **о́бе**

NOM.	о́ба	о́бе
GEN.	обо́их	обе́их
DAT.	обо́им	обе́им
ACC.	о́ба	о́бе
(anim.)	обо́их	обе́их
INSTR.	обо́ими	обе́ими
PREP.	обо́их	обе́их

Usage of Collective Numerals

1. The collective numerals are never used in compound numbers. Cardinal numerals must be used: два́дцать **два** ма́льчика—twenty-two boys.

2. Collective numerals, such as дво́е, тро́е, are followed by the genitive plural of nouns: дво́е ма́льчиков, тро́е студе́нтов.
With personal pronouns, the collective numeral may be in either the nominative or the genitive:

| То́лько мы дво́е бы́ли там. | Only we two were there. |
| Нас бы́ло дво́е. | There were two of us. |

3. These numerals are used chiefly with animate masculine nouns pertaining to persons: дво́е ма́льчиков (*or:* два ма́льчика)—two boys.
With feminine nouns, cardinals are used: две де́вочки—two girls.

4. Feminine persons may be *included* in the number given by the collective numeral:

| У неё тро́е дете́й: два ма́льчика и одна́ де́вочка. | She has three children: two boys and one girl. |

NUMERALS

5. Collective numerals may be used when speaking of kittens, puppies, etc.

    двóе котя́т и трóе щеня́т two kittens and three puppies

But only:

    две кóшки и три собáки two cats and three dogs

6. The only inanimate nouns used with these numerals are those which have no singular. But this usage of collective numerals is limited. One may say: двóе часóв—two watches; трóе санéй—three sleighs; and also: трóе сýток—three days and nights. However, other *abstract* nouns of the same class (вы́боры—elections; кани́кулы—vacations, etc.) do not combine with двóе, трóе, and so forth.

7. The usage of collective numerals with pronouns is again normally limited to male persons:

| Где вáши мáльчики?—Все трóе в шкóле. | Where are your boys?—All three are in school. |

8. To say that the usage of двóе, трóе, etc., is limited to the nominative case would be incorrect. Yet, there is no doubt that in many instances the oblique cases of два, три, четы́ре, etc., are definitely preferred.

 óколо трёх сýток   about three days (and nights)
 стенá с четырьмя́ ворóтами a wall with four gates
 он пришёл с двумя́ детьми́ he came with two children

9. Óба and óбе are followed by the genitive singular of nouns. In the oblique cases, the nouns have plural endings.

NOM.	óба товáрищ**а**	óбе подрýг**и**
GEN.	обóих товáрищ**ей**	обéих подрýг
DAT.	обóим товáрищ**ам**	обéим подрýг**ам**
ACC.	обóих товáрищ**ей**	обéих подрýг
INSTR.	обóими товáрищ**ами**	обéими подрýг**ами**
PREP.	обóих товáрищ**ах**	обéих подрýг**ах**

Note: It may be mentioned here that **óба** and **óбе** mean two similar things or persons: Я купи́л óбе кни́ги.—I bought both books.
But with different objects, **и то и другóе** is used: Я купи́л и то и другóе (крéсло и шкап).—I bought both (the armchair and the cupboard).

Fractional Numerals and Other Numerical Expressions

A. Commonly used fractions are:

$\frac{1}{4}$ (одна́) че́тверть
$\frac{1}{3}$ (одна́) треть
$\frac{1}{2}$ полови́на
$\frac{2}{3}$ две тре́ти
$\frac{3}{4}$ три че́тверти
$1\frac{1}{2}$ полтора́ (*masc.* and *neut.*)
полторы́ (*fem.*)

The numerator одна́ need not be used with че́тверть; it may be used with треть, and is normally used with other fractions $\frac{1}{5}$—одна́ пя́тая, $\frac{1}{6}$—одна́ шеста́я, etc.: че́тверть фу́нта—quarter of a pound; (одна́) треть кило́метра—one-third of a kilometer; одна́ пя́тая ми́ли—one-fifth of a mile. The numerator is always cardinal. The denominator (with fractions other than those above) is ordinal in the genitive plural:

$\frac{2}{5}$—две пя́тых $\frac{5}{9}$—пять девя́тых

B. Declension of че́тверть, треть, полови́на and other fractions.

Че́тверть, треть and полови́на are declined like nouns. In other fractions, both, the numerator and the denominator are declined.

NOM.	че́тверть	треть	полови́на	три пя́тых
GEN.	че́тверти	тре́ти	полови́ны	трёх пя́тых
DAT.	че́тверти	тре́ти	полови́не	трём пя́тым
ACC.	че́тверть	треть	полови́ну	три пя́тых
INSTR.	че́твертью	тре́тью	полови́ной	тремя́ пя́тыми
PREP.	че́тверти	тре́ти	полови́не	трёх пя́тых

Declension of полтора́, полторы́ ($1\frac{1}{2}$) and полтора́ста (150).

NOM.	полтора́	полторы́	полтора́ста
GEN.	полу́тора	полу́тора	полу́тораста
DAT.	полу́тора	полу́тора	полу́тораста
ACC.	полтора́	полторы́	полтора́ста
INSTR.	полу́тора	полу́тора	полу́тораста
PREP.	полу́тора	полу́тора	полу́тораста

C. Other numeral-nouns are:

Единица "one"; unit:

    получить единицу по физике   to get "one" (the lowest grade) in physics
    единица давления   unit of pressure

Двойка, тройка, четвёрка, пятёрка, шестёрка, семёрка, восьмёрка, девятка, десятка mean the two, the three, etc. in cards.

Note: Тройка also means a team of three horses.

десяток	"a ten":	десяток яиц	ten eggs
дюжина	a dozen:	дюжина карандашей	a dozen pencils
сотня	a hundred:	сотня рублей	a hundred rubles

The above words are declined like regular nouns. They may combine with other numerals, and may be used in the plural:

    Две тройки стояли перед домом.   Two troikas stood in front of the house.
    Надо купить два десятка яиц.   We have to buy twenty eggs.
    Я вам это говорил сотни раз.   I have told you that hundreds of times.

Usage of Fractional Numerals and Other Numerical Expressions

1. Agreement of fractional numerals with nouns

(*a*) Nouns which follow fractional numerals (except полтора, полторы and полтораста) are always in the genitive case, regardless of the case of the numeral:

NOM.	половина здания
GEN.	половины здания
DAT.	половине здания
ACC.	половину здания
INSTR.	половиной здания
PREP.	половине здания

(*b*) More often than not, these fractions are followed by a noun in genitive singular:

    одна́ треть са́да   one-third of the garden
    три че́тверти ми́ли   three-quarters of a mile

(*c*) Fractional numerals are followed, of course, by the genitive plural of nouns which have no singular:

    две тре́ти консе́рвов   two-thirds of the canned goods

(*d*) They are followed by the genitive plural when they pertain to separate units which are thought of as an entity:

    две пя́тых на́ших ученико́в   two-fifths of our students

(This is frequently expressed as a percentage: со́рок проце́нтов на́ших ученико́в—forty percent of our students.)

Полтора́ and полтора́ста agree with their nouns in the same manner as cardinal numbers. (See pages 126, 127.)

NOM.	полтора́ рубля́	полтора́ста рубле́й
GEN.	полу́тора рубле́й	полу́тораста рубле́й
DAT.	полу́тора рубля́м	полу́тораста рубля́м
ACC.	полтора́ рубля́	полтора́ста рубле́й
INSTR.	полу́тора рубля́ми	полу́тораста рубля́ми
PREP.	полу́тора рубля́х	полу́тораста рубля́х
	(cf.: два рубля́)	(cf.: пять рубле́й)

2. A number which contains units and fractions is expressed with the aid of the word це́лая (whole):

    1⅖   —одна́ це́лая и две пя́тых
    1,4   —одна́ це́лая, четы́ре деся́тых
    0,3   —ноль це́лых, три деся́тых

Note the use of the comma and the zero (corresponding to English 1.4 and .3).

3. The usage of тро́йка, деся́ток, and дю́жина is very limited. One may say тро́йка лошаде́й (a team of three horses); деся́ток яи́ц (ten eggs); дю́жина карандаше́й (a dozen pencils); but only: три коро́вы (three cows); де́сять дней (ten days); двена́дцать домо́в (twelve houses).

NUMERALS

4. More on the numerals will be found in Chapter VII, in the section Agreement between Subject and Verb Predicate. (See pages 232–34.)

Remark on Rules *vs.* Usage

There are a few cases, with numerals, where common usage digresses from grammatical rules. This is sometimes no more than a matter of personal preference, but the occurrence is not infrequent.
1. The oblique cases of large numbers are often simplified in spoken Russian. Expressions such as "С тремя́ ты́сячами шестьюста́ми пятью́десятью двумя́ рубля́ми" (With three thousand six hundred and fifty-two rubles) are often changed to: "С тремя́ ты́сячами шестьсо́т пятьдеся́т двумя́ рубля́ми." In other words, the first and the last numeral is declined, as well as the "nouns" ты́сяча and миллио́н.*
2. The constructions "Три́дцать оди́н но́вый учени́к" (thirty-one new pupils); "два́дцать оди́н ма́ленький дом" (twenty-one small houses), and the like (i.e., compound number ending in "one," followed by an adjective and a noun) are perfectly correct. Nevertheless many Russians will not use them readily in daily conversation and say, for instance: В шко́ле есть но́вые ученики́. Их три́дцать оди́н. (In the school are new pupils. There are thirty-one of them.)
3. There is a divergence of opinion regarding the correct usage of два, три, четы́ре followed by an adjective and a noun. Most grammarians quote both forms: the adjective in the genitive plural, or in the nominative plural:

> два дубо́вых стола́ or: два дубо́вые стола́—two oak tables; две больши́е доро́ги or: две больши́х доро́ги—two highways †

Usually, however, the genitive plural is preferred with the masculine and the neuter; the nominative plural with the feminine.

* Грамма́тика ру́сского языка́ АН СССР.
† Examples from Грамма́тика ру́сского языка́ АН СССР.

7. VERBS

Structure

Russian verbs have:

Moods—Infinitive, Indicative, Conditional (Subjunctive), and Imperative.
Tenses—Present, Past, Future.
Other forms—Participles and Gerunds.
Aspects—Imperfective and Perfective.

This last notion can be summarized here as follows:

The Imperfective expresses:
    a continuous action
  or, a repeated action
The Perfective usually expresses:
    the completion of an action
    sometimes, the beginning
  or, a duration

The meaning (if not always the translation) is expressed as follows:

Imperfective Infinitive—to be doing something (continuously or repeatedly).
Perfective Infinitive—to do something.
Note: The present tense, the present participle, and the present gerund have no perfective aspect.

Derivation of Verbal Forms

All verbal forms are derived from one of the following stems:
1. The stem of the infinitive

	Infinitive	Past
Example:	писа́ть	писа́л

VERBS

2. The stem of the present (or the perfective future)

              Present   (3d pers. plural)   Imperative
Example: пи́шут   пиши́

Notes:
(*a*) The two stems may coincide:

                  Infinitive нести́   Present (они́) несу́т

(*b*) The following verbal forms have the same stem as the infinitive: the past tense, the past participle, the past gerund, the imperfective future which is formed with the aid of the infinitive, and the conditional mood which is formed with the aid of the past tense.

(*c*) The following verbal forms have the same stem as the present: the imperative, the present participle, the present gerund, and the perfective future.

The Infinitive

The infinitive ends in either one of the following *suffixes*: **-ть**, **-ти**, **-чь**.

           чита́–**ть**   to read
           нес–**ти́**   to carry
           бере́–**чь**   to keep, to safeguard

The *endings* of the infinitive are:

    -ать, -ять, -еть, -уть, -оть, -ыть, -ти, -чь, -зть, -сть, -ить

The ending may concide with the suffix: нести́

Or may not: чита́ть, говори́ть.

The infinitive of verbs ending in **-ть** may be stressed on any syllable: чита́ть, рабо́тать.

The infinitive of verbs ending in **-ти** or **-чь** is stressed on the ending: нести́, бере́чь.

The only exceptions to this are perfective verbs with the prefix **вы-** which is always stressed: вы́нести—to take (to carry) out.

Usage of the Infinitive

A. The following types of constructions do not differ from the English ones:

1. With one subject for both verbs:

Я хочу́ спать.	I want to sleep.
Она́ лю́бит чита́ть.	She likes to read.
Он реши́л уе́хать.	He decided to leave.

2. Sometimes, with different logical subjects for each verb:

Она́ проси́ла меня́ прие́хать.	She asked me to come.
Он всех заставля́ет рабо́тать.	He makes everybody work.

B. The following constructions illustrate the usage of the infinitive characteristic of the Russian language:

1. With verbs denoting the beginning, continuation, or cessation of an action—the verb complement stands in the *imperfective*:

Он начина́ет ходи́ть.	He is beginning to walk.
Я продолжа́л писа́ть.	I continued to write.
Мы ко́нчили есть.	We finished eating.

2. In expressions of purpose, the English *to* is sometimes omitted in translation, especially with verbs of motion:

Он пошёл купи́ть хле́ба.	He went to buy some bread.
Они́ пое́хали за́втракать.	They have gone to have lunch.

Otherwise, two clauses may be joined with **что́бы** or **для того́, что́бы** (see Conjunctions, page 302):

Он пришёл, что́бы всё узна́ть.	He came to find out everything.

3. The infinitive is used with **до́лжен**—must; **обя́зан**—obliged; **гото́в**—ready; **наме́рен**—intend; **рад**—glad:

Он до́лжен идти́.	He must go.
Я рад слы́шать э́то.	I am glad to hear this.

4. The infinitive is used with **на́до**—(one) must; **ну́жно**—(one) must; **необходи́мо**—it is (absolutely) necessary; **мо́жно**—(one) may, it is

possible; **нельзя**—(one) can't, (one) should not; **трудно**—difficult; **хорошо**—good, nice; and other predicative adverbs (see page 270):

Надо учиться.	One must study.
Это трудно понять.	This is difficult to understand.
Хорошо жить в деревне.	It is nice to live in the country.

5. As a subject of a sentence, the infinitive often expresses a business-like or peremptory order:

Выдать гражданину Иванову . . .	Issue to citizen Ivanov . . .
Не курить.	No smoking.
Молчать!	Silence! Quiet!

6. In interrogative sentences, the infinitive may express indecision, emotion, doubt, or a question addressed to oneself or to another person.

Что делать?	What shall I do? (*lit.:* What to do?)
Зачем сердиться на него?	Why be angry with him?
Не сидеть же здесь весь день?	You don't expect (me) to sit here all day?
Пойти или не пойти?	Shall (we) go, or shall we not?
Быть или не быть.	To be or not to be.
Дать вам денег?	Shall I give you some money?
Налить вам молока?	Would you like some milk? (*lit.:* to pour you some milk?)

7. With the particle **бы** the infinitive expresses a wish:

Отдохнуть бы сейчас.	It would be nice to rest now.
Поехать бы куда-нибудь на море.	I would love to go somewhere to the sea.

8. With **не . . . ли** the infinitive expresses a mild suggestion:

Не послать ли ему денег?	Maybe (we) should send him some money.
Не поехать ли в театр?	How about going to the theater?

The Present Tense

There are two conjugations in Russian: the *First* and the *Second*.

Regular Verbs

First conjugation verbs form their present tense by (1) dropping the last *two* letters of the infinitive, and (2) adding the following endings:

	SINGULAR	PLURAL
1st *person*	–ю	–ем
2nd *person*	–ешь	–ете
3rd *person*	–ет	–ют

Examples:

Чита́–ть (to read)　　красне́–ть (to redden, blush)
я чита́ю　　　　　　　я красне́ю
ты чита́ешь　　　　　　ты красне́ешь

он　　　　　　　　　　он
она́ } чита́ет　　　　　она́ } красне́ет
оно́　　　　　　　　　оно́

мы чита́ем　　　　　　мы красне́ем
вы чита́ете　　　　　　вы красне́ете
они́ чита́ют　　　　　　они́ красне́ют

VERBS

Second conjugation verbs form their present tense by (1) dropping the last *three* letters of the infinitive, and (2) adding the following endings:

	SINGULAR	PLURAL
1st person	–ю (у)	–им
2nd person	–ишь	–ите
3rd person	–ит	–ят (–ат)

говор–и́ть (to speak) молч–а́ть (to keep silent)

я говорю́ я молчу́
ты говори́шь ты молчи́шь

он
она́ } говори́т
оно́

он
она́ } молчи́т
оно́

мы говори́м мы молчи́м
вы говори́те вы молчи́те
они говоря́т они молча́т

Remark: Because of the spelling rule, after **ж, ч, ш, щ,** the first person singular ends in **–у**, and the third person plural ends in **–ат**.

Irregular Verbs

An *irregular* verb does not form its present tense according to the rules given above.

Principal rules governing the formation of the irregular present tense are as follows:

1. Verbs ending in **–вать**, preceded by **да, зна,** or **ста,** drop **ва**:

   дава́ть to give: даю́, даёшь . . . даю́т

признавáть to acknowledge, to admit: признаю́, признаёшь . . . признаю́т

вставáть to get up: встаю́, встаёшь . . . встаю́т

Note: This does not apply to other verbs in **–вать** (not preceded by да, зна, or ста):

плáвать to swim: плáваю, плáваешь . . . плáвают

2. Most verbs ending in **–овать** or **–евать** form their present tense with the stem ending in **–у** or **–ю**:

рисовáть to draw: рису́ю, рису́ешь . . . рису́ют
горевáть to grieve: горю́ю, горю́ешь . . . горю́ют
жевáть to chew: жую́, жуёшь . . . жую́т

A few of these verbs do not undergo any change; they have the same stem in the infinitive and in the present.

одевáть to dress (*trans.*): одевáю, одевáешь . . . одевáют
(and the related надевáть, переодевáть, etc.)
здорóваться to greet: здорóваюсь, здорóваешься . . . здорóваются
уповáть to hope (*obs.*): уповáю, уповáешь . . . уповáют

3. *Second* conjugation verbs with a stem ending in a labial (**б, в, м, п, ф**) insert **л** in the present tense, first person singular.

люби́ть to love: люблю́, лю́бишь . . . лю́бят
лови́ть to catch: ловлю́, лóвишь . . . лóвят
корми́ть to feed: кормлю́, кóрмишь . . . кóрмят
торопи́ть to hurry (*trans.*): тороплю́, торóпишь . . . торóпят
графи́ть to draw lines, to rule: графлю́, графи́шь . . . графя́т

(See *Table of Russian Verbs*, Type 37, page 247.)

Four verbs of the *first* conjugation insert an **л** after a labial—and this for *all* persons:

дремáть to doze: дремлю́, дрéмлешь . . . дрéмлют
колебáть to shake, to sway: колéблю, колéблешь . . . колéблют
сы́пать to strew, to pour: сы́плю, сы́плешь . . . сы́плют
трепáть to pull about, to tousle: треплю́, трéплешь . . . трéплют

VERBS

4. Many verbs undergo a mutation of consonants from the infinitive to the present. The last consonant of the infinitive stem changes as follows:

д, з, and г	change to ж
к and т	change to ч
с and х	change to ш
т, ст, and ск	change to щ

The mutation of consonants takes place in the first person singular of second conjugation verbs. It takes place in all persons of first conjugation verbs.

Examples:

Second Conjugation:

ходи́ть	to go, to walk: хожу́, хо́дишь . . . хо́дят
плати́ть	to pay: плачу́, пла́тишь . . . пла́тят
грусти́ть	to be sorry: грущу́, грусти́шь . . . грустя́т
носи́ть	to carry; to wear: ношу́, но́сишь . . . но́сят

First Conjugation:

иска́ть	to look for: ищу́, и́щешь . . . и́щут
пла́кать	to cry: пла́чу, пла́чешь . . . пла́чут
писа́ть	to write: пишу́, пи́шешь . . . пи́шут
пря́тать	to hide: пря́чу, пря́чешь . . . пря́чут
ре́зать	to cut: ре́жу, ре́жешь . . . ре́жут
сказа́ть	to say, to tell: скажу́, ска́жешь . . . ска́жут

(See *Table of Russian Verbs*, pages 238, 243, 247, Types 4, 22, 36.)

Remark: First conjugation verbs ending in **-чь** undergo a mutation of consonants according to the following pattern:

INFINITIVE	1st person singular and 3rd person plural	other persons
чь	г + characteristic ending	ж + characteristic ending
чь	к + characteristic ending	ч + characteristic ending

Examples:

мо_чь_ to be able: могу́, мо́_ж_ешь, мо́_ж_ет, мо́_ж_ем, мо́_ж_ете, мо́гут
пе_чь_ to bake: пе_к_у́, пе_ч_ёшь, пе_ч_ёт, пе_ч_ём, пе_ч_ёте, пе_к_у́т

IRREGULAR VERB ENDINGS

First Conjugation

The endings of irregular verbs are:

Group A.

	SINGULAR	PLURAL
1st person	–ю	–ем or –ём
2nd person	–ешь or –ёшь	–ете or –ёте
3rd person	–ет or –ёт	–ют

Group B.

	SINGULAR	PLURAL
1st person	–у	–ём or –ем
2nd person	–ёшь or –ешь	–ёте or –ете
3rd person	–ёт or –ет	–ут

VERBS

Note: The unstressed **-e** ending prevails in group A. The stressed **-ё** ending prevails in group B:

Examples:

рисова́ть	to draw:	рису́ю, рису́ешь . . . рису́ют
мыть	to wash:	мо́ю, мо́ешь . . . мо́ют
ждать	to wait:	жду, ждёшь . . . ждут
брать	to take:	беру́, берёшь . . . беру́т

Second Conjugation

The endings of irregular verbs are:

	SINGULAR	PLURAL
1st person	**-ю** or **-у**	**-им**
2nd person	**-ишь**	**-ите**
3rd person	**-ит**	**-ят**

Examples:

гнать	to chase:	гоню́, го́нишь . . . го́нят
спать	to sleep:	сплю, спишь . . . спят
лете́ть	to fly:	лечу́, лети́шь . . . летя́т
ходи́ть	to go, to walk:	хожу́, хо́дишь . . . хо́дят

Note: The mutation of consonants in Second Conjugation verbs takes place in the first person singular only; hence the endings **-у** in the first person singular and **-ят** in the third person plural in the last two examples. These verbs should not be confused with regular ones, such as крича́ть: кричу́, кричи́шь . . . крича́т where there is no mutation of consonants. (See *Table of Russian Verbs*, Type 9.)

Verbs Belonging to Both Conjugations

The following verbs have characteristic endings of both conjugations:

бежа́ть	to run: бегу́, бежи́шь, бежи́т, бежи́м, бежи́те, бегу́т
хоте́ть	to want, to wish: хочу́, хо́чешь, хо́чет, хоти́м, хоти́те, хотя́т

To these may be added the two following verbs which have **a** or **e** in the stem:

дать	to give: дам, дашь, даст, дади́м, дади́те, даду́т
есть	to eat: ем, ешь, ест, еди́м, еди́те, едя́т

together with verbs of the same root: зада́ть—to assign; созда́ть—to create; надое́сть—to annoy, to bother.

Usage of the Present Tense

1. The present tense of all Russian verbs—except the verbs of motion, which are discussed later—may be expressed in English by the simple Present or by the Present Continuous: Я чита́ю means *I read, I am reading*, and also *I do read*.

The present is used when referring to an action which is taking place at the present moment:

Я курю́ папиро́су.   I am smoking a cigarette.

Or, when referring to an action of a permanent duration:

Мы живём в го́роде.	We live in the city.
Во́лга впада́ет в Каспи́йское мо́ре.	The Volga flows into the Caspian Sea.

The present may indicate an habitual action:

Мы рабо́таем по суббо́там.   We do work on Saturdays.

2. The *historic present* is used sometimes to make a description more vivid:

Прибежа́ли в и́збу де́ти,	The children came running into the hut,
Второпя́х **зову́т** отца́.	(*They*) *are* hurriedly *calling* their father.
(Пу́шкин.)	

VERBS

3. The *present of anticipation* is sometimes used instead of the future:

Что вы делаете сегодня вечером?	What are you doing tonight?
Завтра кончается мой отпуск.	Tomorrow my vacation ends.
Сегодня мы завтракаем в городе.	Today we are having lunch in town.

This construction, however, cannot be used with just any verb. In fact, it is chiefly used with definite (actual) verbs of motion:

Вечером я иду на лекцию.	Tonight I am going to a lecture.
Летом мы едем в Европу.	In the summer we are going to Europe.

4. The reported speech in subordinate clauses conforms to the direct statement. Note the usage of the present tense in the following example:

Direct Statement	Reported Speech	English Equivalent
Я **знаю** его.	Я сказал, что я **знаю** его.	I said that I knew him.

Compare:

Я сказал, что я знал его.	I said that I used to know him. (I said that I had known him.)

Remark: The logical correctness prevails over grammatical forms not only in reported speech. For instance:

Я живу здесь год.	I have lived here for a year (and I am still living here).

Compare:

Я жил здесь год.	I lived here for a year (once upon a time).

5. The second person is sometimes used in rather indefinite or impersonal phrases.

(a) In the singular it may refer to the speaker or to the person addressed:

Мне не нравится, как он говорит: слушаешь, слушаешь и ничего не понимаешь.	I don't like the way he speaks: one listens, and does not understand anything.
Любишь кататься—люби и саночки возить.	If you like to ride, you had better like to pull the sleigh. (*proverb*)

(b) In the plural the statement is more generalized:

В Аме́рике, е́сли вы зараба́тываете 10.000 до́лларов в год, вы мо́жете жить дово́льно прили́чно.	In America, if one makes $10,000 a year one may live rather comfortably.

The Past Tense

Formation of the Past Tense

The past tense is characterized by gender and number. There is no distinction regarding person.

REGULAR FORMATION

Most verbs form their past tense by dropping the suffix –ть of the infinitive, and adding:

> –л for the masculine
> –ла for the feminine
> –ло for the neuter
> –ли for the plural

Example:

Писа́-ть	MASCULINE	Я (ты, он) писа́л
	FEMININE	Я (ты, она́) писа́ла
	NEUTER	Оно́ писа́ло
	PLURAL	Мы (вы, они́) писа́ли

Many verbs which form their present tense irregularly are regular in the past:

INFINITIVE		PRESENT	PAST
писа́ть	to write	пишу́	писа́л
жить	to live	живу́	жил
брать	to take	беру́	брал
петь	to sing	пою́	пел

IRREGULAR FORMATION

The irregularities are limited to a few classes:

1. Verbs in **-ти**, **-сть**, or **-зть** either have an **л** in the past masculine, or do not:

(a) They do, if the stem of the present (the future, for perfective verbs) ends in **д** or **т**.

Examples:

INFINITIVE		PRESENT	PAST
вести́	to lead	вед-у́	вёл, вела́, вело́, вели́
мести́	to sweep	мет-у́	мёл, мела́, мело́, мели́
класть	to put	клад-у́	клал, кла́ла, кла́ло, кла́ли

(b) They do not, if the stem of the present (the future, for perfective verbs) does not end in **д** or **т**.

INFINITIVE		PRESENT	PAST
нести́	to carry	нес-у́	нёс, несла́, несло́, несли́
лезть	to climb	лез-у	лез, ле́зла, ле́зло, ле́зли

2. The past tense of verbs in **-чь** ends in **-г** or **-к** in the masculine, depending on the stem of the present.

INFINITIVE		PRESENT	PAST
печь	to bake	пек-у́	пёк, пекла́, пекло́, пекли́
мочь	to be able	мог-у́	мог, могла́, могло́, могли́

Note: The verb жечь (to burn) drops the **е** in the feminine, neuter, and plural, in the past: жёг, жгла, жгло, жгли.

3. Verbs ending in **-ереть** in the infinitive drop **-еть** in the past:

| тере́ть | to rub | тёр, тёрла, тёрло, тёрли |
| умере́ть | to die | у́мер, умерла́, у́мерло, у́мерли |

4. Verbs in **-нуть**

(a) As a general rule, the verbs ending in **-нуть**, in the perfective infinitive only, keep **-ну** in the past, that is, they form their past regularly:

Infinitive

IMPERFECTIVE		PERFECTIVE	PAST
крича́ть	to cry	кри́кнуть	кри́кнул, –ла, –ло, –ли
толка́ть	to push	толкну́ть	толкну́л, –ла, –ло, –ли

Exceptions:

IMPERF.	PERF.		PAST
воздвига́ть,	воздви́гнуть	to set up, to erect	воздви́г, –ла, –ло, –ли
достига́ть,	дости́гнуть	to attain, to reach	дости́г, –ла, –ло, –ли
исчеза́ть,	исче́знуть	to disappear	исче́з, –ла, –ло, –ли
отверга́ть,	отве́ргнуть	to reject	отве́рг, –ла, –ло, –ли
привыка́ть,	привы́кнуть	to get used to	привы́к, –ла, –ло –ли
проника́ть,	прони́кнуть	to penetrate	прони́к, –ла, –ло, –ли
умолка́ть,	умо́лкнуть	to become silent	умо́лк, –ла, –ло, –ли

and a few others, including verbs of the same root as those above: Сверга́ть, све́ргнуть—to overthrow; отвыка́ть, отвы́кнуть—to lose the habit.

(b) Verbs which end in **–нуть** both in the imperfective and perfective, discard **–ну** in the past. For example:

Imperfective *Perfective*

INFINITIVE	PAST	INFINITIVE	PAST
мо́кнуть to get wet	мок, –ла, –ло, –ли	промо́кнуть	промо́к, –ла, –ло, –ли
мёрзнуть to freeze	мёрз, –ла, –ло, –ли	замёрзнуть	замёрз, –ла, –ло, –ли

Exceptions

| гнуть to bend | гнул, –ла, –ло, –ли | согну́ть | согну́л, –ла, –ло, –ли |
| тяну́ть to pull | тяну́л, –ла, –ло, –ли | вы́тянуть | вы́тянул, –ла, –ло, –ли |

5. In the following verbs the stem of the past has a **б**.

грести́	to row: грёб, –ла́, –ло́, –ли́
скрести́	to scrape, to scrub: скрёб, –ла́, –ло́, –ли́
ушиби́ть	to bruise, to hurt: уши́б, –ла, –ло, –ли
ошиби́ться	to make a mistake: оши́бся, –лась, –лось, –лись

VERBS

6. The past tense of расти́ (to grow) is: рос, росла́, росло́, росли́.

7. The past tense of идти́ (to go on foot) is: шёл, шла, шло, шли.

Note: The above applies to verbs of the same root, such as зарасти́—to be overgrown (with); дойти́—to go as far as; уйти́—to go away.

The Aspects

The basic principle has been mentioned earlier.
The Imperfective expresses a continuous or repeated action:

Он сиде́л и чита́л.	He was sitting and reading.
Я всегда́ чита́л газе́ту в по́езде.	I always used to read the newspaper in the train.

The Perfective stresses the result, or pertains to the end, the completion of an action:

Она́ прочита́ла ва́ше письмо́.   She read (has read) your letter.

Sometimes, the perfective pertains to the beginning of an action:

Ребёнок запла́кал.   The child started to cry.

Or it pertains to actions of short duration:

Он чихну́л.   He sneezed.

Also to actions of a longer duration:

Мы погуля́ли в па́рке.   We walked (for a while) in the park.

Remarks:

1. An aspect expresses the nature of an action at the moment it takes place. For instance:

В де́тстве я мно́го чита́л.	In my childhood I used to read a lot. (*Imperfective:* at that moment, the action was not completed or single.)
Я прочита́ю э́то за́втра.	I shall read this tomorrow. (*Perfective:* at that moment, the action will be completed.)

2. The basic correspondence between the principal English and Russian verbal forms is shown in the examples below:

ENGLISH		RUSSIAN	
Present Continuous	I am writing	*Present*	Я пишу́
Present	I write	*Present*	Я пишу́
Past Continuous	I was writing	*Past Imperfective*	Я писа́л
Past	I wrote	*Past Imperfective*	Я писа́л
		Past Perfective	Я написа́л
Present Perfect	I have written	*Past Perfective*	Я написа́л
Past Perfect	I had written	*Past Perfective*	Я написа́л
Future Continuous	I shall be writing	*Future Imperfective*	Я бу́ду писа́ть*
Future	I shall write	*Future Imperfective*	Я бу́ду писа́ть*
		Future Perfective	Я напишу́*

Notes:

(a) The translation of *I wrote*, *I shall write* and similar expressions depends on the context (imperfective for continuous or repeated actions; perfective for single and completed actions).

(b) *I used to write*, etc. is translated by я писа́л (*Imperfective*).

(c) The Present Perfect Continuous and the Past Perfect Continuous are frequently translated with the aid of уже́—already.

Я уже́ давно́ здесь живу́.   I have been living here for a long time.
Я уже́ давно́ не́ был там.   I had not been there for a long time.

Formation of the Aspects

The connection between the aspects of most verbs is usually obvious. However, the formation of one aspect from another varies according to the types listed below, as well as within these types.

* See page 168.

VERBS

PREFIXES

Many perfective verbs are formed from the imperfective by adding a prefix:

IMPERFECTIVE		PREFIX	PERFECTIVE
чита́ть	to read	про-	прочита́ть
писа́ть	to write	на-	написа́ть
де́лать	to do, to make	с-	сде́лать
пла́кать	to cry	за-	запла́кать
ре́зать	to cut	раз-	разре́зать
ждать	to wait	подо-	подожда́ть
стро́ить	to build	по-	постро́ить
мыть	to wash	вы-	вы́мыть
красть	to steal	у-	укра́сть
гло́хнуть	to grow deaf	о-	огло́хнуть

Remarks:

1. In addition to these prefixes, there are others which form the so-called "modified perfectives." In these, the basic meaning is altered:

IMPERFECTIVE	BASIC PERFECTIVE	MODIFIED PERFECTIVE	
писа́ть	написа́ть	переписа́ть	to copy, to write over
		вписа́ть	to enter, to write in
		подписа́ть	to sign

Note: Some prefixed verbs remain imperfective:

(*a*) Indefinite verbs of motion, such as **ходи́ть** which forms the imperfectives приходи́ть—to come; уходи́ть—to leave; входи́ть—to enter, etc.

(*b*) A group of verbs with the suffix **-ва**, such as **дава́ть** which forms the imperfectives передава́ть—to hand over, to transmit; отдава́ть—to give back, to return; продава́ть—to sell, etc.

2. The prefixes **по-** and **за-** impart various meanings to the newly formed perfective verbs.

The prefix **по** expresses:

(*a*) Completion of an action: стро́ить—постро́ить (to build); кра́сить—покра́сить (to paint)

Он постро́ил дом. He built a house.

(b) Doing something for a while; occasionally suggesting a certain informality: гуля́ть—погуля́ть (to walk); говори́ть—поговори́ть (to talk)

> Я погуля́л в па́рке.   I took a walk in the park.
> Мы поговори́ли немно́го.   We talked for a while.

(c) The beginning of an action with Definite (Actual) Verbs of Motion: плыть—поплы́ть (to swim); е́хать—пое́хать (to go not on foot), etc.

> Он поплы́л к бе́регу.   He started to swim towards the shore.

(d) A gradual change: старе́ть—постаре́ть (to age); худе́ть—похуде́ть (to lose weight)

> За после́днее вре́мя он   Lately, he has aged quite a lot.
> о́чень постаре́л.

(e) A single action of a short duration:

> Он мне позвони́л у́тром.   He telephoned me in the morning.

Note: покупа́ть is the *imperfective* of купи́ть.

The prefix **за-** expresses:

(a) The beginning of action: петь—запе́ть (to sing); дрожа́ть—задрожа́ть (to tremble):

Она́ запе́ла мою́ люби́мую пе́сню.   She started to sing my favorite song.

This type, however, is limited to a small number of verbs. Normally, the beginning of an action is expressed with auxiliary verbs:

> Он на́чал рабо́тать.   He has begun to work.
> Она́ ста́ла хорошо́ учи́ться.   She is starting to study well.

(b) The completion of an action: мёрзнуть—замёрзнуть (to freeze); со́хнуть—засо́хнуть (to dry up).

> Река́ замёрзла.   The river has frozen.

VERBS

INTERNAL CHANGES

1. Suffixes **-ыва** and **-ива**. With the aid of these suffixes, a *modified perfective* may form a new imperfective of the same meaning and with the same prefix: переписа́ть—перепи́сывать (to copy); подписа́ть—подпи́сывать (to sign); достро́ить—достра́ивать (to finish building).

In contrast to the above, the basic perfectives (such as написа́ть) as a rule do not form a second imperfective with -ыва or -ива. Exceptions are rare: чита́ть—прочита́ть—прочи́тывать.

2. Suffixes **-а, -я** and **-и**.

In any couple of verbs with these suffixes, the one ending in -а(ть) or -я(ть) is the imperfective, the one ending in -и(ть) is the perfective: получа́ть—получи́ть (to receive); реша́ть—реши́ть (to decide); разреша́ть—разреши́ть (to allow); выполня́ть—вы́полнить (to fulfill).

It should not be assumed that the suffix **-и** *alone* means that the verb is perfective. The following verbs, for instance, have -и in both aspects:

Imperfective: говори́ть—to speak; кури́ть—to smoke; пили́ть—to saw
Perfective: поговори́ть, вы́курить, распили́ть

3. The suffix **-ва** is found in a large group of imperfective verbs:

дава́ть—дать (to give); встава́ть—встать (to get up); узнава́ть—узна́ть (to recognize)

and many others where **ва** is preceded by **да**, **зна** or **ста**.

The same occurs with prefixed verbs: передава́ть—переда́ть (to transmit; to give, to hand); отдава́ть—отда́ть (to give back, to return).

4. Suffix **-ну**

(*a*) The suffix **-ну** is found in the perfective aspect of a number of verbs: исчеза́ть—исче́знуть (to disappear); толка́ть—толкну́ть (to push); крича́ть—кри́кнуть (to yell).

(*b*) However, when the verb indicates a more gradual, often "involuntary," action, both aspects may have the suffix **-ну**: мёрзнуть—замёрзнуть (to freeze); мо́кнуть—промо́кнуть (to get wet); ки́снуть—ски́снуть (to become sour).

This class of verbs expresses a state rather than an action.

5. In addition to these four principal types, there are a large number of verbs which undergo various changes in the stem:

        па́дать—упа́сть   to fall
        спаса́ть—спасти́   to save, to rescue

помога́ть—помо́чь	to help
предлага́ть—предложи́ть	to offer, to suggest
начина́ть—нача́ть	to begin
запира́ть—запере́ть	to lock
умира́ть—умере́ть	to die
понима́ть—поня́ть	to understand
собира́ть—собра́ть	to gather, to collect

Likewise, the verbs of the same root: занима́ть—заня́ть (to occupy; to borrow money); выбира́ть—вы́брать (to choose, to elect); убира́ть—убра́ть (to take away; to tidy), etc.

6. Four verbs have the reflexive ending **-ся** in the imperfective only: ложи́ться—лечь (to lie down); сади́ться—сесть (to sit down); станови́ться—стать (to become); ло́паться—ло́пнуть (to burst).

7. Чита́ть has two perfectives: прочита́ть and проче́сть. Likewise возвраща́ть(ся) (to return) has возврати́ть(ся) and верну́ть(ся).

DIFFERENT ROOTS

In a few instances, the imperfective and perfective aspect have different roots: говори́ть—сказа́ть (to say); брать—взять (to take); класть—положи́ть (to put).

CHANGE IN STRESS

Occasionally, the position of the stress changes the aspect. This may take place in the infinitive:

Imperfective: отреза́ть   to cut off (*Present:* отреза́ю, отреза́ешь . . . отреза́ют)

Perfective: отре́зать   (*Future:* отре́жу, отре́жешь . . . отре́жут)

Or, in other tenses:

Present: узнаю́, узнаёшь . . . узнаю́т   (*Infinitive:* узнава́ть —to recognize)

Future Perfective: узна́ю, узна́ешь . . узна́ют(*Infinitive:* узна́ть)

Single Verbs

Not every verb has two aspects.

(*a*) The following verbs occur only in the Imperfective:

VERBS

заве́довать	to manage, to be in charge of	приве́тствовать	to greet
зави́сеть	to depend	принадлежа́ть	to belong
зна́чить	to mean, to signify	пропове́довать	to preach
име́ть	to have	прису́тствовать	to be present
наблюда́ть	to observe	противоре́чить	to contradict
находи́ться	to be located	разгова́ривать	to talk
недоумева́ть	to be perplexed, to wonder	руководи́ть	to be in charge, to direct
нужда́ться	to need		
обита́ть	to dwell	содержа́ть	to contain
облада́ть	to possess	сожале́ть	to regret
обожа́ть	to adore	соотве́тствовать	to correspond
опаса́ться	to fear		
отрица́ть	to deny	состоя́ть	to consist (of)
отсу́тствовать	to be absent	состяза́ться	to compete, to contend
повествова́ть	to narrate		
повинова́ться	to obey, to comply (with)	сочу́вствовать	to sympathize
подозрева́ть	to suspect	сто́ить	to cost
подража́ть	to imitate	уважа́ть	to respect
подразумева́ть	to imply	угнета́ть	to oppress
покрови́тельствовать	to patronize	угрожа́ть	to threaten
		управля́ть	to drive; to rule
предви́деть	to foresee	утвержда́ть	to affirm*
предчу́вствовать	to have a premonition, to feel	уха́живать	to look after; to court
пресле́довать	to pursue	уча́ствовать	to participate

(b) The following verbs occur only in the Perfective:

заблуди́ться	to lose one's way*	очути́ться	to find oneself
гря́нуть	to sound (of thunder); to break out (of war)	понадо́биться	to be needed
		ри́нуться	to rush
		состоя́ться	to take place
очну́ться	to recover, to regain consciousness	стать	to start*

* The verbs marked with an asterisk do have another aspect—but only in a different meaning. Thus, утверди́ть (perf.) means "to approve (something)," заблужда́ться (imperf.) "to err," станови́ться (imperf.) "to become."

устоя́ть	to withstand	хлы́нуть	to gush out, to spout, to rush

(c) The following verbs can be used in either aspect:

веле́ть	to order	минова́ть	to pass, to elapse; to elude
венча́ть	to marry (trans.)		
жени́ться	to marry (intrans.)	насле́довать	to inherit
испо́льзовать	to use, to make use of	ночева́ть	to spend the night
		обеща́ть	to promise
иссле́довать	to investigate, to examine, to study, to explore	обсле́довать	to investigate, to inspect, to explore
		образова́ть	to form
казни́ть	to execute	ра́нить	to wound

And many others borrowed from foreign languages:

арестова́ть	to arrest	ликвиди́ровать	to liquidate
атакова́ть	to charge, to attack		
		организова́ть	to organize
конфискова́ть	to confiscate	телеграфи́ровать	to telegraph

Examples:

Он всегда́ мно́го обеща́ет, а пото́м ничего́ не де́лает.	He always promises a lot and then does nothing. (*imperf.*)
Éсли он обеща́л вам прийти́, я уве́рен, что он придёт.	If he has promised you to come, I am sure he will. (*perf.*)
Пока́ мы атакова́ли . . .	While we were attacking . . . (*imperf.*)
Они́ неожи́данно атакова́ли нас с ты́ла.	They unexpectedly attacked us from the rear. (*perf.*)

Remark: The need for a distinction between two aspects has accounted here for the appearance of another (prefixed) perfective: повеле́ть; повенча́ть; пожени́ть; переночева́ть; унасле́довать; пообеща́ть, etc.

Че́рез два го́да они́ пожени́лись.	Two years later they got married.

Раз он пообеща́л, наве́рно, он придёт.	Since he promised, he surely will come.

Usage of the Past Tense: Imperfective and Perfective

The use of the proper aspect is determined not only by the basic rules. Often, style or fine shades of meaning play a role. It should be kept in mind that the many deviations from normal usage, which are discussed below, are not cut-and-dried rules. Thus, if a Russian will often say "Он проси́л вас прийти́" (He asked you to come) or "Я сего́дня за́втракал в рестора́не" (Today I had lunch in a restaurant), a student (in case of doubt) may well abide by the basic rules and say: "Он попроси́л вас прийти́," "Я сего́дня поза́втракал в рестора́не."

1. The Perfective aspect is sometimes used in the past tense, when one may have expected the Imperfective. This happens when referring to the repetition of identical actions, especially with sentences containing the word раз:

Он не́сколько раз опозда́л на уро́к.	He was late several times for the lesson.
Она́ два ра́за перечита́ла его́ письмо́.	She read his letter over twice.

But, without the word раз:

Он всегда́ опа́здывал на уро́к.	He was always late for the lesson.
Она́ ча́сто перечи́тывала его́ письмо́.	She often read his letter over.

2. The usage of the Imperfective instead of the expected Perfective is more frequent. This may occur:

(*a*) When there is a shade of difference in the meaning of the two aspects, such as in: бежа́ть (*imperf.*)—to run, to flee; побежа́ть (*perf.*)—to run; ви́деть (*imperf.*)—to see; уви́деть (*perf.*)—to see, to notice; хоте́ть (*imperf.*)—to wish, захотéть (*perf.*)—to feel like (suddenly); слы́шать (*imperf.*)—to hear, to learn; услы́шать (*perf.*)—to hear.

Они́ бежа́ли с по́ля би́твы.	They fled from the battlefield.
Я ви́дел его́ сего́дня на у́лице.	I saw him today on the street.
Он хоте́л прийти́ в пять.	He wanted to come at five.
Я слы́шал, что они́ верну́лись.	I heard that they have come back.

(*b*) With some verbs which intrinsically do not contain the idea of completion, and where the distinction between the imperfective and perfective is not sharp. These verbs frequently have the prefix **по–** in the perfective, and imply a duration of an action; for instance: гуля́ть (по–) to walk; спать (по–) to sleep; сиде́ть (по–) to sit; стоя́ть (по–) to stand; жить (по–, про–) to live; ждать (подо–) to wait; служи́ть (про–) to serve, to be employed; рабо́тать (по–) to work.

Also, with a few others, pertaining to eating or drinking, where the idea of completion is not stressed: за́втракать (по–) to have lunch (breakfast); обе́дать (по–) to have dinner; у́жинать (по–) to have supper; пить (вы–) to drink, etc.

Examples:

Сего́дня мы гуля́ли в па́рке.	Today we walked in the park.
Вы хорошо́ спа́ли?	Did you sleep well?
Я ждал его́ мину́т де́сять.	I waited for him for about ten minutes.
Вы уже́ за́втракали?	Have you had lunch already?
Я у́жинал в ру́сском рестора́не.	I had dinner in a Russian restaurant.
Сего́дня мы пи́ли ко́фе без молока́.	Today we had coffee without milk.

(*c*) With verbs pertaining to communications between people, such as: писа́ть (на–) to write; звони́ть (по–) to ring; отвеча́ть (отве́тить) to answer; говори́ть (сказа́ть) to say; жа́ловаться (по–) to complain; встреча́ть (встре́тить) to meet; докла́дывать (доложи́ть) to report; проси́ть (по–) to ask (for)

Я ему́ писа́л насчёт э́того.	I wrote him about it.
Мне кто́-нибудь звони́л?	Did anybody telephone me?

—Да,—отвечал он . . .	—Yes, answered he . . . (*often in literature*)
Он говорил, что он скоро уезжает.	He said that he was leaving soon.
Он жаловался на меня директору.	He complained to the director about me.
Вы их встречали на вокзале?	Did you meet them at the station? (Were you at the station to meet them?)
Сегодня Иванов докладывал.	Today Ivanov gave a report.
Он просил вас прийти утром.	He asked you to come in the morning.

Also, with the verb читать (про–).

Вы читали газету?	Have you read the paper?

These expressions are not as precise, as completed, compared to the more "business-like" below:

Я написал ему про это.	I have written him about it.
Почему вы не позвонили сразу?	Why didn't you telephone right away?
Он не ответил на письмо.	He did not answer the letter.
Она прочитала телеграмму.	She read the telegram (through).

(*d*) With negated verbs. These verbs have anyway a tendency toward the imperfective, but especially so with the verbs of group (*b*) above. Here, the imperfective would be used more frequently—even if not always (as with ждать, подождать):

Мы сегодня не гуляли.	We did not walk today.
Она не спала.	She did not sleep.
Он не работал в субботу.	He did not work on Saturday.
Я долго не ждал.	I did not wait for long.
Почему вы не подождали меня?	Why did you not wait for me?

With many other negated verbs, both aspects are used:

Я не брал ваших денег.	I did not take your money. (*imperf.*)
Он ничего не купил.	He did not buy anything. (*perf.*)

The difference in the usage of one aspect or the other may be illustrated by the following examples:

Я ему́ ничего́ не говори́л.	I didn't tell him anything. (could imply "it so happened")
Я ему́ ничего́ не сказа́л.	I did not tell him anything. (could imply "intentionally")
Я их не приглаша́л, а они́ пришли́.	I didn't invite them but they came.
Я их не пригласи́л.	I did not invite them (intentionally).
Нет, он не приходи́л сего́дня.	No, he didn't come today (he didn't visit us, didn't show up).
Она́ ему́ позвони́ла, но он не пришёл.	She telephoned him but he didn't come.

The Future

Formation of the Future Tense

A. The Imperfective Future is formed with the auxiliary verb **быть** and the infinitive:

Я бу́ду
Ты бу́дешь
Он (она́, оно́) бу́дет
Мы бу́дем
Вы бу́дете
Они́ бу́дут
} + чита́ть, говори́ть, etc.

Note: Бу́ду, бу́дешь, etc. are never added to the perfective infinitive.

B. The Perfective Future has the same endings as the present tense, but it is formed from the perfective infinitive. Those perfectives which are formed by the addition of prefixes belong to the same conjugation as the corresponding imperfective:

VERBS

IMPERFECTIVE INFINITIVE	PRESENT
читáть, говори́ть	я читáю, я говорю́
	ты читáешь, ты говори́шь
	он читáет, он говори́т
	мы читáем, мы говори́м
	вы читáете, вы говори́те
	они́ читáют, они́ говоря́т

PERFECTIVE INFINITIVE	FUTURE
прочитáть, поговори́ть	я прочитáю, я поговорю́
	ты прочитáешь, ты поговори́шь
	он прочитáет, он поговори́т
	мы прочитáем, мы поговори́м
	вы прочитáете, вы поговори́те
	они́ прочитáют, они́ поговоря́т

Non-prefixed perfectives may or may not belong to the same conjugation as their imperfectives:

IMPERFECTIVE	PERFECTIVE	IMPERFECTIVE	PERFECTIVE
Брать	Взять	Решáть	Реши́ть
(*first conj.*)	(*first conj.*)	(*first conj.*)	(*second conj.*)
Я беру́	Я возьму́	Я решáю	Я решу́
Ты берёшь	Ты возьмёшь	Ты решáешь	Ты реши́шь
Он берёт	Он возьмёт	Он решáет	Он реши́т
Мы берём	Мы возьмём	Мы решáем	Мы реши́м
Вы берёте	Вы возьмёте	Вы решáете	Вы реши́те
Они́ беру́т	Они́ возьму́т	Они́ решáют	Они́ решáт

Usage of the Future Tense: Imperfective and Perfective

The basic principle of the aspects (Imperfective: continuous or repeated action; Perfective: single and completed action) applies to the future. The future tense will answer, for example, questions of the following meaning (if not of the exact wording):

Imperfective: "*What will you be doing?*"
Perfective: "*What will you do?*"

Examples:

(a) Imperfective

Я бу́ду вас ждать там.	I will be waiting for you there.
Ле́том мы бу́дем жить в дере́вне.	We are going to live in the country this summer (We will be living).
Я бу́ду учи́ться зимо́й.	I shall study in the winter (I will be studying).

(b) Perfective

Я напишу́ ему́.	I shall write to him.
Я пошлю́ де́ньги сего́дня.	I am going to send the money today (I shall send).
Мы прие́дем в пять.	We will come at five.

In other words, here again, the imperfective stresses the action, and the perfective—broadly speaking—the result, the accomplishment.

IMPERFECTIVE FUTURE

(a) The imperfective future (instead of the perfective) is very often used with the group of verbs (b) (page 166):

Я бу́ду спать в гости́ной.	I will sleep in the living room.
Он бу́дет нас ждать в кафе́.	He will wait for us in the cafe.
Где вы бу́дете у́жинать?	Where will you have supper?
Что вы бу́дете пить?	What will you drink?

(b) The same applies to negated verbs.

| Ну, мы не бу́дем проси́ть вас. | Well, we won't ask you. |
| Я ему́ ничего́ не бу́ду говори́ть. | I won't say anything to him. |

Note: The above expressions are often best translated into English by "We aren't going," "I am not going," etc.

PERFECTIVE AND IMPERFECTIVE FUTURE

(a) With actions which are about to take place right away—the perfective future is used more often than the imperfective.

Я сейча́с запишу́ ваш а́дрес.	I will write down your address (right away).
Мы свернём напра́во.	We are going to turn right.

In some expressions, the perfective future almost merges with present:

Попрошу́ вас . . .	I'll ask you (to . . .)
Позво́лю себе́ заме́тить.	I will take the liberty to point out.
Не суме́ю вам сказа́ть.	I wouldn't be able to tell you.
Как прика́жете.	As you wish.

Similarly in negated sentences with the verb in the 2nd person singular:

Вас не узна́ешь.	One wouldn't recognize you.
Ничего́ не поде́лаешь.	Nothing to be done.
Здесь така́я пу́таница, что ничего́ не разберёшь.	There is such a mix-up here, that one can't understand a thing.

(*b*) Either aspect is used with actions pertaining to more or less distant future:

Я вам напишу́, когда́ я прие́ду в Москву́.	I shall write you when I arrive in Moscow.
Я бу́ду вам писа́ть из Москвы́.	I shall write (be writing) you from Moscow.

PERFECTIVE FUTURE

(*a*) A perfective future may occasionally resemble a wish or a command (depending on the tone and the circumstances):

Вы мне напи́шете, не пра́вда ли?	You will write me, won't you?
Ты сам пойдёшь к нему́ и всё объясни́шь.	You yourself will go to him and explain everything.
Вы начнёте обстре́л в 14.00.	You will open fire at 1400.

(*b*) It may express an action, which in the mind of the speaker always happens, or is likely to happen:

Вот вы всегда́ так, молоды́е лю́ди. . . . Вам что́-нибудь ска́жешь, а вы и . . . (Л. Толсто́й)	That's the way it always is with you young people. . . . One will tell you something, and you just . . .

Он всегда найдёт какую-нибудь ошибку.	He will always find some mistake.

Notes:

(*a*) The usage of всегда with the perfective is most unusual. Here, however, it is possible on account of the "habitual" nature of the action.

(*b*) This type of construction is frequently found in proverbs or sayings, with the verb in the 2nd person singular:

Что посеешь, то и пожнёшь.	What you sow—you will reap.
За двумя зайцами погонишься— ни одного не поймаешь.	If you chase two hares, you won't catch a single one.

(*c*) The future perfective is sometimes found in narratives. Its usage is then similar to the historic present:

Хорошо жить в деревне! Встанешь рано, оденешься, выйдешь в сад . . .	How nice it is to live in the country! You get up early, dress, go out into the garden . . .

(*d*) It is used to express the repetition of a single action on the background of a more lengthy one.

Буря мглою небо кроет,	The storm is covering the sky with a mist,
Вихри снежные крутя,	Whirling and whirling the snow,
То, как зверь, она завоет,	Now howling like a beast,
То заплачет, как дитя.	Now crying like a child.
(Пушкин)	

The Conditional Mood

Formation of the Conditional

In the Conditional (or Subjunctive) the particle **бы** is added to the past tense of any gender, number, or aspect. Sometimes, бы is contracted to **б**:

Я сам написал бы ему.	I would have written to him myself.

Она́ с удово́льствием прочита́ла бы э́ту кни́гу.	She would read this book with pleasure.
Э́то бы́ло бы хорошо́.	That would be fine.
Вы могли́ б прие́хать о́коло трёх?	Could you come around three?

In complex sentences, the particle бы is found in the main clause as well as in the subordinate:

Если я не́ был бы за́нят, я пошёл бы.	If I were not busy, I would go. (*subjunctive*) (*conditional*)

The particle бы usually follows the verb. However, "Если бы я не́ был за́нят, я бы пошёл" is also absolutely correct. Sometimes this particle may emphasize the subject by following it immediately:

<u>Я</u> бы не пошёл.   <u>I</u> wouldn't have gone.

Usage of the Conditional

A. The conditional mood may refer to the past, present or future.
1. *Imperfective Aspect:* Если бы вы приходи́ли к нам ча́ще could refer to the past or present, i.e. "If you would have visited us more often (last summer)" or: "If you would visit us more often."
2. *Perfective Aspect:* Если бы вы пришли́ в сре́ду could refer to the past or future, i.e. "If you would have come on Wednesday," or: "If you would come on Wednesday."
B. Meanings of the Conditional.
Traditionally, the form *past tense* + **бы** is associated with the conditional mood. Yet, this form has a variety of meanings, including many where no "condition" is present. It may express:

1. Condition proper:

Если бы вы наде́ли пальто́, вам не́ было бы хо́лодно.	If you had put on a coat you wouldn't be cold.
Если я не́ был бы бо́лен, я бы пошёл.	If I weren't sick I would go.

2. Wish, desire, request, and sometimes command, i.e. after such verbs as хоте́ть (to want); жела́ть (to wish); проси́ть (to ask); наста́ивать (to insist); смотре́ть (to watch, to see that).

(*a*) In subordinate clauses the particle **бы** is incorporated in **чтобы**:

Он хо́чет, что́бы все зна́ли э́то.	He wants everybody to know it.
Она́ попроси́ла меня́, что́бы я пришёл ра́но.	She asked me to come early.
Он приказа́л, что́бы все собра́лись к восьми́ часа́м.	He ordered everybody to assemble by eight o'clock.
Смотри́те, что́бы они́ не опозда́ли.	See that they aren't late.

The conditional mood, of course, may express the opposite to the above. Then—in the negated sentences—the verb is usually in the imperfective.

Я не хочу́, что́бы вы говори́ли про э́то.	I don't want you to speak about this.
Он попроси́л меня́, что́бы я не приходи́л ра́но.	He asked me not to come early.

(*b*) In simple clauses, the verbs **хоте́ть** and **жела́ть** may be used to express a wish in more polite form:

Я хоте́л бы стака́н воды́.	I would like a glass of water.

Compare:

Я хочу́ стака́н воды́.	I want a glass of water.

Notes:

Проси́ть and **прика́зывать** may be followed by the infinitive:

Она́ попроси́ла меня́ прийти́.	She asked me to come.
Он приказа́л собра́ться к восьми́.	He ordered (us) to assemble by eight.

A suggestion which includes the speaker is translated as follows:

I suggest that we go. Я предлага́ю пое́хать. (*lit.*: I suggest to go.)

3. On certain occasions—an informal suggestion:

Что вы сиди́те до́ма? Пошли́ бы вы погуля́ть.	What are you sitting at home? Why don't you go out for a walk?
Вы бы отдохну́ли немно́го.	Why don't you rest for a while.

4. Thought; doubt; opinion; fear

Уже́ по́здно. Я сомнева́юсь, что́бы он пришёл.	It is late. I doubt that he will come.
Мы не счита́ем, что́бы э́то бы́ло тру́дно.	We don't consider this as difficult.
Я не ду́маю, что́бы она́ прие́хала сего́дня.	I don't think that she will arrive today.
Бою́сь, что́бы он не опозда́л.	I'm afraid he might be late.*

5. Concession. A fairly common usage of this form may be illustrated by the following examples, all of which contain the particles **ни** and **бы**.

Кто бы ни пришёл, меня́ нет до́ма.	Whoever may come, I am not at home.
Что бы вы ни реши́ли, он э́то сде́лает по-сво́ему.	Whatever you decide, he will do it his own way.
Когда́ бы вы ни зашли́, всегда́ бу́дем ра́ды вас ви́деть.	Whenever you can come, we'll always be glad to see you.

6. Purpose. In complex sentences, the purpose may be expressed by **что́бы** + *past tense*:

(*a*) When the subordinate clause has a subject different from the one in the main clause:

Я пришёл, что́бы вы рассказа́ли мне об э́том.	I came so that you would tell me about it.

(*b*) When the subordinate clause is an impersonal sentence:

Она́ откры́ла окно́, что́бы не́ было так жа́рко.	She opened the window so it wouldn't be so hot.

Note: If the two predicates refer to the same subject, the infinitive is used in the subordinate clause:

Я иду́ в конто́ру, что́бы поговори́ть с дире́ктором.	I am going to the office to talk with the director.
Я пришёл, что́бы рассказа́ть вам об э́том.	I came to tell you about it.

* See more detailed explanation in the chapter on conjunctions (page 310).

CONDITION EXPRESSED BY THE IMPERATIVE MOOD

A condition contrary to fact is occasionally expressed by the familiar form of the imperative. The construction is somewhat informal and its usage is rather limited:

Будь я на вашем месте, я не отвечал бы на это письмо.	If I were you, I wouldn't answer this letter.
Знай я ремесло—жил бы я в городе. (Горький)	If I knew a trade I would live in the city.

REPORTED SPEECH

The conditional mood is not used in reported speech, unless a condition is implied. In reported speech, the verb is in the same tense as in the direct statement:

DIRECT STATEMENT	REPORTED SPEECH	ENGLISH EQUIVALENT
Я приду́	Я сказа́л, что я приду́. (will come)	I said that I would come.

Compare:

Я сказа́л, что я пришёл бы, если бы я знал это.	I said that I would have come if I had known this.

The Imperative Mood

Formation of the Imperative

REGULAR FORMATION

The imperative is formed from the third person plural—present tense for the imperfective aspect, future for the perfective aspect—by:

dropping the characteristic endings –ат, –ят, –ут or –ют—and adding

й, и or **ь** for the familiar form,
йте, ите or **ьте** for the polite form.

(*a*) **й** or **йте** is added when the present stem ends in a vowel:

Present: я чита́ю, они́ чита́-ют.   Imperative: чита́й! чита́йте!

(*b*) **и** or **ите** is added when the present stem ends in a consonant, and when the first person singular is stressed on the ending.

Present: я пишу́, они́ пи́ш-ут.   Imperative: пиши́! пиши́те!

(*c*) **ь** or **ьте** is added when the present stem ends in a consonant, and when the first person singular is not stressed on the ending.

Future: я бро́шу, они́ бро́с-ят.   Imperative: брось! бро́сьте!

SPECIAL CASES

1. Verbs ending in –**вать** preceded by да, зна or ста form their imperative by dropping the ending –ть of the infinitive and adding –**й** or –**йте**.
Дава́-ть: дава́й! дава́йте!
Встава́-ть: встава́й! встава́йте!

2. Nine verbs form their imperative quite irregularly:

First group—five verbs in –**ить**.   *Second group*—various verbs.

Бить: бей! бе́йте!	to beat	Лечь: ляг! ля́гте!	to lie down
Вить: вей! ве́йте!	to twine	Есть: ешь! е́шьте!	to eat
Лить: лей! ле́йте!	to pour	Дать: дай! да́йте!	to give
Пить: пей! пе́йте!	to drink	Пое́хать: поезжа́й! поезжа́йте!	to go, to ride
Шить: шей! ше́йте!	to sew		

Note: The imperatives of related verbs, such as разби́ть, переда́ть, are formed similarly.

3. The following four verbs add –**и** (**те**) to stems ending in a vowel:

Крои́ть: крою́, крою́т—кро́йте!   to cut, to cut out (in sewing)
Пои́ть: пою́, по́ят—по́йте!   to give to drink, to water
Дои́ть: дою́, до́ят—до́йте!   to milk
Таи́ть: таю́, та́ят—та́йте!   to conceal; to harbor

4. The imperative ends in –**и** (**те**) regardless of the stress in the first person singular:

(*a*) Practically always, in perfective verbs prefixed with **вы**:

Вы́нести: вы́несу, вы́несут—вы́несите!   to carry out
Вы́учить: вы́учу, вы́учат—вы́учите!   to learn

Exceptions are very rare:

Вы́сунуть: вы́суну, вы́сунут—вы́суньте!	to stick out
Вы́ставить: вы́ставлю, вы́ставят—вы́ставьте! или вы́ставите!	to put out

(b) Usually, when the stem from which it is formed ends in a "cluster of consonants":

Почи́стить: почи́щу, почи́стят—почи́стите!	to clean
Е́здить: е́зжу, е́здят—(не) е́здите!	to ride, to drive

(c) Always, when the last letter of the cluster is an **н**:

Кри́кнуть: кри́кну, кри́кнут—кри́кните!	to shout
Запо́лнить: запо́лню, запо́лнят—запо́лните!	to fill out

5. A few verbs do not form the imperative: ви́деть—to see; слы́шать—to hear; мочь—to be able; хоте́ть—to wish.* Also, a few verbs where simple logic would preclude an imperative mood, such as течь—to flow, ве́сить—to weigh (*intrans.*)

Usage of the Imperative

A. The choice of the proper aspect to use is sometimes a delicate matter. The *basic* principle of the aspects is found again in the imperative: The Imperfective Imperative stresses the action (continuous, repeated, habitual) whereas the perfective stresses rather the result of the (single) action:

Пиши́те нам ча́ще	Write us more often. (imperfective)
Да́йте мне ма́рку, пожа́луйста.	Give me a stamp, please. (perfective)

1. The *Imperfective Imperative* often suggests doing something right away, and therefore may sound peremptory, if not impolite:

Чита́йте э́то!	Read this!
Подмета́йте пол!	Sweep the floor!

* Vinogradov does quote the form захоти́ which he actually no longer considers an imperative (Совреме́нный ру́сский язы́к, p. 460).

VERBS

| Пишите ваш адрес! | Write your address! |
| Убирайте со стола! | Clear the table! |

This, however, is not always the case. Many verbs in which the "imperfective is used instead of the expected perfective" (page 165) are normally used in the imperfective with the imperative mood:

Спите спокойно.	Sleep well. (*lit.:* calmly)
Кушайте сыр.	Eat (some) cheese.
Говорите громче, пожалуйста.	Speak louder, please.

2. The *Negated Imperative* usually stands in the imperfective:

| Не говорите ему насчёт этого. | Don't tell him about this. |
| Не кладите деньги на стол. | Don't put money on the table. |

The so-called "verbs of warning" are exceptions to this rule:

Не простудитесь.	Don't catch cold.
Не упадите.	Don't fall.
Не сломайте; не разбейте.	Don't break.
Не потеряйте.	Don't lose.

Also, the imperative of забывать, забыть is—more often than not—in the perfective:

Не забудьте принести деньги.	Don't forget to bring the money. (*perf.*)
Не забудь позвонить мне завтра.	Don't forget to call me tomorrow. (*perf.*)
Не забывайте нас!	Don't (you) forget us. (*imperf.*)

Note: An additional emphasis may be placed here by adding **смотрите** (**смотри**), the imperative of смотреть (which, of course, loses its literal meaning here):

| Смотрите, не забудьте! | Be sure not to forget! |
| Смотри, не опоздай! | Be sure not to be late! |

3. The *Perfective Imperative* may refer to an immediate, or more distant future. It is usually more polite, since it may imply doing something at a convenient time. This is the case of the examples below, at least as compared to those on page 178, para. 1:

| Прочитайте это. | Read this. |

Подметите комнату.	Sweep the room.
Напишите ваш адрес.	Write down your address.
Напишите нам, когда вы приедете в Париж.	Write us when you come to Paris.

Remark: Oddly enough, the implication is exactly the reverse with intransitive verbs involving motion; for instance, with the imperfectives:

Приходите вечером.	Come tonight.
Садитесь сюда.	Sit here (take a seat).

Here, the perfectives—придите вечером, сядьте сюда—may sound somewhat abrupt (without really being impolite).

THIRD-PERSON IMPERATIVES

Although, strictly speaking, the imperative mood is only used with the second person, the equivalent of an imperative may be found with the third person, singular or plural. In these constructions, **пусть** or **пускай** are added to the future or present.

Пусть он придёт утром.	Let him come in the morning (He should come in the morning).
Пускай мальчики играют там.	Let the boys play there.

JOINT IMPERATIVE

The joint form of the imperative normally coincides with the future perfective, the only difference being the omission of the pronoun **мы**. This form is an invitation for participation:

Напишем ему.	Let's write him.
Сделаем это так.	Let's do it that way.
Пойдём в театр вечером.	Let us go to the theater tonight.

With definite verbs of motion **идти** and **ехать**, the joint imperative may coincide with the present:

Идём скорей.	Let's go quickly.
Ну, едем домой.	Well, let's go home.

Note: The present is not used with the so-called indefinite verbs of motion—ходить, ездить.

VERBS

Adding **те** to the ending of the verb somewhat softens the suggestion without really introducing too much difference in the meaning: Напи́шемте ему́; пойдёмте в теа́тр; идёмте скоре́й.

Remarks:

(*a*) Vinogradov* states that the form without **те** (пойдём) expresses a suggestion directed to one man. The form with **те** (пойдёмте)—to one or more persons:

Пое́дем в го́род.	Let us go to town. (we two)
Пое́демте в го́род.	Let us go to town. ("we two" or "all of us")

(*b*) The form without **те** is usually the only appropriate one at a higher intellectual or emotional level. A teacher would say at a lecture:

Рассмо́трим тепе́рь осо́бый слу́чай.	Let us examine now a special case.
Допу́стим, что э́ти ли́нии паралле́льны.	Let us assume that these lines are parallel.

Similarly:

Вы́полним свой долг!	Let us fulfill our duty!
Отстои́м на́шу свобо́ду!	Let us defend (safeguard) our freedom!

Another way of expressing the joint imperative is with the aid of **дава́йте** (let us). This construction suggests a proposal and has nothing of a command:

Дава́йте напи́шем ему́. (*perf.*)	Let us write him.
Дава́йте писа́ть ча́ще друг дру́гу. (*imperf.*)	Let us write each other more often.

It will be seen from the above examples, that when the meaning of a sentence calls for the perfective—the future perfective is used: напи́шем. When the meaning calls for the imperfective—the infinitive must be used: писа́ть. (In other words, дава́йте can not be followed by пи́шем or написа́ть.)

Note: **Да́йте я** means *let me.*

* В. В. Виногра́дов. Совреме́нный ру́сский язы́к.

Remarks:

(*a*) The usage of personal pronouns with the imperative is infrequent. It usually emphasizes a contrast:

Я пойду направо, а ты иди налево.	I'll go to the right and you go to the left.
Я буду работать, а вы отдохните.	I shall work and you have a rest.

(*b*) Adding **да** to the imperative expresses impatience:

Да уходите же!	Go away (this minute)!
Да говорите, в чём дело!	Come on, say what's the matter!

(*c*) Adding **-ка** to the imperative makes the sentences rather familiar or informal:

Поставь-ка это сюда.	How about putting it here?
Пойдёмте-ка на пляж.	Why don't we go to the beach?

(*d*) Another, quite informal, way of expressing "let's" is with the past perfective. This usage is practically limited to the following types:

Ну, поéхали.	Well, let's go (let's get off).
Пошли домой.	(Come on) let's go home.

Reflexive Verbs

Preliminary Remark on Transitive and Intransitive Verbs

1. A transitive verb takes a direct object which is normally in the accusative case (without prepositions):

Он читает письмо.	He is reading a letter.
Она видела сестру.	She saw (her) sister.

It may be recalled that sometimes the object following a transitive verb is followed by the genitive:

Дайте мне хлеба.   Give me some bread. (*partitive genitive*)

VERBS

Я не чита́л э́тих книг.   I did not read these books. (*negated sentence*)

Certain transitive verbs are not necessarily followed by a direct object. When this happens, the verb often refers to occupation:

По вечера́м мы чита́ем.   In the evenings we read.
Он мно́го пи́шет.   He writes a lot.

2. An intransitive verb is not directly aimed at an object or a person. It never answers the questions кого́? что? (whom? what?).

Мы гуля́ли в па́рке.   We walked in the park.
Он рабо́тает на фа́брике.   He works at the factory.

Only in one type of construction is it followed by an object in the accusative case, without prepositions. This happens in sentences referring to time, distance, weight or price:

Они́ разгова́ривали всю доро́гу.   They talked all the way.
Он спал час.   He slept for an hour.
Ка́мень ве́сит то́нну.   The rock weighs one ton.
Кни́га сто́ит рубль.   The book costs one ruble.

3. A large group of intransitive verbs is formed by adding the particle –ся to transitive verbs. The distinction between these two types of verbs should be carefully observed in Russian:

Transitive   to meet (somebody, something)   встреча́ть, встре́тить
Intransitive   to meet (with)   встреча́ться, встре́титься
Transitive   to wash (somebody, something)   мыть, вы́мыть
Intransitive   to wash (oneself)   мы́ться, вы́мыться

> *Note:* The verbs ending in –ся are often called reflexive verbs, a traditional and convenient—if not quite accurate—term.

Formation and Conjugation of Reflexive Verbs

The particle (or affix) –ся is an abbreviation of the reflexive pronoun **себя́**. As mentioned above, it may be added to the infinitive of transitive verbs. Only occasionally is it added to intransitive ones, as, for example, in Мне не спи́тся—I don't feel like sleeping.

-Ся follows verbal forms ending in a consonant, **-ь** or **-й**: мы́ться—to wash; я мы́лся—I washed; ты мо́ешься—you wash; мо́йся!—wash (yourself).

-Сь follows verbal forms ending in a vowel: я мо́юсь—I wash; она́ мы́лась—she washed (herself).

Note: Participles of reflexive verbs always end in –ся
after a consonant:

Я ви́дел люде́й, верну́вших<u>ся</u> из Москвы́.	I saw (some) people who have returned from Moscow.

or after a vowel:

Я ви́дел да́му, верну́вш<u>ую</u>ся из Москвы́.	I saw a lady who has returned from Moscow.

CONJUGATION OF A REFLEXIVE VERB

	IMPERFECTIVE	PERFECTIVE
Infinitive	одева́ться (to dress)	оде́ться
Present	я одева́ю**сь**	
	ты одева́ешь**ся**	
	он одева́ет**ся**	
	мы одева́ем**ся**	
	вы одева́ете**сь**	
	они́ одева́ют**ся**	
Past	(*m.*) одева́л**ся**	(*m.*) оде́л**ся**
	(*f.*) одева́ла**сь**	(*f.*) оде́ла**сь**
	(*n.*) одева́ло**сь**	(*n.*) оде́ло**сь**
	(*pl.*) одева́ли**сь**	(*pl.*) оде́ли**сь**
Future	я бу́ду одева́ть**ся**	я оде́ну**сь**
	ты бу́дешь одева́ть**ся**	ты оде́нешь**ся**
	он бу́дет одева́ть**ся**	он оде́нет**ся**
	мы бу́дем одева́ть**ся**	мы оде́нем**ся**
	вы бу́дете одева́ть**ся**	вы оде́нете**сь**
	они́ бу́дут одева́ть**ся**	они́ оде́нут**ся**

Conditional	(*m.*) одева́лся бы	(*m.*) оде́лся бы
	(*f.*) одева́лась бы	(*f.*) оде́лась бы
	(*n.*) одева́лось бы	(*n.*) оде́лось бы
	(*pl.*) одева́лись бы	(*pl.*) оде́лись бы
Imperative	одева́й**ся**!	оде́нь**ся**!
	одева́йте**сь**!	оде́ньте**сь**!

Classification and Usage of Reflexive Verbs

PRELIMINARY REMARK

The formation of a reflexive verb from a transitive one is not always possible:

Some transitive verbs (начина́ть, продолжа́ть, etc.) form a reflexive in the third person only:

Уро́к начина́ется.	The lesson is beginning.
Рабо́та продолжа́лась.	Work continued.

Others seldom or never form reflexives: знать (to know); купи́ть (to buy); etc.

CLASSIFICATION*

1. Reflexive proper

In these verbs the action is directed towards the person performing it:

Я одева́юсь.	I am dressing (myself).
Он мы́лся.	He was washing (himself).

2. Neuter-Reflexive

Here the action is contained within the agent, rather than being reflected upon it.† The effect of adding –**ся** is merely to change the verb from transitive to intransitive, as illustrated below.

(*a*) Transitive

Мы останови́ли авто́бус.	We stopped the bus.

---

* This classification is a simplified version from Vinogradov's Совреме́нный ру́сский язы́к.

† "The subject, remaining the performer of the action, is not thought of as such"—Ша́хматов.

Они́ ко́нчили рабо́ту.	They finished the work.
Профе́ссор на́чал ле́кцию в два часа́.	The professor began his lecture at two o'clock.
Э́то беспоко́ит меня́.	This worries me.

(b) Intransitive (Reflexive)

Мы останови́лись на углу́.	We stopped at the corner.
Рабо́та ко́нчилась ра́но.	The work finished early.
Ле́кция начала́сь в два часа́.	The lecture began at two o'clock.
Она́ беспоко́ится.	She is worrying.

3. Reciprocal

The action here pertains to two or more people (sometimes objects).

(a) Transitive:

Я ча́сто ви́дел его́.	I often saw him.
Он познако́мил меня́ со свое́й сестро́й.	He introduced me to his sister.
Мы встре́тили та́нки неприя́теля.	We met the enemy's tanks.

(b) Intransitive:

Мы ви́делись не́сколько раз ле́том.	We saw each other a few times in the summer.
Мы познако́мились на конце́рте.	We met (made acquaintance) at a concert.
На́ши та́нки встре́тились за ле́сом.	Our tanks met beyond the wood.

Note: It should not be assumed that all verbs involving a reciprocal action end in –ся, for example: Мы разгова́ривали—We were talking. Они́ лю́бят друг дру́га.—They love each other.

4. Passive

These verbs are used chiefly or only with the third person.

Здесь продаётся вино́.	Wine is sold here.
На собра́нии обсужда́лись ва́жные вопро́сы.	At the meeting some important questions were discussed.

This type of construction may be replaced (and often is) by an impersonal one, with the subject omitted:

    Здесь продаю́т вино́.
    На собра́нии обсужда́ли ва́жные вопро́сы.

5. Qualitative

These verbs express a quality, an habitual characteristic:

Э́та па́лка не сгиба́ется.	This stick does not bend.
Э́ти таре́лки не бью́тся.	These plates are unbreakable.
Соба́ка куса́ется.	The dog bites.
Земля́ враща́ется.	The Earth spins.

6. Impersonal

The impersonal reflexive belong to a small group of verbs, which, as a rule, lack intensity of expression:

Мне хо́чется.	I feel like.
Нам не ве́рилось.	We couldn't believe (somehow).
Мне не спи́тся.	I can't sleep (I don't feel like sleeping).

Compare the examples above to the more forceful expressions:

Я хочу́.	I want.
Мы не ве́рим.	We don't believe.
Я не сплю.	I don't sleep.

The verbs каза́ться (to seem), and нра́виться (to appeal, to please) which do not have a corresponding form without –ся also express a rather mild idea.

7. Verbs pertaining to a result carried out to a full extent:

Я хорошо́ вы́спался.	I slept well (I had a really good sleep).
Де́вочка распла́калась.	The girl burst into tears.
Наконе́ц я дожда́лся того́ дня.	Finally, the day (for which I waited so long) came.
Все разъе́хались на кани́кулы.	Everybody left for their vacation.
Они́ разошли́сь	They parted (they separated).

8. Neuter Verbs

These verbs have no corresponding form without –ся. The most commonly used are listed below.

боя́ться, по-	to be afraid	пости́ться	to fast
горди́ться, воз-	to be proud (of)	появля́ться, появи́ться	to appear
догáдываться, догадáться	to guess	распоряжáться, распоряди́ться	to direct, to give orders
здорóваться, по-	to greet, to say how do you do	расставáться, расстáться	to part, to separate
кáяться, рас-	to repent	случáться, случи́ться	to happen
лени́ться, раз-	to be lazy	смея́ться, по-	to laugh
любовáться, по-	to admire	старáться, по-	to try
мчáться, по-	to rush	стреми́ться	to strive
надéяться	to hope	толпи́ться	to crowd, to form a crowd
нуждáться	to need		
наслаждáться, наслади́ться	to enjoy (very much)	труди́ться, по-	to labor
оставáться, остáться	to remain, to stay	улыбáться, улыбну́ться	to smile
очути́ться	to happen to be, to find oneself	явля́ться, яви́ться	to appear

Remark: As mentioned previously (page 162) the following verbs end in –ся in the imperfective aspect only:

станови́ться, стать	to become
ложи́ться, лечь	to lie down
сади́ться, сесть	to sit down
лóпаться, лóпнуть	to burst

9. A few verbs acquire a different meaning with the addition of –ся.

договáривать, договори́ть	to finish saying something
договáриваться, договори́ться	to negotiate, to come to an agreement
находи́ть	to find
находи́ться	to be located

проща́ть, прости́ть	to forgive
проща́ться, прости́ться	to say farewell, goodbye
слу́шать, послу́шать	to listen
слу́шаться, послу́шаться	to obey
состоя́ть	to consist (of)
состоя́ться	to take place

Impersonal Verbs

Impersonal verbs occur in two types of sentences.

1. When the sentence has no subject:

Темне́ть: темне́ет.	It is getting dark.
Света́ть: света́ет.	It is getting light; dawn is breaking.
Моро́зить: моро́зит.	It is freezing.

2. When the sentence has a logical subject but no grammatical one. This logical subject may be in the dative or in the accusative.

(*a*) In the dative case:

Хоте́ться: мне хо́чется	I feel like.
Каза́ться: вам ка́жется.	It seems to you.
Нездоро́виться: ему́ нездоро́вится.	He does not feel well.

(*b*) In the accusative case:

Тошни́ть: меня́ тошни́т.	I feel sick (to the stomach).
Зноби́ть: меня́ зноби́т.	I have chills.
Лихора́дить: её лихора́дит.	She has a fever.

Usage of Impersonal Verbs

1. Impersonal verbs are used only in the third person singular. In the past tense they take the neuter ending:

Уже́ света́ет.	It is already getting light.
Всю ночь моро́зило.	It was freezing all night.

2. The logical subject may be any person, singular or plural:

   Мне хоте́лось. I felt like.
   Вам нездоро́вилось. You didn't feel well.
   Им каза́лось. It seemed to them.

3. Impersonal verbs are used in the infinitive, indicative, and conditional moods. They are not used in the imperative.

4. There are some verbs which occur in both personal and impersonal constructions:

  Ве́тер ду́ет.   The wind is blowing. (*personal*)
  В коридо́ре ду́ет. There is a draft in the corridor. (*impersonal*)
  Не́бо темне́ет.   The sky is getting dark. (*personal*)
  На дворе́ темне́ет. It is getting dark outside. (*impersonal*)

5. Many verbs, when they become impersonal, acquire a figurative meaning:

  Бу́дет с вас!   You've had enough. (быть, *lit*. to be)
  Мне не везёт.   I have no luck. (везти́, *lit*. to drive, to cart)
  Не сто́ит спо́рить. There's no use arguing. (сто́ить, *lit*. to cost)

Verbs of Motion

Basic Verbs of Motion

1. Russians always distinguish between going *on foot*: идти́ (итти́), ходи́ть and *not on foot*: е́хать, е́здить.

2. Another basic distinction is made in 15 pairs of verbs between definite (actual) motion, and indefinite (habitual). A list of these verbs follows:

	DEFINITE	INDEFINITE
to go (on foot)	идти́	ходи́ть
to go (not on foot)	е́хать	е́здить
to run	бежа́ть	бе́гать
to wander, to stroll	брести́	броди́ть

VERBS

	DEFINITE	INDEFINITE
to drive (trans.), to take, to cart	везти́	вози́ть
to lead, to take	вести́	води́ть
to chase	гнать	гоня́ть
to roll	кати́ть	ката́ть
to climb	лезть	ла́зить
to fly	лете́ть	лета́ть
to carry	нести́	носи́ть
to swim	плыть	пла́вать
to crawl	ползти́	по́лзать
to plant	сади́ть	сажа́ть
to pull, to drag	тащи́ть	таска́ть

Definite verbs may be translated *"to be going, to be running,"* etc. They pertain to motion actually taking place:

| Я иду́ в шко́лу. | I am going to school. |
| Пти́цы летя́т на юг. | The birds are flying south. |

Indefinite verbs may pertain to

(*a*) Habitual action or motion:

| Я хожу́ в шко́лу. | I go to school. |

(*b*) Motion in different directions:

| Он ходи́л по ко́мнате. | He was walking in the room (around the room; back and forth). |
| Пти́цы лета́ют над са́дом. | The birds are flying above the garden (in all directions). |

(*c*) An action which could be called characteristic:

| Мой сын уже́ хо́дит. | My son already walks (can walk). |
| Пти́цы лета́ют. | Birds fly. |

Remark: Thus, the actual and habitual verbs differ—as far as translation is concerned—from all other verbs. Whereas, for example: "I read" (*present*) and "I am reading" (*present continuous*) are both translated by "Я чита́ю"—in contrast, "I drive" and "I am driving" are translated respectively by "Я е́зжу" and "Я е́ду."

The example below gives the English equivalent of two pairs of verbs in the present, past, and future.

	DEFINITE (ACTUAL)		INDEFINITE (HABITUAL)	
	on foot	*not on foot*	*on foot*	*not on foot*

Infinitive

To be going — To go

идти́ (пойти́)　ехать (пое́хать)　ходи́ть (походи́ть)　е́здить (пое́здить)

Present

I am going, etc. — I go, etc.

я иду́	я е́ду	я хожу́	я е́зжу
ты идёшь	ты е́дешь	ты хо́дишь	ты е́здишь
он идёт	он е́дет	он хо́дит	он е́здит
мы идём	мы е́дем	мы хо́дим	мы е́здим
вы идёте	вы е́дете	вы хо́дите	вы е́здите
они́ иду́т	они́ е́дут	они́ хо́дят	они́ е́здят

Past Imperfective

I was going, etc. — I used to go, etc.

шёл	е́хал	ходи́л	е́здил
шла	е́хала	ходи́ла	е́здила
шло	е́хало	ходи́ло	е́здило
шли	е́хали	ходи́ли	е́здили

Past Perfective

I went, etc. — I walked, etc.* — I drove (rode), etc.*

пошёл	пое́хал	походи́л	пое́здил
пошла́	пое́хала	походи́ла	пое́здила
пошло́	пое́хало	походи́ло	пое́здило
пошли́	пое́хали	походи́ли	пое́здили

* These forms are encountered infrequently (see page 195).

VERBS

Future Imperfective

I will be going, etc.*		I shall go, I will be going, etc.	
я бу́ду идти́	я бу́ду е́хать	я бу́ду ходи́ть	я бу́ду е́здить
ты бу́дешь идти́	ты бу́дешь е́хать	ты бу́дешь ходи́ть	ты бу́дешь е́здить
он бу́дет идти́	он бу́дет е́хать	он бу́дет ходи́ть	он бу́дет е́здить
мы бу́дем идти́	мы бу́дем е́хать	мы бу́дем ходи́ть	мы бу́дем е́здить
вы бу́дете идти́	вы бу́дете е́хать	вы бу́дете ходи́ть	вы бу́дете е́здить
они́ бу́дут идти́	они́ бу́дут е́хать	они́ бу́дут ходи́ть	они́ бу́дут е́здить

Future Perfective

I shall go, etc.		I will walk, etc.*	I will drive, etc.*
я пойду́	я пое́ду	я похожу́	я пое́зжу
ты пойдёшь	ты пое́дешь	ты похо́дишь	ты пое́здишь
он пойдёт	он пое́дет	он похо́дит	он пое́здит
мы пойдём	мы пое́дем	мы похо́дим	мы пое́здим
вы пойдёте	вы пое́дете	вы похо́дите	вы пое́здите
они́ пойду́т	они́ пое́дут	они́ похо́дят	они́ пое́здят

THE PERFECTIVE OF VERBS OF MOTION

The perfective aspect of the verbs of motion is formed by adding **по–** to the imperfective: пое́хать, пое́здить; поплы́ть, попла́вать. The perfective of **идти́** is **пойти́**.

With definite verbs, **по–** often indicates the beginning of an action:

| Он пошёл напра́во. | He went to the right. |
| Мы поплы́ли к бе́регу. | We started to swim towards the shore. |

However, frequently the beginning of the action is only more or less implied:

| Она́ пойдёт к до́ктору. | She will go to the doctor. |
| Он пое́хал на вокза́л. | He has gone to the station. |

With indefinite verbs, **по–** merely indicates that the action has lasted for a while:

| Мы походи́ли по го́роду | We walked (for a while) in the town. |

* These forms are encountered infrequently (see pages 194, 195).

Usage of Basic Verbs of Motion

The verbs of motion will be discussed in regard to their literal meaning (motion on foot, or not on foot) and to their figurative meaning.

LITERAL MEANING

1. Definite Verbs of Motion

(a) The imperfective future of definite verbs (идти́, е́хать, etc.) places emphasis on the motion itself—not on the destination:

Мы бу́дем идти́ по э́той доро́ге, пока́ мы вас не встре́тим.	We will be going along this road until we meet you.
Я вам обеща́ю, что я бу́ду е́хать ме́дленно.	I promise you that I shall drive (will be driving) slowly.

(b) The definite (actual) verb is occasionally used to express an habitual action. This happens when the motion clearly suggests only one direction:

Ка́ждый день, ро́вно в де́вять часо́в, я иду́ в гара́ж, сажу́сь в маши́ну и е́ду на фа́брику.	Every day, at exactly nine o'clock, I go to the garage, take seat in the car and drive to the factory.
Утром я снача́ла мо́юсь, пото́м иду́ на ку́хню, гото́влю за́втрак, иду́ в столо́вую и сажу́сь пить чай.	In the morning, first of all, I wash, then go to the kitchen, prepare breakfast, go to the dining room and sit down to have tea.

Note: The above statement and examples should be regarded as exceptions to the general rule.

(c) The present tense of идти́ and е́хать is sometimes used to express future:

За́втра я е́ду на вы́ставку.	Tomorrow I am going to the exhibition.
Сего́дня ве́чером мы идём в теа́тр.	Tonight we are going to the theater.

Note: Similar constructions are not possible with ходи́ть or е́здить.

(d) The joint imperative is used with definite verbs only:

    Ну, едем.   Well, let's go.
    Идём скорей.   Come along quickly.

(e) Definite verbs of motion may express approaching. They are then translated "to come":

    Идите сюда.   Come here.
    Кто-то едет навстречу.   Somebody is coming towards (us).

2. Definite and Indefinite Verbs of Motion

(a) Идти (or ходить) пешком may seem redundant, since the word пешком itself means "on foot." However, there is a difference between Он идёт пешком which *emphasizes* going on foot and Он идёт в магазин, which simply mentions it (the logical stress being on the destination).

(b) When the purpose or destination are stressed, and when the manner of locomotion is unknown (or unimportant)—then usually идти or ходить are used, in preference to ехать or ездить.

    Вам надо пойти к доктору.   You should go (and see) a doctor
    Вы часто ходите в театр?   Do you often go to the theater?

3. Indefinite Verbs of Motion

(a) The past and future perfectives of indefinite verbs are used rather infrequently. They indicate a cessation of an action which lasts for a while.

    Он походил по комнате, остановился и сказал . . .   He walked around the room, stopped and said . . .
    Если хотите, мы полетаем завтра.   If you wish, we will go flying for a while tomorrow.

(b) The past imperfective of indefinite verbs of motion is also used to express a motion back and forth, such as a round-trip:

    Вчера я ездил в город.   Yesterday I went to the city.
    Утром мы ходили на почту.   In the morning we went to the post-office.

Compare the above examples to:

    Он поехал в город.   He went (has gone) to the city.
    Они пошли на почту.   They went (have gone) to the post-office.

An *habitual action* may refer to something which never takes place. It contains then a negative idea of repetition:

Она́ никогда́ не хо́дит к до́ктору.	She never goes to see a doctor.
Я ни ра́зу не лета́л на самолёте.	I have never (not a single time) flown in an airplane.

The Imperative Mood of Verbs of Motion

As a rule, both definite and indefinite verbs are used in the imperative mood.

Normally, the *definite* verb will be used with the simple (non-negated) imperative:

Иди́те на уро́к.	Go to your lesson.
Плыви́те к бе́регу!	Swim towards the shore!
Поезжа́йте пря́мо.	Go straight.

An *indefinite* verb would refer to motion in various directions:

Пла́вайте здесь.	Swim here.

With negated imperatives, the *indefinite* verb is used more frequently:

Не ходи́те туда́.	Don't go there. (Don't ever go there.)
Не пла́вайте здесь.	Don't swim here.
Не е́здите к нему́.	Don't go to (see) him.
Не гоня́йте кур по двору́.	Don't chase the chickens around the yard.

A definite negated verb rather stresses the action itself:

Не плыви́те так бы́стро.	Don't swim so fast.
Ямщи́к, не гони́ лошаде́й!	Coachman, don't drive (hurry) the horses.

Verbs of Motion Pertaining to Travel and Transportation

1. The *on-foot* verbs идти́ and ходи́ть are used to express travel or motion of public conveyances. The habitual verb ходи́ть suggests a regular schedule (motion back and forth).

Э́тот парохо́д идёт в Евро́пу.	This boat is going to Europe.
По́езд шёл на се́вер.	The train was going north.

VERBS

Автобус идёт в центр города.	The bus is going to the center of the town.
Пароходы ходят из Одессы в Ялту.	Boats run between Odessa and Yalta.
Поезда не ходили зимой.	The trains did not run in the winter.
Автобусы ходят каждые два часа.	Buses run every two hours.

2. The *not-on-foot* going verbs ехать, ездить and the couple плыть, плавать are used:

(a) When the stress is not on the destination, but on the motion itself:

Наш автобус едет быстро.	Our bus is going fast.
Баржи плывут по реке.	Barges are sailing down the river.

(b) With private cars, carriages, etc.:

Автомобиль едет через мост.	A car is going across the bridge.
Экипаж ехал по улице.	A carriage was going along the street.

(c) When referring to transportation, i.e. to persons traveling *in* a public conveyance:

Мы ехали на пароходе.	We were traveling by steamship.
Зимой они всегда ездили в город на поезде.	In the winter they always went to town by train.
Мы плыли в Европу.	We were going (sailing) to Europe.
Он плавал на разных кораблях.	He sailed on different ships.

3. The verbs лететь, летать are used with airplanes, helicopters, etc.:

Самолёт летит на юг.	The plane is flying south.
Вертолёт летал над городом.	A helicopter was flying above the town.

FIGURATIVE MEANING

Both definite and indefinite verbs are used in figurative speech. However, with few exceptions only <u>one</u> verb will be used in any particular type of expression (in contrast to prefixed verbs of motion, where verbs of both roots are used in any set expression):

Там всегда идут хорошие пьесы.	They always show good plays there.
Она ходила за больным.	She was taking care of the patient.
Я несу ответственность за это.	I am responsible for this.
Он носит очки.	He wears glasses.
Она ведёт занятия.	She is conducting the lessons (studies).
Он всех водит за нос.	He deceives (fools) everybody.

The above examples may be regarded as set expressions. The definite (actual) verbs are of a wider usage: they are frequently found in figurative speech, even with habitual actions:

Его дети всегда себя хорошо ведут.	His children always behave well.
Там часто идёт снег.	It often snows there.

In particular, the verbs идти and ходить have a variety of figurative meanings. These deserve a separate mention.

Идти may express:

1. Traveling, being en route. It is used then with nouns, such as письмо, телеграмма, почта, etc.

Телеграмма шла два дня.	The telegram was en route for two days.
Почта здесь идёт медленно.	The mail here goes slowly.

2. "Working." It is used when speaking of watches, clocks and other mechanisms:

Мои часы не идут.	My watch isn't running.
Идти на холостом ходу.	To idle (to be in neutral, to run on no load work).

3. Certain weather conditions:

Вчера шёл дождь.	Yesterday it rained.
Снег идёт (падает).	It is snowing.

4. The starting of work, of an activity:

    Идти́ в реме́сленное учи́лище.   To enter a trade school.
    Пойти́ доброво́льцем.   To go as a volunteer.

5. Taking place:

    Сейча́с иду́т экза́мены.   The examinations are taking place now.
    Иду́т бой.   Battles are going on (taking place).

6. Approaching:

    Весна́ идёт.   Spring is coming.

7. The motion of some masses, substances. It is used with nouns, such as дым—smoke; ту́чи—clouds; облака́—(heap) clouds; лёд—ice; вода́—water:

    Дым идёт из трубы́.   Smoke is coming out of the chimney.
    Лёд идёт вниз по реке́.   Ice is going down the river.

Ходи́ть may express:

1. Visiting, attending:

    ходи́ть к кому́-нибудь   to visit somebody
    ходи́ть в шко́лу   to attend (to go to) school

2. Motion in different directions, at different times:

    Мы ходи́ли по магази́нам.   We went around all the shops.
    ходи́ть на охо́ту   to go hunting

3. Motion back and forth:

    По́ршень хо́дит взад и вперёд.   The piston is moving back and forth.

4. Wearing:

    ходи́ть без шля́пы   to go without a hat (not to wear a hat)
    Отчего́ вы всегда́ хо́дите в чёрном? (Че́хов)   Why do you always wear black?

The verbs **Видáть** and **Слыхáть**

These two verbs sometimes function as the indefinite forms of ви́деть and слы́шать. Their usage is rather limited:

1. Слыхáть is used only in the past tense:

   Я слыхáл э́то.   I heard this.

2. Видáть is found in all three tenses, past, present, and future:

   Мы их чáсто видáли.   We used to see them often.
   Мы их рéдко видáем.   We see them seldom.
   Надéюсь, что мы бу́дем видáть друг дру́га.   I hope that we will be seeing each other.

3. These verbs may convey a rather vague idea, something happening by chance:

   Вы не видáли моего́ сы́на?   You haven't seen my son (by any chance)?
   Я был на балу́ и слыхáл молву́.   I was at a ball and heard a rumor. (An opening sentence of a parlor game.)

4. In the actual, physical sense, only ви́деть and слы́шать are used:

   Я ничего́ не ви́жу в такóй темнотé.   I can't see anything in this darkness.
   В стáрости он плóхо слы́шал.   When he was old, he couldn't hear very well.

5. In the figurative meaning of *to see* (*to realize, to feel*), only ви́деть is used:

   Я ви́жу, что вы меня́ не понимáете.   I see that you don't understand me.
   Мы ви́дели, что э́то ни к чему́.   We felt that all this was of no use.

Prefixed Verbs of Motion

1. Characteristics of Prefixed Verbs of Motion

Adding a prefix to a basic verb of motion has the following effects:

   (*a*) A direction is imparted to the motion.

VERBS

(*b*) Indefinite verbs become imperfective.
(*c*) Definite verbs become perfective.

Example:

Basic verb of motion		Prefix	Direction of motion	Prefixed verb of motion		
INDEFINITE	DEFINITE			IMPERFECTIVE	PERFECTIVE	
носи́ть	нести́	при– у–	toward away	приноси́ть уноси́ть	принести́ унести́	to bring to carry away

Example of a prefixed verb of motion

IMPERFECTIVE *Infinitive:* уноси́ть
Present: я уношу́, ты уно́сишь . . . они́ уно́сят
Past: уноси́л, уноси́ла, уноси́ло, уноси́ли
Future: я бу́ду уноси́ть, ты бу́дешь уноси́ть . . . они́ бу́дут уноси́ть

PERFECTIVE *Infinitive:* унести́
Past: унёс, унесла́, унесло́, унесли́
Future: я унесу́, ты унесёшь . . . они́ унесу́т

The prefixed verbs of motion—unlike the basic ones—make no distinction between indefinite and definite motion. In other words, я уношу́ means both "I take away" and "I am taking away."

2. Irregular Formation of Prefixed Verbs of Motion

(*a*) Eight types of imperfective verbs are formed from stems which are different from indefinite basic verbs:

Indefinite Basic	New Stem	Prefixed Verb (Examples)	
е́здить	–езжа́ть	выезжа́ть	to drive out, to leave
ла́зить	–леза́ть	влеза́ть	to climb onto; into

Indefinite Basic	New Stem	Prefixed Verb (Examples)	
катáть	–кáтывать	скáтывать	to roll down (trans.)
сажáть	–сáживать	обсáживать	to plant around
таскáть	–тáскивать	перетáскивать	to move, to drag (over)
бéгать	–бéгать	прибегáть	to run up to
плáвать	–плывáть	уплывáть	to swim away
пóлзать	–ползáть	подползáть	to crawl up to

(b) A few *perfective* verbs are formed from the *basic indefinite* above:

съéздить	to go somewhere and return: Мы съéздили на óзеро.
объéздить	to travel all around: Он объéздил весь свет.
сбéгать	to run quickly somewhere and return: Я сбéгаю в магазúн.
слáзить	to climb and return: Мáльчик слáзил за шлянпой.
укатáть	to roll—*trans.*: Надо укатáть тéннисную площáдку.
прокатáть	to take for a drive: Он прокатáл нас по гóроду.
затаскáть	to wear out, to soil: Дéвочка затаскáла плáтье.
проплáвать	to swim, to sail: Мы проплáвали год.
запóлзать	to begin to crawl: Ребёнок запóлзал пó полу.

Note: These verbs should not be confused with the *imperfectives*, such as съезжáть—to drive down; объезжáть—to drive around; сбегáть—to run down.

(c) When the verb идтú takes a prefix ending in a vowel, a change of stem occurs in the infinitive and in the future perfective.

Examples:

Infinitive: уйтú
Future perfective: я уйдý, ты уйдёшь . . . онú уйдýт
Infinitive: перейтú
Future perfective: я перейдý, ты перейдёшь . . . онú перейдýт

Note: The й does not appear in the future perfective of прийтú: я придý, ты придёшь . . . онú придýт.

VERBS

3. List of prefixes added to basic verbs of motion

Prefix	Motion (principal meaning)	Examples	
в	into	входи́ть в дом	to enter the house
вз, вс	upward	взбежа́ть по ле́стнице	to run up the stairs
вы	out of	вы́ехать из го́рода	to drive out of town
до	as far as	дое́хать до реки́	to drive as far as the river
за	with a stop (on the way)	зае́хать к друзья́м (по доро́ге домо́й)	to drop in at some friends (on the way home)
о, об	around	облете́ть вокру́г де́рева	to fly around a tree
от	away	отнести́ куда́-нибудь	to take somewhere
пе́ре	over	перейти́ (че́рез) у́лицу	to cross the street
под	up to	подплы́ть к ло́дке	to swim up to the boat
при	towards	прие́хать домо́й	to come home
про	by, through	проезжа́ть ми́мо ста́нции	to ride past the station
у	away	уе́хать из го́рода	to leave town
с	downward	сходи́ть с горы́	to walk down the hill

4. Variation in the spelling of prefixes

(a) The six prefixes which end in a consonant (**в, вз, под, об, от, с**) add a **ъ** when they precede any form of **-езжа́ть** or **-е́хать**:

Examples:

Infinitive: въезжа́ть   *Present:* я въезжа́ю, ты въезжа́ешь . . . они́ въезжа́ют

Infinitive: съезжа́ть   *Past Imperf.:* съезжа́л, съезжа́ла, съезжа́ли

Infinitive: отъе́хать   *Past Perf.:* отъе́хал, отъе́хала, отъе́хали

Infinitive: объезжа́ть   *Fut. Imperf.:* я бу́ду объезжа́ть, ты бу́дешь объезжа́ть . . . они́ бу́дут объезжа́ть

Infinitive: подъе́хать   *Fut. Perf.:* я подъе́ду, ты подъе́дешь . . . они́ подъе́дут

(b) The same prefixes become **во, взо, подо, обо, ото, со** when they precede any form of **идти́**.

Examples:

Infinitive: войти́   *Past Perf.:* вошёл, вошла́, вошли́
Infinitive: подойти́   *Fut. Perf.:* я подойду́, ты подойдёшь . . . они́ подойду́т

(c) The verb гнать is preceded by the same prefixes **во, взо, подо, обо, ото,** and **со** in the infinitive and in the past—but not in the future:

Infinitive: вогна́ть   *Past Perf.:* вогна́л, вогна́ла, вогна́ли
                          Fut. Perf.: я вгоню́, ты вго́нишь . . . они́ вго́нят

5. Prefixed verbs with dual meaning. Some prefixed verbs—derived from the indefinite ones—have different meanings and belong to different aspects. For instance:

Сходи́ть (*perf.*)—to go somewhere and return

    На́до к нему́ сходи́ть.   (We) will have to go and see him.

Сходи́ть (*imperf.* of сойти́)—to go down

    Здесь нельзя́ сходи́ть.   You can't go down (descend) here.

Проводи́ть (*perf.* of провожа́ть)—to accompany, to see off

    Мы проводи́ли её на вокза́л.   We saw her off at the station.

Проводи́ть (*imperf.* of провести́)—to spend (time)

    Мы проводи́ли ка́ждое ле́то на берегу́ мо́ря.   We spent each summer at the seashore.

6. Prefixes with multiple meaning

   (a) The prefix **пере-** may have the meaning of:

      —*over* (as in "to cross over")

      Мы перешли́ мост.   We crossed over the bridge.

VERBS

    —*to, over* (as in "to move")

перее́хать в друго́й го́род	to move to another city
перее́хать на но́вую кварти́ру	to move to a new apartment
перее́хать вниз	to move downstairs (Here, of course, е́хать no longer means motion by vehicle.)

(*b*) **про–** may have the meaning:

    —*by, past*

  пройти́ ми́мо до́ма to go past the house

    —*through*

пройти́ сквозь кусты́.	to pass through the bushes
прое́хать че́рез парк	to go through the park

    —(with distances)

пройти́ три киломе́тра	to go (to walk) three kilometers
прое́хать со́рок миль	to drive 40 miles

    —(with "to come," "to go," cf. French "*passer*")

  Пройди́те ко мне в кабине́т. Come into my office.

(*c*) **о–** (**об–, о́бо–**) may have the meaning:

    —*around, round*

  Мы объе́хали вокру́г о́зера. We drove around the lake.

    —*around, past*

  Мы объе́хали го́род. We drove around the city (to avoid the traffic, for instance).

    —*to, (one after another)*

  Он обошёл все магази́ны. He went to all the shops.

(*d*) **за** may express:

    —motion behind an object

  зайти́ за дом to go behind (round) the house

    —motion in depth

Он завёл нас в лес.	He led us far into the wood.
Мы забрели́ в го́ры.	We wandered into the mountains.

—a motion taking place conjointly with the main one

| Зайди́те к нам по доро́ге домо́й. | Drop in to see us on your way home. |
| Подъезжа́я к го́роду, мы реши́ли зае́хать в рестора́н. | When we were approaching the town, we decided to stop at a restaurant. |

—"to drop in," without specifying any other destination

| Я зашёл к ним. | I dropped in to see them. |
| Вчера́ мы зашли́ к Ива́новым. | We dropped in to see the Ivanovs yesterday. |

7. Various combinations of prefixes and verbs

(a) Other verbs may combine with the prefixes discussed above:

Examples:

игра́ть—to play
- вы́играть—to win (a game, a battle)
- проигра́ть—to lose (a game, a battle)

бить—to beat
- уби́ть—to kill
- переби́ть—to interrupt

де́лать—to do, to make
- подде́лать—to counterfeit
- приде́лать—to attach, to fix

(b) Conversely, other prefixes may combine with verbs of motion:

Examples:

на-: находи́ть, найти́	to find
из-: изводи́ть, извести́	to annoy, to aggravate
рас-, раз-: расходи́ться, разойти́сь	to separate, to disperse

In either of the groups, however, the newly formed prefixed verb no longer necessarily suggests motion, and the connection with the basic verb of motion may be quite remote.

Usage of Prefixed Verbs of Motion

LITERAL MEANING

1. Prefixed verbs of motion formed from an indefinite basic verb may signify a motion back and forth, a return trip. This, however, is limited to just a few verbs, chiefly to the compounds of **ходи́ть** and **-езжа́ть**:

| Она́ приезжа́ла к нам в сре́ду. | She visited us on Wednesday. |

VERBS

Сюда́ кто́-то входи́л, пока́ нас не́ было до́ма. — Somebody was here while we were away.

2. The imperfective aspect is used with negated verbs.

Я не хочу́ уезжа́ть так ра́но. — I don't want to leave so early.
Не уходи́те. — Don't go away.

3. Not all verbs of motion combine with every prefix.

(*a*) The following verbs do so: ходи́ть—идти́; -езжа́ть—е́хать; -бе́гать—бежа́ть; вози́ть—везти́; води́ть—вести́, -ка́тывать—кати́ть; лета́ть—лете́ть; носи́ть—нести́.

(*b*) The verbs броди́ть—брести́ combine with few.

(*c*) As regards other verbs, their usage with certain prefixes would simply be seldom warranted, as, for instance with сплыва́ть—сплыть (to swim, to sail, to float down) or with ополза́ть—оползти́ (to crawl around). It is, in other words, the difference between current usage and existence. (Both couples of verbs are listed with examples in Слова́рь ру́сского языка́. АН СССР.)

Figurative Meaning

It may be recalled that with basic (non-prefixed) verbs of motion only one form either *definite* or *indefinite* is used with a certain set expression, as for example: иду́т пье́сы (plays are shown) and хо́дят слу́хи (rumors circulate). With prefixed verbs of motion, verbs of both roots are used. It amounts to the difference between the imperfective and perfective aspects.

приноси́ть, принести́ по́льзу	to be of use
выходи́ть, вы́йти за́муж	to marry (said of a woman)
приходи́ть, прийти́ в у́жас	to be horrified
доноси́ть, донести́	to report, to inform (on somebody)

The number of verbs having a figurative meaning is quite large. Sometimes, the figurative meaning occurs in speech as often as the literal; sometimes, even more frequently.

(*lit.*) Он подвёл меня́ к свое́й ба́бушке. — He led me up to his grandmother.

(*fig.*) Он стра́шно подвёл меня́. — He put me in a awkward position ("He played a bad trick on me").

(*lit.*)	Она́ перехо́дит мост.	She is crossing the bridge.
(*fig.*)	Вода́ перехо́дит в пар.	Water changes into steam.
(*lit.*)	Он с трудо́м донёс чемода́н до вокза́ла.	He hardly could carry the suitcase as far as the station.
(*fig.*)	Он донёс на э́того подозри́тельного челове́ка.	He informed on that suspicious man.
(*fig.*)	Мы вас догна́ли.	We caught up with you.
(*fig.*)	Его́ прогна́ли со слу́жбы.	He was fired from the job.

Participles

Russian participles are classified as follows:

ACTIVE PARTICIPLES	Example:	Meaning:
Present	чита́ющий	(one) who is reading
Past: Imperfective	чита́вший	(one) who was reading
Past: Perfective	прочита́вший	(one) who has read

PASSIVE PARTICIPLES	Example:	Meaning:
Present	чита́емый	(something) which is being read
Past: Imperfective	чи́танный	(something) which was being read
Past: Perfective	прочи́танный	(something) which has been read

Note: The meaning, of course, may admit variants as regards *translation* into English: чита́ющий (one who reads), прочи́танный (something which was read), etc.

VERBS

Characteristics of Participles

Participles are verbal adjectives. They possess characteristics of both of these parts of speech.

1. Adjectival characteristics are the following:

    (*a*) Endings: Participles have typical adjectival endings.

    читáющ**ий**, прочи́танн**ый**, напи́санн**ая**.

    (*b*) Genders: Participles have three genders.

    | MASC. | читáющ**ий** |
    | FEM. | читáющ**ая** |
    | NEUT. | читáющ**ее** |

    (*c*) Numbers: Participles have two numbers.

    | *Singular:* | читáющ**ий** |
    | *Plural:* | читáющ**ие** |

    (*d*) Cases: Participles are declined regularly, like adjectives.

    | NOM. | читáющ**ий** |
    | GEN. | читáющ**его** |
    | DAT. | читáющ**ему** |
    | ACC. (anim.) | читáющ**его** |
    | INSTR. | читáющ**им** |
    | PREP. | читáющ**ем** |

2. Verbal characteristics are the following (as indicated in the table above):

    (*a*) Participles can be active or passive:

    | ACT. | человéк, стрóящий дом | the man (who is) building the house |
    | PASS. | дом, пострóенный им | the house which was built by him |

    (*b*) Participles have two tenses, present and past (no future):

    | PRES. | человéк, пи́шущий письмó | the man (who is) writing the letter |
    | PAST | дáма, писáвшая письмó | the lady who was writing the letter |

(c) Participles have two aspects in the past tense:

| IMP. | челове́к, чита́вший кни́гу | the man who was reading the book |
| PERF. | челове́к, прочита́вший кни́гу | the man who (has) read the book |

Furthermore:

(d) Participles can be transitive or intransitive (including reflexive):

TRANS.	де́вочка, купи́вшая шля́пу.	the girl who bought the hat
INTRANS.	лю́ди, иду́щие по у́лице.	the people who are going down the street
REFL.	уро́к, нача́вшийся в три часа́.	the lesson which began at three o'clock

(e) Participles govern the same case as the verb from which they are formed:

| кома́ндовать а́рмией (*instr.*) | to command an army |
| генера́л, кома́ндующий а́рмией (*instr.*) | the general who is commanding the army |

(f) In certain constructions, participles call for the same preposition as the verb from which they are formed:

| игра́ть **на** скри́пке | to play the violin |
| ма́льчик, игра́ющий **на** скри́пке | the boy who was playing the violin |

Formation of Active Participles

PRESENT ACTIVE PARTICIPLES

Present active participles are formed from the third person plural, present tense, by dropping the ending –**т** and adding –**щий** (–**щая**, –**щее**, –**щие**).

| чита́ть | чита́ю–т | чита́ю**щий** |
| говори́ть | говоря́–т | говоря́**щий** |

VERBS

PAST ACTIVE PARTICIPLES

1. Regular Formation

Past active participles are formed from the past tense, masculine, by dropping the ending –л and adding –вший (–вшая, –вшее, –вшие).

начинáть	начинá–л	начинá**вший**
начáть	нáча–л	начá**вший**

2. Irregular Formation

(*a*) From verbs not ending in –л in the past tense, past active participles are formed by adding –ший to the stem of the past:

нестú (to carry):	нёс	нёс**ший**
погúбнуть (to perish):	погúб	погúб**ший**
печь (to bake):	пёк	пёк**ший**
заперéть (to lock):	зáпер	зáпер**ший**

Exceptions:

исчéзнуть (to disappear):	исчéз	исчéзнувший
подвéргнуть (to expose, to subject):	подвéрг	подвéргнувший

And, similarly, with verbs of the same root, such as отвéргнуть—to reject, to repudiate; свéргнуть—to depose, to overthrow.

(*b*) From verbs ending in –л in the past tense, and having the suffixes –д or –т in the present (or future perfective), past active participles are formed by adding the ending –ший to the stem of the present:

вестú (to lead):	ведý	вёл	вéд**ший**
подместú (to sweep)	подметý	подмёл	подмéт**ший**

Exceptions:

сесть (to sit down):	сяду	сел	сéв**ший**
класть (to lay down):	кладý	клал	клáв**ший**
красть (to steal):	крадý	крал	крáв**ший**
упáсть (to fall):	упадý	упáл	упáв**ший**
есть (to eat):	ем (едя́т)	ел	éвший

(An "exception within an exception," this group forms past active participles regularly—similarly to читáть: читáл **читáвший**.)

(*c*) The past active participle of идтú is **шéдший**. Similarly, with related verbs: уйтú: ушéдший, найтú: нашéдший, etc.

(d) The past participle of прочéсть is formed from the synonymous verb прочитáть: Прочéсть: прочтý, прочёл, **прочитáвший**.

(e) The verb пасть (to fall) has two different participles: **пáвший** and **пáдший**, the latter used figuratively:

<blockquote>

пáвший на пóле бúтвы   fallen on the battlefield
пáдший человéк   a (morally) fallen man

</blockquote>

(f) The verbs приобрестú (to acquire) and изобрестú (to invent, to devise) have two forms for their past participles: приобрéтший, изобрéтший and—in conversational Russian—приобрёвший, изобрёвший.

PARTICIPLES FORMED FROM REFLEXIVE VERBS

Active participles can be formed from reflexive verbs. The participle always ends in –ся regardless of the preceding letter (vowel or consonant).

Declension of Active Participles

The following examples illustrate declensions of participles formed from transitive verbs, and of participles formed from reflexive verbs.

	Transitive verb		Reflexive verb	
	Imperfective	*Perfective*	*Imperfective*	*Perfective*
	встречáть	встрéтить	встречáться	встрéтиться
	(to meet)		(to meet with; to be encountered)	

Present Participle

NOM.	встречáющий	встречáющийся
GEN.	встречáющего	встречáющегося
DAT.	встречáющему	встречáющемуся
ACC.	встречáющий	встречáющийся
(*anim.*)	встречáющего	встречáющегося
INSTR.	встречáющим	встречáющимся
PREP.	встречáющем	встречáющемся

Past Participle—Imperfective

NOM.	встречáвший	встречáвшийся
GEN.	встречáвшего	встречáвшегося
DAT.	встречáвшему	встречáвшемуся

Past Participle—Imperfective

ACC.	встреча́вший	встреча́вшийся
(*anim.*)	встреча́вшего	встреча́вшегося
INSTR.	встреча́вшим	встреча́вшимся
PREP.	встреча́вшем	встреча́вшемся

Past Participle—Perfective

NOM.	встре́тивший	встре́тившийся
GEN.	встре́тившего	встре́тившегося
DAT.	встре́тившему	встре́тившемуся
ACC.	встре́тивший	встре́тившийся
(*anim.*)	встре́тившего	встре́тившегося
INSTR.	встре́тившим	встре́тившимся
PREP.	встре́тившем	встре́тившемся

Formation of Passive Participles

With very rare exceptions, passive participles are formed only from transitive verbs.

PRESENT PASSIVE PARTICIPLES

1. Regular Formation

Present passive participles are formed from the first person plural, present tense, by adding to it the adjectival endings **–ый (–ая, –ое, –ые)**:

чита́ть	чита́ем	чита́ем**ый**
люби́ть	лю́бим	люби́м**ый**

2. Irregular Formation

(*a*) Present passive participles <u>retain</u> the suffix **–ва** when this suffix is dropped in the present tense (with verbs ending in **–вать** preceded by **да–, зна–** or **ста–**). The participle is then formed from the infinitive:

Infinitive	Present	Participle
задава́-ть (to assign)	мы задаём	задава́емый
признава́-ть (to recognize)	мы признаём	признава́емый

(*b*) Four verbs form their present passive participle with the suffix **–ом**:

вести́ (to lead)	ведо́мый
нести́ (to carry)	несо́мый

иска́ть (to look for)   иско́мый
влечь (to attract)   влеко́мый

These four participles are hardly ever used in modern Russian.

(c) The present passive participle of дви́гать (to move) is дви́жимый.

(d) Only very few *intransitive* verbs (formerly transitive) may form a present passive participle:

Infinitive	Participle
кома́ндовать (to command)	кома́ндуемый
предше́ствовать (to precede)	предше́ствуемый
руководи́ть (to direct, to conduct)	руководи́мый
управля́ть (to rule; to drive)	управля́емый

PAST PASSIVE PARTICIPLES

1. Regular Formation

Past passive participles are formed from the past tense:

(a) The ending –л is dropped, and the ending –нный (–нная, –нное, –нные) is added:

чита́ть	чита́–л	чи́танный
ви́деть	ви́де–л	ви́денный

(b) With verbs ending in –ить, the ending –ил is dropped, and the ending –енный (–енная, –енное, –енные) is added: получи́ть—получ–и́л—полу́ченный.

Note: The mutation of consonants in the present or future perfective of verbs ending in –ить (page 149) is also observed in the formation of participles:

носи́ть (to carry)	ношу́	носи́л	но́шенный
встре́тить (to meet)	встре́чу	встре́тил	встре́ченный

(c) The ending –ённый (–енный) is added to the past tense which does not end in –л (except with verbs in –ереть such as запере́ть below).

принести́ (to bring)	принёс	принесённый (*colloq.* прине́сенный.)
увезти́ (to drive away)	увёз	увезённый (*colloq.* увезенный.)

VERBS

(d) The ending –л (or fem. –ла) is dropped, and **–тый, –тая, –тое, –тые** are added to form the past passive participle of verbs ending in –уть, –оть, –ыть, –ереть and of most monosyllabic verbs, prefixed or not:

разду́ть (to blow up)	разду́–л	разду́**тый**
расколо́ть (to split, to chop)	расколо́–л	раско́ло**тый**
мыть (to wash)	мы–л	мы́**тый**
запере́ть (to lock)	за́пер–ла	за́пер**тый**
петь (to sing)	пе–л	пе́**тый**
бить (to beat)	би–л	би́**тый**
взять (to take)	взя–л	взя́**тый**
оде́ть (to dress) (*trans.*)	оде́–л	оде́**тый**
нача́ть (to begin)	на́ча–л	на́ча**тый**

The formation of past passive participles is the same with verbs related to the ones above: уби́ть (to kill): уби́тый; заня́ть (to occupy): за́нятый; наде́ть (to put on): наде́тый.

Exception: The monosyllabic verb дать (and the prefixed вы́дать to hand out, зада́ть to assign, etc.) form their participle with the suffix **–нн**: **да́нный**.

2. Irregular Formation

In one type of verbs, the past passive participle is formed from the present or future perfective when the stem of these tenses ends in **–д** or **–т**.

привести́ (to bring, to lead)	привед–у́	привёл	приведённый
укра́сть (to steal)	украд–у́	укра́л	укра́денный
подмести́ (to sweep)	подмет–у́	подмёл	подметённый

THE SHORT FORM OF PASSIVE PARTICIPLES

The short passive participles have the same endings as short adjectives. They are used only predicatively and are not declined.

Examples:

	Masculine	Feminine	Neuter	Plural
Pres. Pass.	люби́м	люби́ма	люби́мо	люби́мы
Past Pass.:				
IMPERF.	ви́дан	ви́дана	ви́дано	ви́даны
	бит	би́та	би́то	би́ты

	Masculine	Feminine	Neuter	Plural
PERF.	прочи́тан	прочи́тана	прочи́тано	прочи́таны
	напи́сан	напи́сана	напи́сано	напи́саны
	вы́мыт	вы́мыта	вы́мыто	вы́мыты

Note: In participles ending in **-нный** in the long form, only one **н** is retained in the short form.

Nouns and Adjectives Derived from Participles

A few nouns and many adjectives were formerly participles. They may function as both. In some instances there is a difference in spelling.

1. Nouns

The words—заве́дующий; управля́ющий; ра́ненный—and some others may be used as participles:

челове́к, заве́дующий библиоте́кой	the man in charge of the library
же́нщина, управля́ющая маши́ной	the woman who is driving the car
бойцы́, ра́не<u>нны</u>е во вчера́шнем бою́	the soldiers wounded in yesterday's battle

The same words may be used as nouns:

заве́дующий	the manager
управля́ющий	superintendent, manager (of an estate)
ра́не<u>н</u>ый	the wounded (man)

2. Adjectives

Adjectives derived from participles constitute a larger class.

(*a*) The distinction between adjectives and participles centers around the following points:

An adjective has a less "active" character than a participle. The notion of time is not clearly present in an adjective.

| Adjective: | Зна́ющий челове́к. | An educated man, a man having knowledge. |
| Participle: | Челове́к, зна́ющий доро́гу. | The man who knows the way. |

Adjectives originating from passive participles make no reference to the agent performing the action:

Уважа́емый граждани́н	Dear Sir (*lit.* "Respected Citizen")
разру́шенный дом	a destroyed house
ра́неные бойцы́	wounded soldiers

Passive participles indicate the agent (in the instrumental case) or have qualifying words:

челове́к, уважа́емый все́ми	a man respected by everybody
дом, разру́шенный неприя́телем	a house destroyed by the enemy
бойцы́, ра́ненные при отступле́нии	soldiers wounded during the retreat

Frequently, an adjective derived from a participle has a figurative meaning:

блестя́щие результа́ты	brilliant (outstanding) results
цвету́щее предприя́тие	a flourishing enterprise
потеря́нное вре́мя	lost (wasted) time

Note: Adjectives and participles may occasionally have different endings (and different meanings):

вися́щий на стене́	hanging on the wall (*participle*)
вися́чий мост	suspension bridge (*adjective*)
пла́чущая де́вочка	a crying girl (*participle*)
плаку́чая и́ва	a weeping willow (*adjective*)

(The ending **щий** is Church Slavonic; **чий** is Russian.)

(*b*) Reflexive participles may also become adjectives:

небью́щаяся посу́да	unbreakable dishes
враща́ющийся вал	a rotating shaft

(*c*) Many adjectives with the suffix –л historically belong to past active participles: взро́слый—grown up; про́шлый—last, former; уста́лый—tired.

(*d*) A large number of *negated* adjectives have the suffix of present passive participles –мый. These adjectives are formed from imperfective or perfective verbs, transitive or intransitive.

незабыва́емое впечатле́ние	unforgettable impression
несгора́емый шкап	safe (*lit.:* non-combustible closet)

непромока́емое пальто́	waterproof coat
необходи́мые ме́ры	necessary (unavoidable) measures
непроходи́мые доро́ги	impassable roads
невозмути́мое споко́йствие	imperturbable calmness (placidity)
невыполни́мый план	impracticable plan
Непобеди́мая арма́да	invincible Armada
неулови́мый звук	elusive (barely perceptible) sound
неутоми́мый рабо́тник	indefatigable worker

THE SPELLING OF PAST PASSIVE PARTICIPLES AND RELATED ADJECTIVES

1. Participles are spelled with two **н**'s:

письмо́, полу́ченное вчера́	the letter which was received yesterday
де́ньги, по́сланные по по́чте	the money sent by mail

2. Adjectives are spelled with two **н**'s when they have a prefix, or when they have one of the suffixes **-ирова** or **-ова**:

запу́танное де́ло	a confused (entangled) business
аннекси́рованная террито́рия	annexed territory
марино́ванная ры́ба	marinated fish

Otherwise, adjectives formed from participles are spelled with one **н**:

пу́таный отве́т	a confused answer
ра́неный офице́р	a wounded officer
копчёная ветчина́	smoked ham

Exceptions: The non-prefixed adjectives **да́нный** and **жела́нный** are spelled with two **н**'s:

в да́нный моме́нт	at the present moment
жела́нный гость	a welcome guest

3. The spelling rule regarding the *short form* of past passive participles and corresponding adjectives is different: In the feminine, neuter and plural, the participle takes one **н**, the adjective takes two **н**'s:

PARTICIPLE: Здесь образо́вана коми́ссия.   A commission has been formed here.

VERBS

PARTICIPLE: Они́ бы́ли воспи́таны тётей. They were brought up by their aunt.
ADJECTIVES: Она́ о́чень образо́ванна. She is very well educated.
Они́ хорошо́ воспи́танны. They are well brought up.

The Usage of Participles

Participles are used both in written and in spoken Russian, more or less frequently and depending on the type of participle.

1. Often the following constructions are used instead of participles:

Ма́льчик, кото́рый чита́ет кни́гу   The boy who is reading the book

instead of: Ма́льчик, чита́ющий кни́гу

Ма́льчик, кото́рый чита́л кни́гу   The boy was reading the book

instead of: Ма́льчик, чита́вший кни́гу

Де́вочка, кото́рая прочита́ла письмо́   The girl who read the letter

instead of: Де́вочка, прочита́вшая письмо́

Письмо́, кото́рое де́вочка прочита́ла   The letter which the girl read

instead of: Письмо́, прочи́танное де́вочкой

2. Constructions with кото́рый can be replaced with participles only when кото́рый is in the nominative, or in the accusative without prepositions. Thus, the two sentences below:

челове́к, кото́рый подари́л мне кни́гу   the man who gave me the book
кни́га, кото́рую он написа́л   the book which he wrote

may be reworded as follows:

челове́к, подари́вший мне кни́гу   the man who gave me the book
кни́га, напи́санная им   the book which was written by him

This would not be possible with sentences, such as:

челове́к, кото́рому я подари́л кни́гу	the man to whom I gave the book
кни́га, про кото́рую он написа́л	the book about which he has written

3. On the other hand, a participle may be used to avoid a *succession* of constructions with кото́рый: Челове́к, кото́рый говори́л со мной—инжене́р, прие́хавший из Москвы́. (The man who spoke with me is an engineer who arrived from Moscow.) is stylistically better than: Челове́к, кото́рый говори́л со мной—инжене́р, кото́рый прие́хал из Москвы́.

4. There is a difference between the usage of a participle *preceding* a noun and that of a subordinate clause: The participle *describes* the noun, whereas the construction with кото́рый places an emphasis on the subordinate clause. Thus:

Мать подошла́ к спа́вшему ребёнку—describes the child as *sleeping*.

Мать подошла́ к ребёнку, кото́рый спал—may emphasize the contrast between this child who *was sleeping* and another one who was not.

USAGE OF ACTIVE PARTICIPLES

Active participles, present or past, are used fairly often. The tense of the active participle may be the same as the one of the main verb:

(a) Я ви́жу челове́ка, стоя́щего на углу́. I see a man who is standing on the corner.

(b) Я уви́дел челове́ка стоя́вшего на углу́. I saw a man who was standing on the corner.

Or, it may be different:

(c) Я зна́ю ученика́, написа́вшего э́ту рабо́ту. I know the pupil who has written this work.

These constructions present no difficulty. However, example (d) below should be particularly noted because of the apparent oddity of its literal translation:

(d) Я уви́дел челове́ка стоя́щего на углу́.

VERBS

This example has the same meaning as (b) above, yet here the literal translation would appear to be "I saw a man who *is* standing on the corner."

USAGE OF PASSIVE PARTICIPLES

1. The Imperfective aspect of passive participles is seldom used.
2. The tense of the passive participle may be the same as the one of the main verb:

    (a) Мы покупа́ем това́р, импорти́руемый из Евро́пы. — We buy goods imported from Europe.

    (b) Я прочита́л письмо́, напи́санное ва́ми. — I have read the letter written by you.

Or, it may be different:

    (c) Я чита́ю письмо́, напи́санное ва́ми. — I am reading the letter written by you.

These constructions present no difficulty; however, here again the following example (d) should be particularly noted on account of its literal translation.

    (d) Мы ви́дели челове́ка, обвиня́емого в кра́же. (*lit.* "We saw a man who *is* accused of theft.")

3. The Present Passive Participle is either not formed at all from many verbs, or practically never used. This applies to: бить—to beat; брать—to take; говори́ть—to say; ждать—to wait; корми́ть—to feed; лить—to pour; мыть—to wash; писа́ть—to write; пить—to drink; плати́ть—to pay; проси́ть—to ask, to request; стро́ить—to build; учи́ть—to study, to teach, and a few others.

From many other verbs, these participles are used—even if not too frequently. For example: чита́ть—чита́емый; дава́ть—дава́емый.

Among the verbs forming present passive participles currently in use are:

    (a) Certain prefixed ones, such as: привлека́ть—to attract; создава́ть—to create; вытесня́ть—to force out; to crowd out, to dislodge; изобража́ть—to picture, to portray; обвиня́ть—to accuse; опи́сывать—to describe; ожида́ть—to await.

    (b) Verbs of foreign origin having the suffixes **-ировать** or **-овать**, as for example: аннекси́ровать—to annex; аннули́ровать—to annul; импорти́ровать—to import; оккупи́ровать—to occupy; реквизи́ровать

—to requisition; формули́ровать—to formulate; экспорти́ровать—to export; критикова́ть—to criticize; организова́ть—to organize.

4. The Past Passive Participles formed from *imperfective* verbs are used very seldom (at least with most verbs). They are found with a few non-prefixed verbs, such as: вида́ть—ви́данный; слы́шать—слы́шанный; красть—кра́денный; носи́ть—но́шенный; бить—би́тый; жа́рить—жа́ренный. These participles easily become adjectives (spelled with one **н**):

кра́деные де́ньги	stolen money
жа́реная ры́ба	fried fish

5. The Past Passive Participles formed from *perfective* verbs are used frequently, both in spoken and in written Russian:

чек, подпи́санный ва́ми	a check signed by you
статья́, прочи́танная в кла́ссе	an article read in class

USAGE OF THE SHORT FORM OF THE PASSIVE PARTICIPLE

The short form of a passive participle may express the present, the past or the future:

Всё сде́лано.	Everything is done.
Письмо́ бы́ло по́слано вчера́.	The letter was sent yesterday.
За́втра магази́ны бу́дут закры́ты.	Tomorrow the shops will be closed.

Often the short form, used without the auxiliary verb быть, indicates merely the result of an action, viewed at the present moment:

Э́тот дом хорошо́ постро́ен.	This house is built well.
Э́то письмо́ напи́сано по-ру́сски.	This letter is written in Russian.

With **был** (**была́, бы́ло, бы́ли**) the action is entirely viewed in the past:

Э́та кни́га была́ напи́сана в два го́да.	This book was written in two years.

It may refer to a condition no longer present:

Дом был постро́ен мои́м отцо́м.	The house was built by my father. (The house may no longer even exist.)

VERBS

Likewise, with **будет** (**будут**) the result is viewed in the future:

Всё будет сделано вовремя.   Everything will be done on time

Gerunds

Russian gerunds are classified as follows:

	Example	Meaning
Present	читая	(while) reading
Past Imperfective	не имев	not having (had)
Past Perfective	написав	having written

Note: There are no passive gerunds.

Characteristics of Gerunds

Gerunds are verbal adverbs. They possess characteristics of both of these parts of speech.

1. Adverbial characteristics:

   (*a*) Gerunds never change. They have no gender, number, or case.

   (*b*) Gerunds answer the same types of questions as adverbs, i.e. когда, как, почему, etc.

2. Verbal characteristics:

   (*a*) Gerunds, as indicated above, have two aspects.

   | IMPERFECTIVE | читая газету | (while) reading the paper |
   | PERFECTIVE | прочитав газету | having read the paper |

   (*b*) They are formed from transitive and intransitive verbs, and express correspondingly a transitive or intransitive action.

   | TRANSITIVE | читая книгу | (while) reading the book |
   | INTRANSITIVE | сидя в кресле | (while) sitting in an armchair |

(c) They govern the same case as the verb from which they are formed.

| VERB | кома́ндовать полко́м (*instr.*) | to command a regiment |
| GERUND | кома́ндуя полко́м (*instr.*) | (while) commanding a regiment |

(d) In certain constructions, gerunds call for the same preposition as the verb from which they are formed.

| VERB | игра́ть в ша́хматы | to play chess |
| GERUND | игра́я в ша́хматы | (while) playing chess |

Formation of Present Gerunds

Present gerunds are formed from the third person plural, present tense, by dropping the endings –ут, –ют or –ат, –ят and adding –я or –а to the stem. The ending **а** is added to stems ending in –**ж, ч, ш, щ**.

Жить	жив–у́т	живя́
Чита́ть	чита́–ют	чита́я
Держа́ть	де́рж–ат	держа́
Сиде́ть	сид–я́т	си́дя

IRREGULAR FORMATION

1. The group of verbs ending in –**вать** preceded by да-, зна- or ста- form their gerund from the infinitive.

| дава́–ть | (даю́т) | дава́я |
| встава́–ть | (встаю́т) | встава́я |

2. Present gerunds may end occasionally in –**учи** or –**ючи**. This is usually limited to colloquial speech, folksongs or set expressions.

Examples:

е́дучи	going, driving (the only form used)
"Че́рез по́ле и́дучи, Ру́су ко́су плету́чи."	"Walking through the field, Braiding (her) blond braids."
жить припева́ючи	to live gaily (*lit.* to live and sing along)

Note: Only **бу́дучи**, the present gerund of быть, belongs entirely to literary Russian.

3. From many verbs, the present gerund is either not formed at all, or practically never used. To these belong:

(*a*) The verbs with no vowel in the stem of the present tense, such as: ждать (to wait)—жду, ждёшь; врать (to tell lies)—вру, врёшь.

(*b*) The verbs ending in **-чь**, such as: мочь—to be able; жечь—to burn (*transitive*).

(*c*) The verbs with the suffix **-нуть**, such as: ги́бнуть—to perish; мо́кнуть—to get wet.

(*d*) The verbs below, and a few others:

бежа́ть	to run	лезть	to climb
бить	to beat	ма́зать	to daub, to spread
вить	to twine, to spin	петь	to sing
вяза́ть	to tie; to knit	писа́ть	to write
лить	to pour	пляса́ть	to dance
каза́ться	to seem, to appear	пить	to drink
шить	to sew	чеса́ть	to scratch

Formation of Past Gerunds

Past gerunds are formed from the past tense in the following ways:

1. When the stem of both the infinitive and the past ends in a vowel, **-л** is dropped from the past and **-в** is added to the stem:

    написа́-ть (to write)   написа́-л   написа́**в**
    спроси́-ть (to ask)   спроси́-л   спроси́**в**

The alternate forms написа́вши, спроси́вши, etc. are seldom used.

2. When the stem of both the infinitive and the past ends in a consonant, the ending **-ши** is added to this stem.

    принес-ти́ (to bring)   принёс   принёс**ши**

3. When the stem of the infinitive ends in a vowel, and the stem of the past ends in a consonant other than -л, two endings are possible for the past gerund.

запере́–ть (to lock)	за́пер	запере́в or	за́перши
привы́кну–ть (to get used to)	привы́к	привы́кнув or	привы́кши

IRREGULAR FORMATION

1. A few verbs form their past gerunds from the perfective future, third person plural. To these belong:

(*a*) The compounds of идти́

прийти́ (to come)	прид–у́т	придя́
зайти́ (to drop in)	зайд–у́т	зайдя́
перейти́ (to cross)	перейд–у́т	перейдя́
найти́ (to find)	найд–у́т	найдя́

These gerunds resemble the present gerunds by *form*, that is by the ending **–я**. The parallel forms in **–ши** (прише́дши, наше́дши, etc.) are used less frequently.

(*b*) A few verbs which admit two (sometimes three) variant forms:

Привести́ (to lead to, to bring to)	привед–у́т	приведя́ (or приве́дши)
Принести́ (to bring)	принес–у́т	принеся́ (or принёсши)
Услы́шать (to hear)	услы́ш–ат	услы́ша (also услы́шав or услы́шавши)
Уви́деть (to see)	уви́д–ят	уви́дя (also уви́дев or уви́девши)
Предви́деть (to foresee)	предви́д–ят	предви́дя (also предви́дев or предви́девши)

Note: Проче́сть forms the gerund прочтя́ (of the same meaning as прочита́в and прочита́вши—which are formed from прочита́ть).

2. Finally, the past gerund in **–а** or **–я** is encountered in a few set expressions.

положа́ ру́ку на се́рдце	frankly, honestly (*lit.* "with the hand on the heart")
спустя́ рукава́	carelessly (*lit.* "with sleeves down")
сиде́ть сложа́ ру́ки	to do nothing (*lit.* to sit with arms folded)

VERBS

These adverbialized forms are limited to the expressions given above. Otherwise, the ending is regular: положи́в де́ньги в карма́н (having put the money in the pocket), сложи́в платóк (having folded a handkerchief), etc.

Gerunds Formed from Verbs Ending in -ся

Gerunds are formed from reflexive verbs according to the basic rules given above (see pages 224, 225.) Two additional rules follow:
 All reflexive gerunds end in **-сь**.
 Past reflexive gerunds are formed with the suffixes **-вши** and **-ши** (not в).

Present Gerund:	одева́ться	одева́-ются	одева́-**ясь**
Past Gerunds:	оде́ться	оде́-лся	оде́-**вшись**
	запере́ться	за́пер-ся	за́пер-**шись**

Exceptions: A few reflexive past gerunds have a variant form which resembles the present gerund. (Cf. para. 1, page 226.)

оби́деться (to get offended)	оби́дясь	or	оби́девшись
прищу́риться (to squint)	прищу́рясь	or	прищу́рившись
прислони́ться (to lean against)	прислоня́сь	or	прислони́вшись
прости́ться (to say goodbye)	простя́сь	or	прости́вшись
встре́титься (to meet)	встре́тясь	or	встре́тившись

Usage of Gerunds

A. Gerunds versus Subordinate Clauses

1. The same idea may be expressed by a gerund or by a subordinate clause containing когда́, пока́, в то вре́мя как, потому́ что, так как, etc.

Когда́ я прие́хал домо́й, я нашёл его́ письмо́.   When I arrived home I found his letter.

Or: Прие́хав домо́й, я нашёл его́ письмо́.

Пока́ он одева́лся, он слу́шал но́вости по ра́дио.	While he was dressing he was listening to the news on the radio.

Or: Одева́ясь, он слу́шал но́вости по ра́дио.

Я пошёл пешко́м, потому́ что я опозда́л на авто́бус.	I went on foot because I was late for the bus.

Or: Опозда́в на авто́бус, я пошёл пешко́м.

Студе́нт сдал экза́мены и уе́хал домо́й.	The student passed his examinations and went home.

Or: Сдав экза́мены, студе́нт уе́хал домо́й.

2. Sometimes a subordinate clause is preferred to a gerund. For instance:

Опозда́в на авто́бус, я реши́л идти́ пешко́м—can be replaced by:

Когда́ я опозда́л на авто́бус, я реши́л идти́ пешко́м.	When I missed the bus, I decided to walk.

Or, by:

Я реши́л идти́ пешко́м, потому́ что я опозда́л на авто́бус.	I decided to walk because I missed the bus.

The subordinate clause clarifies the statement.

3. When a gerund acquires the meaning of an adverbial expression of manner, it cannot be replaced with a subordinate clause:

Она́ смотре́ла на меня́, как бы не понима́я, в чём де́ло.	She was looking at me, as if she didn't understand what was it about.
Он вошёл в ко́мнату, стуча́ сапога́ми.	He entered the room stamping his feet (*lit.* his boots).

4. Since the gerund expresses an action which qualifies the main one, both actions must refer to the same subject. In other words, it is impossible to replace with a gerund a sentence such as:

Когда́ я верну́лся домо́й, у меня́ боле́ла голова́.	When I returned home, my head was aching.

VERBS

Exceptions to the above rule are rare. They may be found, however, in some impersonal sentences, when the subject is clearly implied:

Вспоминáя об э́том, мне всегдá хо́чется смея́ться.	When I think of it, I always feel like laughing.
Хорошо́ плыть по Во́лге осе́нней но́чью, си́дя на корме́ ба́ржи. (Го́рький)	It is good to sail down the Volga on an autumn night, sitting on the stern of a barge.*

Or in constructions with a predicative infinitive:

Моя́ цель—око́нчив университе́т, приня́ться за рабо́ту.	My aim is, after I finish my college studies, to start working.

B. Intrinsically, a gerund does not express any definite time. *Present Gerunds* express an action which takes place simultaneously with the principal one. It may refer to the present, past, or future.

Example:

Си́дя в ваго́не, он читáет (читáл, бу́дет читáть) кни́гу.

The use of the gerund establishes a certain perspective between the main and the accompanying actions.
Thus, both verbs are equally important in:

Мы слу́шали его́ и смея́лись.	We listened to him and laughed.

But the main verb is смея́ться in "Слу́шая его́, мы смея́лись"—and the main verb is слу́шать in "Смея́сь, мы слу́шали его́."

C. *Past gerunds* can be formed from both imperfective and perfective verbs.

1. Past gerunds are *formed* from imperfective verbs but are hardly ever *used* in current speech. They are found sometimes in negated constructions, with verbs which have no perfective, or with verbs which are used in both aspects:

не име́в возмо́жности	not having (had) the opportunity
обеща́в мно́го раз	having promised many times

2. Past gerunds formed from perfective verbs are used frequently. They,

---

* Example from А. Н. Гвоздёв: Очерки по стили́стике ру́сского языка́.

as a rule, express an action which *precedes* the main one; they may refer to the past, present or future:

Око́нчив ле́кцию, он пошёл (идёт, пойдёт) домо́й.	After finishing the lecture he went (goes, will go) home.

Very rarely, there may be found a digression from this rule of antecedence. In the following sentences (seemingly anachronistic) the gerund indicates the *consequence* of the main action:

Ва́за упа́ла, разби́вшись на куски́.	The vase fell and broke into pieces (*lit.* having broken into pieces).
Где́-то вблизи́ уда́рил гром, напуга́в всех.	Somewhere in the vicinity, thunder struck and frightened everybody (*lit.* having frightened everybody).

D. A clause may contain both a past and a present gerund. The past gerund will refer to an action preceding the one expressed by the present gerund:

Пове́сив пальто́ и снима́я шля́пу,	Having hung his coat and taking off his hat	(precedes main action) (simultaneous with main action)
он сказа́л . . .	he said . . .	(main action)
Сняв шля́пу и ве́шая пальто́,	Having taken off his hat and hanging his coat	(precedes main action) (simultaneous with main action)
он сказа́л . . .	he said . . .	(main action)

Agreement of Verb Predicates with Subjects

In certain instances, the agreement of verb predicates with subjects is governed by rather complex rules. Those given below should not be regarded as rigid; they are given merely as guidance.

VERBS

Agreement in Number

1. With two or more subjects and one predicate, the general rules are:

   (*a*) When the predicate follows the subjects, it is normally in the plural:

Кни́га и газе́та **лежа́т** на столе́.	The book and the paper are lying on the table.
Шум и крик **раздава́лись** везде́. (Пу́шкин)	Noise and shouts were sounding everywhere.*

   (*b*) When the predicate precedes the subjects, it is usually in the singular:

На столе́ **лежи́т** кни́га и газе́та.	On the table are lying a book and a paper.
В дере́вне **послы́шался** то́пот и кри́ки. (Л. Толсто́й)	In the village were (suddenly) heard stamping and shouts.*

   (*c*) When the subjects are persons, the predicate is in the plural, regardless of its position in the sentence.

Ве́чером **пришли́** Па́вел и Ива́н.	In the evening came Paul and John.
Брат и сестра́ **уезжа́ют** за́втра.	My brother and my sister are leaving tomorrow.

2. When the compound subject includes мно́го, немно́го, ма́ло, ско́лько, or сто́лько, the predicate is in the singular:

Ско́лько ученико́в **пришло́** на уро́к?	How many pupils came to the lesson?
Мно́го люде́й **пришло́** на собра́ние.	Many people came to the meeting.

   But:

Мно́гие лю́ди ушли́ ра́но.	Quite a few people (among them) left early.

3. When the compound subject includes—большинство́, меньшинство́, or не́сколько, the predicate is either in the singular or (sometimes) in the plural.

---

* As quoted by Добромы́слов и Розента́ль: Тру́дные вопро́сы грамма́тики и правописа́ния.

(*a*) The construction with the predicate in the singular expresses a somewhat passive idea:

| Большинство́ ученико́в **бы́ло** отпра́влено в ла́герь. | Most pupils were sent to the camp. |
| Большинство́ э́тих пи́сем **пришло́** у́тром. | Most of these letters arrived in the morning. |

(*b*) The predicate in the plural may be found in sentences which express a more active idea (and therefore is used with persons as subjects):

| Большинство́ ученико́в **уе́хали** в ла́герь. | Most of the pupils left for camp. |

(*c*) The same idea of a passive action versus an active one is true of не́сколько:

| За две́рью **находи́лось** не́сколько челове́к и как бу́дто кого́-то **отта́лкивали**. | Behind the door were a few people, who, it seemed, were pushing someone away.* |

Note: When **большинство́** or **меньшинство́** function as independent subjects, the predicate must be in the singular:

| Большинство́ **голосова́ло** за резолю́цию. | The majority voted for the resolution. |
| Меньшинство́ **голосова́ло** про́тив. | The minority voted against. |

4. When the subject is expressed by a numeral and noun, the following rules govern the agreement:

(*a*) With *one*, the predicate is, of course, in the singular:

        Прошла́ одна́ неде́ля.   One week passed.

(*b*) With *two*, *three*, or *four*, the predicate is usually in the plural:

| Три ма́льчика **пришли́** у́тром. | Three boys came in the morning. |
| Две кни́ги **лежа́т** на столе́. | Two books are lying on the table. |

---

* Добромы́слов и Розента́ль: Тру́дные вопро́сы грамма́тики и правописа́ния.

However, the singular predicate is used in impersonal constructions:

У него **было** два чемодана.   He had two suitcases.

(c) With numerals from five up, a subtle distinction is made, depending on whether the subject is thought of as an entity, or as consisting of separate units.

In the first case, the predicate is in the singular:

Прошло пять минут.   Five minutes passed. (a length of time)

Сюда **войдёт** восемь вёдер воды.   This will hold eight buckets of water. (a measure)

In the second case, the predicate is in the plural:

Пять человек **принесли** подарки.   Five people brought presents. (independent actions by different persons)

Sometimes the choice is less obvious:

В классе **сидело** десять учеников.   There were ten pupils sitting in the classroom.

is very close to:

Десять учеников **сидели** в классе.   Ten pupils were sitting in the classroom.

Sometimes the choice is a delicate matter, no longer confined to grammar. The speaker actually determines whether *one* word or a *group* of words should be considered the "primary" or "secondary" part of a sentence (in the sense these terms are used by O. Jespersen).*

(d) The predicate is in the singular when the subject expresses approximation:

Получено около сорока книг.   About forty books were received.
Там **работает** человек тридцать.   About thirty people work there.

* Otto Jespersen, The Philosophy of Grammar, Chapter VII ("The Three Ranks").

(e) The predicate is in the singular when the subject expresses limitation:

| Только шесть домов **было** построено. | Only six houses were built. |
| Пришло́ всего́ де́сять студе́нтов. | Only ten students came. |

(f) When two nouns are joined by the preposition **с**, the predicate may be either in the singular or in the plural. The plural suggests a certain equality between the two nouns.

| Муж с жено́й **пошли́** на конце́рт. | The husband and (with) the wife went to the concert. |
| Оте́ц с детьми́ **гуля́л** в па́рке. | The father walked in the park with the children. |

Agreement in Gender

When the subject and the predicate are of different genders, there is a difficulty (or awkwardness) as regards the agreement of auxiliary verbs.

1. As a rule, the auxiliary verb agrees with the subject:

Его́ **сестра́ была́** о́чень ми́лое существо́.	His sister was a very nice creature.
Пе́рвый челове́к, прише́дший на голосова́ние, **была́ стару́шка** из сосе́днего до́ма.	The first person who came to vote, was an old woman from the house next door.*
Это бы́ло для меня́ тру́дный по́двиг.	This was for me a difficult exploit.†

2. Sometimes, the auxiliary verb agrees with the predicate. This happens when the predicate carries a logical stress:

| Всё э́то споко́йствие **была́** чи́сто одна́ **личи́на**. (Пи́семский) | All this calmness was just a mask.** |
| Мно́гое из э́того **была́ пра́вда**. | Much of this was the truth.†† |

* Example from Совреме́нный ру́сский язы́к. Си́нтаксис. Под реда́кцией проф. Е. М. Га́лкиной-Федору́к.
† As quoted by А. Н. Гво́здев. Очерки по стили́стике ру́сского языка́.
** As quoted in Грамма́тика ру́сского языка́. Си́нтаксис. АН СССР.
†† As quoted by Добромы́слов и Розента́ль. Тру́дные вопро́сы грамма́тики и правописа́ния.

VERBS

Note: In certain instances, it is not always easy to differentiate between the subject and the predicate. The distinction is not clear, for instance, in the following sentence:

Пе́рвый учени́к был мой друг.

However, by rewording the sentence and putting the predicate in the instrumental case, the meaning is clarified:

SUBJECT	PREDICATE
Пе́рвый учени́к был мои́м дру́гом. *(instrumental)*	The number-one pupil was a friend of mine.

PREDICATE	SUBJECT
Пе́рвым ученико́м был мой друг. *(instrumental)*	My friend was the number-one pupil.

Similarly, as regards the examples given above:

Его́ сестра́ была́ о́чень ми́лым существо́м.

Пе́рвым челове́ком, прише́дшим на голосова́ние, была́ стару́шка из сосе́днего до́ма.

Agreement in Case

1. If a sentence contains two verb predicates, both of them governing the same case, the agreement presents no problem:

Он мне меша́ет и надоеда́ет. *(dative)* He disturbs me and annoys me.

2. When the two verbs of a predicate govern different cases, then two objects (direct or indirect) are used:

Она́ люби́ла э́тот портре́т и дорожи́ла им.
(accusative) *(instrumental)* She loved this portrait and valued it.

Она́ не люби́ла её и зави́довала ей.
(accusative) *(dative)* She did not like her and envied her.

Table of Russian Verbs

Table Guide

1. Verb endings

In the following Table the verbs are listed according to the eleven types of endings of their infinitives:

–ать, –ять, –еть, –уть, –оть, –ыть, –ти, –сть, –зть, –чь, –ить

(*a*) Most verbs ending in **–ать, –ять**, and **–еть** belong to the First Conjugation.

(*b*) All verbs ending in **–уть, –оть, –ыть, –ти, –сть, –зть,** and **–чь** belong to the First Conjugation.

(*c*) The great majority of verbs ending in **–ить** belong to the Second Conjugation.

2. Order of verb listing

Under each type of ending the verbs are listed as follows:

> First Conjugation
>> Regular (when applicable)
>> Irregular

> Second Conjugation
>> Regular (when applicable)
>> Irregular

Remark: It will be remembered that regular verbs form their present tense by dropping the last two letters of their infinitive (in the first conjugation) or the last three letters of their infinitive (in the second conjugation) and then by adding the corresponding characteristic endings.

чита́–ть: я чита́–ю, ты чита́–ешь ... они́ чита́–ют
говор–и́ть: я говор–ю́, ты говор–и́шь ... они́ говор–я́т

The past tense is formed by dropping the last two letters of the infinitive and by adding –л, –ла, –ло or –ли to the stem.

чита́–ть: чита́л, чита́ла, чита́ло, чита́ли

Verbs classified here as "irregular" are those which form their present or past tense differently.

3. Productive types of verbs
Only one typical example is given for each *productive* type (regular or irregular). The number of these verbs is not only very large but is, in fact, constantly increasing. For example:

красне́ть	a verb derived from an adjective
влия́ть	a "translation" of the French "in-fluencer"
телефони́ровать	a newly formed verb with a foreign root

4. Personal endings
The first and second person singular and the third person plural, present tense, or future perfective, are given with every verb that heads a group of similar ones, which is given immediately below. (Sometimes, a verb within a group will not be *used* in the 1st person, e.g., течь—to flow.)

5. Unstable letters
The symbols —**a**, +**e**, etc. which are given in the Notes, draw attention to letters which are dropped or which appear in the stem of the present tense (or future perfective):

—**a**	with ждать: жду, ждёшь . . . ждут
—**a**, +**e**	with брать: беру́, берёшь . . . беру́т

6. Mutation of letters
A mutation of letters is indicated in the *Notes* by д → ж (for ви́деть: ви́жу), с → ш (for носи́ть: ношу́), е → о (for петь: пою́), etc.

7. Only irregularly formed past tense or imperative moods are listed.

8. Prefixed verbs are conjugated similarly to verbs of the same root given in the Table, that is **вы**дава́ть similar to **дава́ть**; **у**каза́ть similar to сказа́ть.

9. The first verb within a group gives the stress pattern for other verbs. Exceptions within the group are listed.

Table of Verbs

FIRST CONJUGATION	ENDING: –ать	Notes
Regular		
1. *to read*	чита́ть: чита́ю, чита́ешь, чита́ют	(Productive)
Irregular		
2. *to draw*	рисова́ть: рису́ю, рису́ешь, рису́ют	(Productive) —ова; +у
to be at war	воева́ть: вою́ю, вою́ешь, вою́ют	(Productive) —ева; +ю The following verbs retain –ова and –ева: *to greet* здоро́ваться *to hope* упова́ть (*obs.*) *to intend* намерева́ться *to doubt* сомнева́ться *to dress* одева́ть (*trans.*)
3. *to give*	дава́ть: даю́, даёшь, даю́т	—ва in verbs ending in -вать preceded by да, зна, and ста
to find out, to recognize	узнава́ть	
to get up	встава́ть	
4. *to knit; to tie*	вяза́ть: вяжу́, вя́жешь, вя́жут	—а; з → ж
to lick	лиза́ть	
to spread, to rub with	ма́зать	
to say, to tell	сказа́ть	
to cut	ре́зать	
to dance (a folk dance, etc.)	пляса́ть: пляшу́, пля́шешь, пля́шут	—а; с → ш
to write	писа́ть	
to scratch	чеса́ть	
to send (to)	присла́ть: пришлю́, пришлёшь, пришлю́т	
to mumble	бормота́ть: бормочу́, бормо́чешь, бормо́чут	—а; т → ч
to hide	пря́тать	
to trample	топта́ть	
to (take) trouble, to solicit	хлопота́ть	
to laugh loudly	хохота́ть	
to whisper	шепта́ть	
to tickle	щекота́ть	

VERBS

FIRST CONJUGATION	ENDING: -ать	Notes
to splash	брызгать: брызжу, брызжешь, брызжут (*Also*: брызгаю, брызгаешь, брызгают)	—а; г → ж
to move (*trans.*)	двигать (*Also*: двигаю, двигаешь, двигают)	
to tell lies	лгать: лгу, лжёшь, лгут	—а; г → ж (except in 1st pers. sing. and in 3d pers. pl.)
to cry	плакать: плачу, плачешь, плачут	—а; к → ч
to jump, to gallop	скакать	
to slander	клеветать: клевещу, клевещешь, клевещут	—а; т → щ
to tremble, to palpitate	трепетать	
to whistle, to hiss	свистать:* свищу, свищешь, свищут	—а; ст → щ
to wave	махать: машу, машешь, машут (*Also*: махаю, махаешь, махают)	—а; х → ш
to look for	искать: ищу, ищешь, ищут	—а; ск → щ
to splash, to splatter	плескать (*Also*: плескаю, плескаешь, плескают)	
to rinse	полоскать (*Also*: полоскаю, полоскаешь, полоскают)	

Note: Verbs with similar endings not listed here are regular. For example:
кусать to bite: кусаю, кусаешь, кусают
пускать to let (go): пускаю, пускаешь, пускают

5.
to tell lies	врать: вру, врёшь, врут	—а
to wait	ждать	
to glut, to devour	жрать	
to yell	орать	
to tear	рвать	
to suck	сосать	
to weave	ткать	
to thirst for, to crave	жаждать: жажду, жаждешь, жаждут	*
to moan	стонать: стону, стонешь, стонут	
to take	брать, беру, берёшь, берут	—а; +е
to tear, to flog	драть	
to call, to name	звать: зову, зовёшь, зовут	—а; +о

* Not to be confused with **свистеть**, Type 22.

FIRST CONJUGATION	ENDING: –ать	Notes
6. to doze	дрема́ть: дре́млю, дре́млешь, дре́млют	–а; +л
to agitate, to sway	колеба́ть	
to strew, to pour	сы́пать	
to pull about	трепа́ть	

7. to press, to squeeze	жать: жму, жмёшь, жмут	–а; +м
to begin	нача́ть: начну́, начнёшь, начну́т	–а; +н
to become	стать: ста́ну, ста́нешь, ста́нут	+н

8. to go, to drive, to ride	е́хать: е́ду, е́дешь, е́дут	–ха; +д

SECOND CONJUGATION	ENDING: –ать	Notes

Regular

9. to howl	визжа́ть: визжу́, визжи́шь, визжа́т	
to grumble	ворча́ть	
to hold	держа́ть: держу́, де́ржишь, де́ржат	
to tremble	дрожа́ть	
to breathe	дыша́ть: дышу́, ды́шишь, ды́шат	
to sound	звуча́ть	
to cry, to yell	крича́ть	
to lie (down)	лежа́ть	
to be silent	молча́ть	
to squeak	пища́ть	
to hear	слы́шать: слы́шу, слы́шишь, слы́шат	
to knock	стуча́ть	
to stick out, to protrude	торча́ть	
to crack, to rattle	треща́ть	
to race, to dash	мча́ться	

Irregular

10. to chase	гнать: гоню́, го́нишь, го́нят	+о
to sleep	спать: сплю, спишь, спят	+л, (1st pers. sing.)

VERBS

	FIRST CONJUGATION	ENDING: –ять	Notes
	Regular		
11.	to walk	гуля́ть: гуля́ю, гуля́ешь,	(Productive)

	Irregular		
12.	to bark	ла́ять: ла́ю, ла́ешь, ла́ют	—я
	to melt	та́ять	
	to devise, to undertake	зате́ять	
	to sow	се́ять	
	to blow softly, to wave	ве́ять	
	to repent	ка́яться: ка́юсь, ка́ешься, ка́ются	
	to hope	наде́яться	
	to laugh	смея́ться: смею́сь, смеёшься, смею́тся	

13.	to take	взять: возьму́, возьмёшь, возьму́т	—я; +о; +ьм
	to understand	поня́ть: пойму́, поймёшь, пойму́т	—ня; +йм
	to occupy; to borrow (money)	заня́ть	
	to hire; to rent	наня́ть	
	to raise, to lift	подня́ть: подниму́, подни́мешь, подни́мут	—я; +им
	to take away	отня́ть	
	to embrace	обня́ть	
	to take off	снять	
	to receive	приня́ть: приму́, при́мешь, при́мут	—ня; +м
	to rumple, to crumple	мять: мну, мнёшь, мнут	—я; н

	SECOND CONJUGATION	ENDING: –ять	
	Regular		
14.	to stand	стоя́ть: стою́, стои́шь, стоя́т	
	to be afraid	боя́ться: бою́сь, бои́шься, боя́тся	

	FIRST CONJUGATION	ENDING: –еть		Notes
	REGULAR			
15.	*to redden*	краснéть: краснéю, краснéешь, краснéют		(Productive)

	IRREGULAR		Past	Notes
16.	*to rub*	терéть: тру, трёшь, трут	тёр	–е; –е
	to die	умерéть	ýмер	
	to lock	заперéть	зáпер	
	to unlock	отперéть: отопрý, отопрёшь, отопрýт	óтпер	–е; –е; +о (prefix)

17.	*to roar, to yell*	ревéть: ревý, ревёшь, ревýт	–е

18.	*to put, to leave* *to dress* (trans.)	деть: дéну, дéнешь, дéнут одéть	+н

19.	*to sing*	петь: пою́, поёшь, пою́т	е → о

	SECOND CONJUGATION	ENDING: –еть	Notes
	REGULAR		
20.	*to order, to decree*	велéть: велю́, вели́шь, веля́т	
	to burn (intrans.)	горéть	
	to ring	звенéть	
	to look	смотрéть: смотрю́, смóтришь, смóтрят	
	to ache	болéть: . . . боли́т . . . боля́т	3rd person only. Not to be confused with: болéть: болéю, болéешь, болéют— to be sick (Type 15)

	IRREGULAR		
21.	*to grieve, to mourn*	скорбéть: скорблю́, скорби́шь, скорбя́т	+л
	to creak	скрипéть	
	to suffer, to endure	терпéть: терплю́, тéрпишь, тéрпят	
	to snore	храпéть	
	to speak hoarsely	хрипéть	
	to thunder, to rattle, to raor	гремéть	

VERBS

			Notes
SECOND CONJUGATION	ENDING: **–еть**		
to boil (intrans.)	кипе́ть		
to hiss	шипе́ть		
to make noise	шуме́ть		

			Notes
22. to see	ви́деть: ви́**жу**, ви́**дишь**, ви́**дят**		д → ж
to hate	ненави́деть		
to offend	оби́деть		
to look at, to gaze	гляде́ть: гляжу́, гляди́шь, глядя́т		
to sit	сиде́ть: сижу́, сиди́шь, сидя́т		
to turn (trans.)	верте́ть: верчу́, ве́ртишь, ве́ртят		т → ч
to fly	лете́ть: лечу́, лети́шь, летя́т		
to pant, to puff	пыхте́ть		
to depend	зави́сеть: зави́**шу**, зави́**сишь**, зави́**сят**		с → ш
to hang (intrans.)	висе́ть: вишу́, виси́шь, вися́т		
to shine, to glisten	блесте́ть: блещу́, блести́шь, блестя́т		ст → щ
	Also: блещу́, бле́щешь, бле́щут		
to whistle	свисте́ть		

			Notes
FIRST CONJUGATION (only)	ENDING: **–уть**		
Regular			
23. to blow	дуть: ду́**ю**, ду́**ешь**, ду́**ют**		
to blow up	наду́ть		
Irregular			
24. to move (trans.)	дви́нуть: дви́**ну**, дви́**нешь**, дви́**нут**		(Productive) ну → н

		Past	Notes
25. to erect, to build	воздви́гнуть: воздви́гну, воздви́гнешь, воздви́гнут	воздви́г*	ну → н —нуть (in the past)
to resurrect	воскре́снуть		
to grow deaf	гло́хнуть		
to reach, to attain	дости́гнуть		

* Some verbs admit a variant form in the past, considered at present obsolete. For example, избе́г**нул**, дости́г**нул**.

FIRST CONJUGATION (only)	ENDING: –уть	Notes
to become silent	замо́лкнуть	
to become quiet	зати́хнуть	
to avoid	избе́гнуть	
to disappear	исче́знуть	
to get sour	ки́снуть	
to freeze (intrans.)	мёрзнуть	
to get wet	мо́кнуть	
to get stronger	окре́пнуть	
to become blind	осле́пнуть	
to smell (intrans.)	па́хнуть	
to start hanging (intrans.)	пови́снуть	
to perish	поги́бнуть	
to subject to	подве́ргнуть	
to go out, to be extinguished	пога́снуть	
to go out, to be extinguished	поту́хнуть	
to get used to	привы́кнуть	
to swell	распу́хнуть	
to dry (intrans.)	со́хнуть	

Note: Some verbs have two imperfectives—one of them formed from the perfective. Examples: мо́кнуть, промока́ть; ги́бнуть, погиба́ть.

FIRST CONJUGATION (only)	ENDING: –оть	Notes
IRREGULAR		
26. to stab, to pierce	коло́ть: колю́, ко́лешь, ко́лют	—о
to weed	поло́ть	
to rip; to whip	поро́ть	
to struggle, to fight	боро́ться: борю́сь, бо́решься, бо́рются	
to grind, to mill	моло́ть: мелю́, ме́лешь, ме́лют	о → е; —о

FIRST CONJUGATION (only)	ENDING: –ыть	Notes
IRREGULAR		
27. to howl	выть: во́ю, во́ешь, во́ют	ы → о
to cover	крыть	
to wine	ныть	
to wash	мыть	
to dig	рыть	

VERBS

	FIRST CONJUGATION (only)	ENDING: –ыть		Notes
28.	to swim	плыть: плыву́, плывёшь, плыву́т		+в
	to be reputed, to pass for	слыть		
	to get cold	стыть, сты́ну, сты́нешь, сты́нут		+н

			Future	Notes
29.	to be	быть: ... есть ... (суть)	бу́ду, бу́дешь, бу́дут	Only 3rd pers. used in present

	FIRST CONJUGATION (only)	ENDINGS: –ти, –сть, –зть		

IRREGULAR

			Past	Notes
30. (a)	to drive, to transport	везти́: везу́, везёшь, везу́т	вёз	
	to gnaw	грызть		
	to climb	лезть: ле́зу, ле́зешь, ле́зут	лез	
	to crawl	ползти́		
	to carry	нести́: несу́, несёшь, несу́т	нёс	
	to herd, to shepherd	пасти́		
	to shake	трясти́		
(b)	to wander	брести́: бреду́, бредёшь, бреду́т	брёл	–с; +д
	to lead, to take	вести́		
	to put	класть	клал	
	to steal	красть		
	to fall	упа́сть		
	to sit down	сесть: ся́ду, ся́дешь, ся́дут	сел	е → я; –с; +д
(c)	to sweep	мести́: мету́, метёшь, мету́т	мёл	–с; +т
	to braid, to twine, to wreathe	плести́		
	to acquire	приобрести́		
	to blossom	цвести́		
	to read	проче́сть: прочту́, прочтёшь, прочту́т		–е; –с; +т

			Past	Notes
(d)	to row	грести́: гребу́, гребёшь, гребу́т	грёб	–с; +б
	to scrape, to claw	скрести́		
	to grow	расти́: расту́, растёшь, расту́т	рос	а → о (past)
	to go (on foot)	идти́: иду́, идёшь, иду́т	шёл, шла, шло, шли	

	FIRST CONJUGATION (only)	ENDING: **-чь**			

IRREGULAR

31.
				Past	Notes
(a)	to bake	печь: пе**ку́**, пе**чёшь**, пе**ку́т**		пёк	+к (1st pers. sing., 3d pers. pl.) and ч (other persons)
	to attract	привле́чь			
	to whip, to thrash	сечь			
	to flow	течь			
	to abdicate	отре́чься: отре**ку́сь**, отре**чёшься**, отре**ку́тся**		отрёкся	

(b)	to take care of, to save	бере́чь: берегу́, бережёшь, берегу́т		берёг	+г (1st pers. sing., 3d pers. pl.) and ж (other persons)
	to neglect, to disregard	пренебре́чь			
	to watch over	стере́чь			
	to be able	мочь: могу́, мо́жешь, мо́гут		мог	
	to cut, to clip	стричь		стриг	

(c)	to burn (trans.)	жечь: жгу, жжёшь, жгут		жёг, жгла, жгло, жгли	−e; +г (1st pers. sing., 3d pers. pl.) and ж (other pers.)

			Imperative	Past	Notes
(d)	to lie down	лечь: ля́гу, ля́жешь, ля́гут	ляг, ля́гте	лёг	e → я; +г (1st pers. sing., 3d pers. pl.) and ж (other pers.)

VERBS

	FIRST CONJUGATION	ENDING: –ить		
	REGULAR			
32.	*to rot*	гнить: гнию́, гниёшь, гнию́т		

			Imperative	*Notes*
	IRREGULAR			
33.	*to beat*	бить: бью, бьёшь, бьют	бей, бе́йте	–и; +ь
	to twist, to twine	вить		
	to pour	лить		
	to drink	пить		
	to sew	шить		

			Past	*Notes*
34.	*to shave*	брить: бре́ю, бре́ешь, бре́ют		–и; +е
	to live	жить: живу́, живёшь, живу́т		+в
	to hurt, to bruise	ушиби́ть: ушибу́, ушибёшь, ушибу́т	уши́б	–и

	SECOND CONJUGATION	ENDING: и́ть	*Notes*
	REGULAR		
35.	*to speak, to say*	говори́ть: говорю́, говори́шь, говоря́т	(Productive)
	to decide	реши́ть: решу́, реши́шь, реша́т	Endings –у, –ат after sibilants

	IRREGULAR		*Notes* (Productive) Mutation of consonant in 1st person singular:
36.	*to load*	грузи́ть: гружу́, гру́зишь, гру́зят	з → ж
	to carry	носи́ть: ношу́, но́сишь, но́сят	с → ш
	to pay	плати́ть: плачу́, пла́тишь, пла́тят	т → ч
	to stop, to cease	прекрати́ть: прекращу́, прекрати́шь, прекратя́т	т → щ
	to forgive	прости́ть: прощу́, прости́шь, простя́т	ст → щ
	to go (on foot, habitually)	ходи́ть: хожу́, хо́дишь, хо́дят	д → ж

37.	*to draw lines, to rule*	графи́ть: графлю́, графи́шь, графя́т	(Productive) +л in the 1st person singular (after labials)
	to catch	лови́ть: ловлю́, ло́вишь, ло́вят	

SECOND CONJUGATION	ENDING: –и́ть	Notes
to love	люби́ть: любл**ю́**, лю́б**ишь**, лю́б**ят**	
to hurry (trans.)	торопи́ть: торопл**ю́**, торо́п**ишь**, торо́п**ят**	
to feed	корми́ть: кормл**ю́**, ко́рм**ишь**, ко́рм**ят**	

The following verbs have characteristic endings of both conjugations:

38. *to give*   дать: **дам, дашь, даст, дади́м, дади́те, даду́т***

     to eat   есть: **ем, ешь, ест, еди́м, еди́те, едя́т***

     to want, to wish   хоте́ть: хочу́, хо́чешь, хо́чет, хоти́м, хоти́те, хотя́т

     to run   бежа́ть: бегу́, бе**жи́шь**, бе**жи́т**, бе**жи́м**, бе**жи́те**, бегу́т   —ж; +г (1st pers. sing., 3d pers. pl.)

Note: Related verbs, such as прода́ть (to sell), надое́сть (to annoy, to bother) have the same type of endings.

* The endings are characteristic of an ancient type of formation.

8. ADVERBS

An adverb is a non-inflected part of speech. Adverbs do not have gender, case or number. They never change—except qualitative adverbs in **o** or **e** which have a comparative and a superlative degree.

Formation of Adverbs

Adverbs are formed from various parts of speech, among which adjectives figure most prominently.

Adverbs Formed from Adjectives

(*a*) Adverbs ending in **o** or **e**.
They coincide with the neuter short form of an adjective, and usually have the same stress. This is a very large class of adverbs:

    Это о́зеро краси́во. (*adj.*)   This lake is beautiful.
    Она́ краси́во (*adv.*) поёт.   She sings beautifully.

Occasionally, the stress will vary:

    Это о́зеро глубо́ко. (*adj.*)   This lake is deep.
    Вы глубоко́ (*adv.*) непра́вы.   You are completely (*lit.* deeply) wrong.

> *Notes:*
> (*a*) Not all qualitative adjectives can form adverbs. The following do not:
>
> Certain adjectives pertaining to colors: голубо́й—blue, sky-blue; кори́чневый—brown; ро́зовый—pink, etc.
> Adjectives with the suffix **-ов**: даровой—free (of charge), gratis; передово́й—foremost, advanced.

(*b*) There are very few adverbs ending in **-e** and formed from soft adjectives. To name some: крайне—extremely; внешне—outwardly; излишне—unnecessarily; неуклюже—awkwardly; искренне (also: искренно)—sincerely.

Examples:

крайне интересно	most (extremely) interesting
внешне спокойный	outwardly calm
искренне ваш	sincerely yours

(*c*) Some soft adjectives form adverbs ending in **-o**: ранний—рано (early); поздний—поздно (late); давний—давно (a long time ago, for a long time).

(*d*) As a rule, adverbs in **-o** or **-e** are not formed from relative adjectives. Exceptions are a few prefixed adverbs, referring to time, sequence, order: поминутно—each minute; досрочно—before term; поочерёдно—in turn; ежемесячно—every month, etc.

(*b*) Adverbs in **-ски** and **-цки**.
These adverbs are formed from adjectives ending in –ский or –цкий. They may, or may not have the prefix по-: иронически—ironically; страдальчески—painfully; по-женски—woman-like; по-русски—(in) Russian; по-турецки—(in) Turkish.

(*c*) Adverbs formed from the once existing oblique cases of short adjectives: надолго—for a long time; направо—to (on) the right; слева—from (on) the left; понемногу—gradually; вполне—entirely, and many others.

(*d*) Adverbs formed from the long form of various adjectives (mostly with the prefix по-):

From qualitative adjectives: по–старому—as before; по–новому—in a new way.
From relative adjectives: по–летнему—in a summer fashion; по–зимнему—in a winter fashion.

(*e*) Some adverbs are formed from adjectives-participles: вызывающе—challengingly; раздражающе—irritatingly, etc.

Adverbs Formed from Nouns

(*a*) *Non-prefixed* adverbs are formed mostly from the instrumental *singular:* утром—in the morning; днём—in the afternoon; весной—in the spring; кругом—around; etc.

These adverbs are very numerous, while those formed from the instrumental *plural* are infrequent: временами—every now and then; вечерами—in the evenings; местами—here and there.

A few adverbs are formed from cases other than the instrumental: дома—at home (from the *genitive*); сейчас—now (from the *accusative*); правда—truly (from the *nominative*); etc.

> *Note:* A few adverbs were formed from nouns which no longer exist: босиком—barefoot; без умолку—(talking) ceaselessly; без ведома—without knowledge, etc.

Other adverbs are only loosely connected with the original noun. Thus: даром (free, gratis) does not really imply a gift (дар); рядом (next, nearby) does not necessarily mean "in a row" (ряд), etc.

(*b*) *Prefixed* adverbs have been readily formed from various cases.

Examples:

GEN.	издали—from afar; снизу—from below
DAT.	кстати—by the way; посредине—in the middle
ACC.	наконец—finally; вперёд—forward
INSTR.	замужем—married (of a woman)
PREP.	вместе—together; внизу—below

(*c*) Finally, there are quite a few combinations of nouns (or phraseological units) which are regarded as adverbs:

день за днём	day after day
шаг за шагом	step after step
лицом к лицу	face to face
слово в слово	word for word
время от времени	from time to time
со дня на день	any day (now)
изо дня в день	day after day
вверх дном	upside down
раз навсегда	once and for all

Adverbs Formed from Numerals

A few adverbs are formed from ordinal numerals: сперва́—at first; впервы́е—for the first time; во-пе́рвых—in the first place; во-вторы́х—secondly; etc.

Some are formed from cardinal and collective numerals: наедине́—in private, alone; одна́жды—once; два́жды—twice; вдво́е—double, twice; etc.

Adverbs Formed from Verbs

(a) These adverbs may be formed from participles: умоля́юще—imploringly; вызыва́юще—defiantly

(b) Others are formed from gerunds: шутя́—easily, without effort (*lit.* jokingly); неме́для—without delay; мо́лча—silently

These adverbs include a few set expressions, such as спустя́ рукава́, сложа́ ру́ки. (See page 226, para. 2.)

(c) Мо́жет быть and почти́ are adverbs of verbal origin. [Почти́ is the imperative mood of the verb—поче́сть to count, to consider. Thus, почти́ два часа́ (almost two hours) meant "consider: two hours."]

Adverbs Formed from Pronouns

(a) The origin of these adverbs is readily visible in the following types:
Adverbs formed from possessive pronouns, such as: по-мо́ему; по-ва́шему; по-свое́му.
Adverbs formed from the pronouns что, тот and сей, such as: почему́ (from по чему́); отчего́ (from от чего́); оттого́ (from от того́); зате́м (from за тем); тепе́рь (from то пе́рво); сейча́с (from сей час)

(b) In other instances, the derivation is not obvious and presents mainly a historical interest. These pronominal adverbs are also called *primary* or *simple*: везде́; здесь; туда́

Adverbs Formed from Other Adverbs

These adverbs are formed with the aid of particles or prepositions: где́-нибудь; куда́-то; никогда́; послеза́втра; позавчера́, etc.

Classification and Usage of Adverbs

Adverbs are classified into two types: Qualifying and Specifying.

Qualifying Adverbs

These adverbs refer to the intrinsic characteristics of a notion which they qualify. They may pertain to verbs, adjectives, other adverbs and sometimes to nouns.

		Part of speech qualified
Он **хорошо́** говори́т.	He speaks *well*.	verb
Это **о́чень** интере́сная кни́га.	This book is *very* interesting.	adjective
Вы е́дете **сли́шком** бы́стро.	You are driving *too* fast.	adverb
Чте́ние **вслух** о́чень поле́зно.	Reading *aloud* is very beneficial.	noun

Qualifying adverbs are sub-divided into *adverbs of quality*, *adverbs of quantity* (or *measure*), and *adverbs of manner*.

ADVERBS OF QUALITY

These adverbs answer the question как? (how). For instance: хорошо́—well; пло́хо—badly; бы́стро—fast; ме́дленно—slowly; гро́мко—loudly; ти́хо—softly; стра́нно—strangely; ве́село—gaily; ирони́чески—ironically; саркасти́чески—sarcastically; ка́к-нибудь—somehow; наотре́з—flatly, categorically.

Мы е́хали бы́стро.	We were driving fast.
Это звучи́т стра́нно.	This sounds strange.
сказа́ть саркасти́чески	to say sarcastically
отказа́ться наотре́з	to refuse flatly

Usage of Adverbs of Quality

(*a*) These adverbs usually qualify actions, as shown above. However, occasionally, they may not pertain to verbs:

Это сто́ило необыча́йно до́рого.	This was unusually expensive.
Он удиви́тельно ми́лый челове́к.	He is an awfully nice man (*lit*. amazingly nice).

(*b*) Comparative degree

Adverbs of quality which end in **-о** or **-е** may have a comparative degree. Its formation follows the rules given with the comparative degree of adjectives (page 90). There are two forms of the comparative: the simple, formed with the suffixes **-ее (-ей)**, **-ше**, or **-е** and the compound, formed with the addition of **бо́лее**.

бы́стро—быстре́е (быстре́й)	or	бо́лее бы́стро
краси́во—краси́вее (краси́вей)	or	бо́лее краси́во
высо́ко—вы́ше	or	бо́лее высо́ко
про́сто—про́ще	or	бо́лее про́сто

Adverbs in **-ски** have only the compound form:

Он отнёсся к э́тому бо́лее крити́чески, чем други́е прису́тствующие.	He treated it more critically than any other people present.

The distinction between the comparatives of adverbs and adjectives is in their syntactical functions; the comparative of adverbs qualifies verbs—not nouns:

ADJECTIVE:	Э́та кни́га **лу́чше**, чем та.	This book is better than that one.
ADVERB:	Он чита́ет **лу́чше**, чем пи́шет.	He reads better than he writes.

The addition of **по-** to the short form of some comparatives, mollifies the idea by implying "somewhat":

Э́то мо́жно сде́лать попро́ще.	One could do it somewhat simpler.
Пиши́те нам поча́ще.	Write us more often (won't you?).

Remark: Some comparative degrees admit two variant forms.

поздне́е	and	по́зже	
ра́нее	and	ра́ньше	(the latter is used more frequently).
да́лее	and	да́льше	(the latter is used more frequently).

(*c*) Superlative degree

The superlative degree of adverbs is formed from the superlative degree of adjectives by adding the suffix **-е** to their stem.

ADVERBS

Superlative of adjective	*Superlative of adverb*	
строжа́йший	строжа́йше	—most strictly.

The superlative degree proper is used very seldom in current speech. It is found in a few isolated expressions:

Покорне́йше прошу́	I humbly request
строжа́йше запрещено́	(most) strictly forbidden
Он все подро́бнейше объясни́л.	He explained everything in greatest details.

The superlative degree is much more often conveyed with the aid of всего́ and всех added to the comparative.

Examples:

Я бо́льше всего́ люблю́ чте́ние.	I like reading better than anything else.
Он пришёл по́зже всех.	He came later than anybody else.

ADVERBS OF QUANTITY OR MEASURE

These adverbs answer the questions: ско́лько? (how much? how many?); как мно́го? (how much? how many?); наско́лько? (how much? to what extent?); до како́й сте́пени? (how much? how far? up to what degree?). Frequently, the question is not stated but just implied:

—Вы уста́ли? —Are you tired?
—Да, я о́чень уста́л. —Yes, I am very tired.

Some frequently used adverbs of quantity follow:

весьма́	extremely	необыча́йно	unusually
гора́здо	much more, far more	ниско́лько	not at all
		о́чень	very
доста́точно	enough, sufficient	почти́	almost
		слегка́	slightly
е́ле–е́ле	barely, hardly	сли́шком	too, too much
исключи́тельно	exceptionally	соверше́нно	completely, entirely
ма́ло	(very) little		
мно́го	a lot, (very) much	совсе́м	quite, entirely
		стра́шно	frightfully

удиви́тельно	amazingly	чересчу́р	too, too much,
ужа́сно	terribly		excessively
		чуть-чуть	a little bit

Also: вдво́е—double, twice as; втро́е—thrice as; два́жды—twice; три́жды—thrice; etc.

Usage of Adverbs of Quantity or Measure

(a) As a general rule, these adverbs may qualify verbs, adjectives, or other adverbs.

		Part of speech qualified
Я о́чень люблю́ её.	I like her very much.	verb
Это о́чень краси́во.	This is very pretty.	adjective
Сейча́с о́чень ра́но.	It is very early (now).	adverb
Я соверше́нно не понима́ю.	I don't understand at all.	verb
Рестора́н соверше́нно пусто́й.	The restaurant is quite empty.	adjective
соверше́нно я́сно напи́сано	quite clearly written	adverb

(b) Мно́го, ма́ло, два́жды, три́жды qualify only verbs, as a rule;* мно́го is occasionally used with the comparative degree of adjectives. (See page 257).

Я мно́го рабо́таю.	I work a lot.
Вы ма́ло спи́те.	You sleep very little.
Он два́жды звони́л мне.	He telephoned me twice.

(c) Adverbs of quantity or measure very rarely qualify nouns. Sentences, such as the following are encountered infrequently:

Мы с ним немно́го прия́тели.	We are on rather friendly terms.
Он почти́ стари́к.	He is almost an old man (by now).

* Unlike the numerals ("indefinite-cardinals") мно́го and ма́ло which do qualify nouns: мно́го книг; ма́ло вре́мени.

ADVERBS

(d) The usage of a few selected adverbs deserves comments:

Гораздо, вдвое, втрое are used only with the comparative degree.

Этот дом гораздо лучше, но он стоит вдвое дороже.	This house is far better but it costs twice as much.
Он говорит гораздо лучше, чем я.	He speaks much better than I.

Совсем, вполне, очень, and **много** are used in the following ways:

Совсем means *quite, completely, entirely*.

Это совсем близко.	This is quite near.
Я совсем забыл.	I quite (completely) forgot.
Это совсем другое дело..	This is an entirely different matter.

Note: Frequently, совсем will be used in a negative statement, whereas вполне or очень will be used with a positive one:

Я совсем не понимаю.	I do not understand at all.
Я вполне понимаю.	I quite understand.
Я совсем не согласен.	I don't agree at all.
Я вполне согласен.	I quite agree.
Это совсем недалеко.	It is not far at all.
Это очень далеко.	It is quite far.

Очень may qualify adjectives, adverbs, and verbs. It expresses a degree, a certain intensity:

очень милый	very nice
очень далеко	very far
Я её очень люблю.	I like her very much.

Много, when functioning as an adverb, qualifies verbs. In contrast to очень, it expresses an amount, a quantity:

Он много работает.	He works a lot.
Они много сделали для нас.	They did a lot (very much) for us.

Много is also used with the comparative degree. It has then the same meaning as гораздо:

Ему много лучше сегодня.	He is much better today.
Это много дороже.	This is much more (far more) expensive.

Довольно—достаточно

Довольно means *rather* or *enough*. Достаточно means *enough, sufficient*. *Not enough* is usually translated by **недостаточно, мало, слишком мало**.

Он довольно хорошо говорит по-русски.	He speaks Russian rather well.
Так довольно?	Is this enough (sufficient)?
У вас достаточно денег?	Do you have enough money?
Я не еду в Европу. У меня недостаточно денег для этого и слишком мало времени.	I am not going to Europe. I don't have enough money for that and I don't have enough time.

Почти—чуть не

Почти means *almost* and refers to something which is still to be attained:

Она почти готова.	She is almost ready.
Я почти всё кончил.	I have finished almost everything.
Уже почти семь часов.	It is already almost seven.

Чуть не means *almost* and refers to something avoided:

Мы чуть не опоздали.	We were almost late.
Он чуть не умер от этого.	He almost died from it.

ADVERBS OF MANNER

These adverbs answer the questions: как? (how?); каким образом? (how? in what manner?); каким способом? (in what way? by what method?).

They do not imply a characteristic which may exist to a greater or lesser extent and, therefore, do not have a comparative degree. Therein lies the difference between them and adverbs of quality in **-o** and **-e** (which also answer the question: как?).

Some currently used adverbs of manner and two examples follow:

бегом	running	вполголоса	in an undertone
вдруг	suddenly	вслух	aloud
верхом	on horseback	наизусть	by heart
вплавь	swimming	начисто	clean, fair
вплотную	close, close up to	пешком	on foot
		шёпотом	in a whisper

ADVERBS

Они говори́ли шо́потом. — They spoke in a whisper.
Я люблю́ е́здить верхо́м. — I like horseback riding.

These adverbs pertain to verbs, and sometimes to nouns related to verbs:

говори́ть вполго́лоса; чита́ть вслух; е́здить верхо́м.
разгово́р вполго́лоса; чте́ние вслух; езда́ верхо́м.

Very closely related to adverbs of manner are *adverbs of comparison*. Most of them have the prefix **по–**:

встре́тить по–бра́тски	to meet as a brother (in a brotherly way)
выть по–во́лчьи	to howl as a wolf
одева́ться по–ле́тнему	to dress in summer clothes (as if it were summer)
шни́цель по–ве́нски	wienerschnitzel (veal steak as made in Vienna)
ко́фе по–туре́цки	coffee Turkish-style
суда́к по–по́льски	pike-perch Polish fashion (à la polonaise)

Note: In contrast to the last two examples, **по–** pertaining to the language of a country no longer means "in the manner of":

говори́ть по–туре́цки	to speak Turkish
чита́ть по–по́льски	to read Polish
письмо́ по–ру́сски	a letter in Russian

Finally, one more *sub-type of adverbs of manner* are those formed from the instrumental case of nouns:

поднима́ть пыль столбо́м	to raise dust (in a column)
лете́ть стрело́й	to fly like an arrow

Usage of Adverbs in –ски

Some adverbs in –**ски** may be used with or without the prefix **по–**. The use of prefix softens the adverb somewhat:

Мы дру́жески расста́лись.	We parted friends.
Он при́нял меня́ по–дру́жески.	He received me as a friend.
де́тски беспо́мощный	childishly helpless
Вы рассужда́ете по–де́тски.	You reason as if you were a child.

Note: Adverbs having the suffix **-ич** do not take the prefix **по-**:

физи́чески невозмо́жно physically impossible
теорети́чески, э́то так theoretically, this is so

Specifying Adverbs

Specifying adverbs refer to extrinsic characteristics of a notion (time, location, etc.). They usually pertain to verbs, sometimes to adverbs and nouns, and, less frequently, to adjectives. For example:

		Part of speech to which adverb pertains
Я е́ду **туда́**.	I am going *there*.	verb
ра́но **у́тром**	*early* in the morning	adverb
в до́ме **напро́тив**	in the house *across*	noun
всегда́ весёлый	*always* gay	adjective

These adverbs are subdivided into *adverbs of time*, *adverbs of place*, *adverbs of cause* (or *reason*) and *adverbs of purpose*.

ADVERBS OF TIME

They answer the questions: когда́? (when?); с каки́х пор? (since when?); до каки́х пор? (up to when? until when?); ско́лько вре́мени? (how long? how much time?); как ча́сто? (how often?):

Он прие́хал вчера́.	He arrived yesterday.
Я живу́ здесь давно́.	I have lived here for a long time (since long ago).
Мой конь и доны́не носи́л бы меня́. (Пу́шкин)	My steed would be carrying me up to this day.
Мы недо́лго жда́ли.	We did not wait for long.
Он ре́дко прихо́дит.	He seldom comes (visits us).

A list of currently used adverbs of time follows. The majority of these answer когда́?

ADVERBS

сего́дня	today	иногда́	sometimes
вчера́	yesterday	тогда́	then
позавчера́	the day before yesterday	пото́м	afterwards
		сперва́	at first
тре́тьего дня	the day before yesterday	снача́ла	at first
		сра́зу	right away
за́втра	tomorrow	ско́ро	soon
послеза́втра	the day after tomorrow	то́тчас	immediately, right away
ра́но	early	впосле́дствии	later, thereafter
по́здно	late	обы́чно	usually
у́тром	in the morning	по́сле	afterwards; after (more often, a preposition)
днём	in the afternoon		
ве́чером	in the evening		
но́чью	at night		
весно́й	in the spring	с тех пор	from then on
ле́том	in the summer	смо́лоду	since youth
о́сенью	in the fall	и́здавна	since long ago
зимо́й	in the winter	до сих пор	until now, until here
сейча́с	now		
тепе́рь	now, at present	надо́лго	for a long time
давно́	long ago	ненадо́лго	not for long
неда́вно	recently	навсегда́	forever
ра́ньше	before, earlier	доны́не	until this day
пре́жде	before, formerly	до́лго	long, a long time
на–дня́х	one of these days	недо́лго	not long, not a long time
одна́жды	once		
накану́не	on the eve	ча́сто	often
во́время	on time	ре́дко	seldom
всегда́	always	ежедне́вно	daily

A few set expressions function as adverbs of time:

чуть свет	at daybreak	не по дням, а по часа́м	very rapidly (*lit.* not by days, but by hours)
со дня на́ день	any day (now)		
и́зо дня в день	from day to day		

Usage of Adverbs of Time

The following adverbs, which express duration or repetition, are used with the imperfective aspect of verbs: всегда́; никогда́; обыкнове́нно;

иногда; всё время; часто; долго; ежедневно. However, никогда may be followed by the perfective when it expresses a single action which never took, or never will take place.

Она никогда не ответила на это письмо.	She never answered this letter.
Он никогда не узнает об этом.	He will never find out about this.

Note: Occasionally, some of these adverbs will be followed by the future perfective (when the tense implied is really the present).

Она всегда скажет что-нибудь неприятное.	She will always say something disagreeable.
Иногда он придёт в восемь, иногда в девять.	Sometimes he will come at eight, sometimes at nine.

Сейчас, теперь, сегодня

Сейчас means "now," "just," "shortly," "right away." It is used with the present, past, and future:

Я сейчас пью кофе.	I am drinking coffee now.
Он сейчас звонил.	He just called up (a moment ago).
Она сейчас вернётся.	She will return shortly (right away).

Теперь means "now," "at present." It is used chiefly with the present tense, but sometimes with the past or future:

Я теперь работаю в банке.	I am working at present in a bank.
Теперь он решил уехать.	(And) now he decided to leave.
Он теперь уж не вернётся.	He will not return now (any more).

Сегодня means "today" (rarely "at present"). Thus, "Where are they living today (at present)?" is translated "Где они живут теперь?"

Всегда, всё время

Всегда means "always"; **всё время** means "all the time," "constantly." Sometimes these adverbs are practically interchangeable:

Он всегда жалуется.	He always complains.
Он всё время жалуется.	He complains all the time.

ADVERBS

But normally, they express different ideas:

Я всегда́ сплю по́сле обе́да.	I always sleep after dinner.
Мы всегда́ говори́м с ним по-ру́сски.	We always speak Russian with him.
Вы всё вре́мя спа́ли?	Did you sleep all this time?
Мы всё вре́мя говори́ли по-ру́сски.	We spoke Russian all the time.

До́лго, давно́

До́лго means "for a long time," "long." It is used with the present, past, and future:

Я до́лго жил там.	I lived there for a long time.
Как до́лго он говори́т!	How long he is speaking!
Я там до́лго не оста́нусь.	I won't remain there for long.

Давно́ means "a long time ago," and also "for a long time"—when the action is carried into the present:

Это бы́ло давно́.	That was long ago.
Мы здесь давно́ живём.	We have lived here for a long time (and we still are living here).

ADVERBS OF PLACE

Adverbs of place answer the questions: где? (where?); куда́? (where to?); отку́да? (from where?); доку́да? (how far? up to where?):

Он до́ма.	He is at home.
Они́ пошли́ домо́й.	They went home.
Отсю́да всё ви́дно.	You can see everything from here.
Мы е́дем доту́да.	We are driving that far (up to there).

A list of currently used adverbs of place follows. The majority of these answer где? and куда́?

здесь	here	внизу́	below, down(stairs)
тут	here		
там	there	наверху́	above, up(stairs)
везде́	everywhere		
всю́ду	everywhere	впереди́	in front, ahead
повсю́ду	all around	позади́	behind

вокру́г	around	вперёд	forward, ahead
нигде́	nowhere	вниз	down (motion)
не́где	nowhere to	наве́рх	up (motion)
где́-то	somewhere	куда́-то	somewhere (motion)
где́-нибудь	anywhere		
где́-либо	anywhere (you wish)	куда́-нибудь	anywhere (motion)
ко́е-где	here and there	куда́-либо	anywhere you wish (motion)
до́ма	at home		
напра́во	on (to) the right	ко́е-куда́	somewhere (motion)
нале́во	on (to) the left		
спра́ва	on (from) the right	впра́во	to the right
		вле́во	to the left
сле́ва	on (from) the left	домо́й	home(ward)
		отсю́да	from here
напро́тив	across, opposite	отту́да	from there
далеко́	far	отовсю́ду	from everywhere
недалеко́	not far	издалека́	from far away
бли́зко	near	и́здали	from afar
побли́зости	in the vicinity	ниотку́да	from nowhere
ря́дом	beside, next (to)	не́откуда	from nowhere to
о́коло	near, nearby	отку́да-то	from somewhere
ми́мо	past, by	отку́да-нибудь	from anywhere
туда́	there (motion)	отку́да-либо	from anywhere (you wish)
сюда́	here (motion)		
наза́д	back(wards)	доту́да	up to there
обра́тно	back(wards)	досю́да	up to here

Note: Several adverbs among those listed above frequently function as prepositions: впереди́; позади́; напро́тив; ми́мо; вокру́г; and especially о́коло.

Adverb	Я живу́ **напро́тив**.	I live across.
Preposition	**Напро́тив** вокза́ла есть рестора́н.	Opposite the terminal there is a restaurant.
Adverb	Посмотре́ть **вокру́г**.	To look around.
Preposition	Путеше́ствие **вокру́г** све́та.	A trip around the world.

ADVERBS

Usage of Some Adverbs of Place

Напра́во and **нале́во** answer both где? and куда́?

Парк напра́во. (где?)	The park is on the right.
Он пошёл напра́во. (куда́?)	He went to the right.

Све́рху and **сни́зу** may answer где?, куда́?, and отку́да?

Све́рху лежа́ло одея́ло. (где?)	On the top lay a blanket.
Положи́те э́то све́рху. (куда́?)	Put it on the top.
Све́рху что́-то упа́ло. (отку́да?)	Something fell from the top.

Здесь and **тут** are synonymous (тут being a trifle more informal).*

Рестора́н здесь (тут).	The restaurant is here.
Ва́ши де́ти тут, а мои́ там.	Your children are here, mine are there.
Дире́ктор заво́да здесь.	The director of the plant is here.

Note: See usage of the demonstrative particle **вот** (here is, there is, here's, there's), page 317.

Там, тут and **здесь** are essentially adverbs of place. Occasionally, however, they function as adverbs of time:

Тут он мне и говори́т . . .	(And) then he tells me . . .
Ну, там ви́дно бу́дет.	Well, we'll see (then).
Но здесь председа́тель останови́л говори́вшего. (А. Н. Толсто́й)	But then (here) the chairman stopped the man who was speaking.

Туда́ and **сюда́** express motion (These adverbs are used constantly in Russian—in contrast to their English equivalents "thither" and "hither"). The motion expressed is motion from one locality to another:

Кто е́дет туда́?	Who is going there?
Мы прие́хали сюда́.	We arrived here.

When the motion is contained within the same locality, **там** and **здесь** are used:

Кто там е́дет?	Who is driving there? (Who is that man driving over there?)
Мы гуля́ем здесь.	We are walking here.

---

* Слова́рь ру́сского языка́ АН СССР qualifies тут as "разг." (*colloq.*).

Отсю́да and **отту́да** are used with motion or to express a distance.

Я уезжа́ю отсю́да.	I am leaving this place.
Отту́да де́сять киломе́тров до го́рода.	It's ten kilometers from there to the city.

Куда́ occasionally may function as an adverb of quantity or measure. It is used with the comparative degree:

Э́то куда́ лу́чше.	This is much (far) better.
Э́тот дом куда́ доро́же.	This house is much more ("way" more) expensive.

Далеко́ не may mean "far from" in the figurative sense:

Он далеко́ не глуп.   He is far from stupid.

ADVERBS OF CAUSE OR REASON

These adverbs answer the questions почему́? (why?); отчего́? (why? because of what?).

There are not many adverbs of cause:

неспроста́—for some (special) reason; понево́ле—against one's will, willy-nilly; потому́—therefore; почему́—why; поэ́тому—therefore; сгоряча́—rashly, in anger; сду́ру—foolishly, out of stupidity, etc.

ADVERBS OF PURPOSE

These adverbs answer the questions заче́м? (why? what for?); для чего́? (what for?); с како́й це́лью? (with what purpose?).

There are few adverbs of purpose: зате́м—therefore; заче́м-то—for some reason; назло́—for spite; наро́чно—on purpose; на́ смех (на́смех) —for fun, to make fun of; неча́янно—unintentionally, by chance.

Primary Adverbs

The primary adverbs, it will be recalled, are derived from *pronouns*. (See p. 252.) For this reason they are referred to as "pronominal adverbs." Belonging to the different types of adverbs discussed on the preceding pages (adverbs of place, adverbs of time, etc.), they have different meanings within each type (an interrogative, an indefinite, etc.).

Examples of Primary Adverbs*

	INTERROGATIVE ADVERBS	DEMONSTRATIVE ADVERBS	NEGATIVE ADVERBS	INDEFINITE ADVERBS
Adv. of Place	где? куда?	здесь, там	нигде́, никуда́ не́где, не́куда	где́-то, куда́-то где́-нибудь, куда́-нибудь где́-либо, куда́-либо ко́е-где, ко́е-куда́
Adv. of Time	когда́?	тогда́	никогда́ не́когда	когда́-то когда́-нибудь когда́-либо ко́е-когда́
Adv. of Manner	как?	так	ника́к	ка́к-то ка́к-нибудь ка́к-либо ко́е-как
Adv. of Quantity	ско́лько?	сто́лько	ниско́лько	ско́лько-нибудь не́сколько
Adv. of Reason	почему́?	потому́		почему́-то почему́-нибудь почему́-либо
Adv. of Purpose	заче́м?	зате́м	не́зачем	заче́м-то заче́м-нибудь

* The following Table is based on the one given by И. М. Пу́лькина and Е. Б. Заха́ва-Некра́сова in «Уче́бник ру́сского языка́ для студе́нтов-иностра́нцев.»

Formation and Usage of Some Primary Adverbs

1. *Negative adverbs* formed with the particle **ни** always combine with negated verbs:

Я нигде́ его́ не нашёл.	I did not find him anywhere.
Он никогда́ не рабо́тает.	He never works.
Вы меня́ ниско́лько не беспоко́ите.	You don't trouble me at all.
Мы никуда́ не е́дем.	We aren't going any place.

2. *Negative adverbs* formed with the particle **не́** are *not* followed by negated verbs. These adverbs are used in *impersonal sentences*. The verb is always in the *infinitive*. The logical subject (if there is one) stands in the *dative case*:

Нам не́куда пойти́.	We have no place to go.
Мне не́когда разгова́ривать.	I have no time to talk.
Здесь не́где сесть.	There is no place to sit here.

3. *Indefinite adverbs* are formed with the particles **-то**, **-нибудь**, **-либо** and **кое-**. The remarks given in connection with indefinite pronouns (page 118) apply here: The particle **-то** suggests one unknown (X). The particle **-нибудь** admits a choice between several unknown factors, including the absence of any (Y_1 Y_2 . . . O). The adverbs formed with the particle **-либо** are close to those with the particle **-нибудь**; however, they are even somewhat more indefinite, indicating a freer choice.

The following examples will illustrate the marked difference between the **-то** and the **-нибудь** adverbs on the one hand, and the very slight one between the **-нибудь** and the **-либо** ones on the other hand:

Он **где́-то** рабо́тает.	He is working *somewhere*.
Он **где́-нибудь** рабо́тает?	Is he working *somewhere (anywhere)*?
А он **где́-либо** рабо́тает сейча́с?	But is he working *anywhere (at all)* now?
Я **когда́-то** говори́л с ним об э́том.	I spoke with him *once* about it.
Я **когда́-нибудь** скажу́ ему́ про э́то.	*Sometime* I will tell him about it.

ADVERBS

Если вы **когда-либо** скажете ему об этом, мне будет очень неловко.
If you ever *tell him about it, I will be very embarrassed.*

Он **почему-то** не пришёл.
For some reason he didn't come.

Если вы **почему-нибудь** не сможете прийти, пожалуйста дайте мне знать.
If, for some reason, you will not be able to come, please let me know.

Если вы **почему-либо** опоздаете, пожалуйста позвоните мне.
If, for any reason (whatsoever) you may be late, please telephone me.

4. **Кое-где** means *here and there*; **кое-когда** *now and then, from time to time*; **кое-куда** *somewhere, to a couple of places*; **кое-как** *somehow*, often suggesting *carelessly*.

Кое-где растаял снег.
Here and there the snow had melted.

Он **кое-когда** заходит сюда.
He drops in now and then.

Мне нужно **кое-куда** пойти.
I have to go to a couple of places.

Он **кое-как** окончил школу.
He somehow finished his school (without any distinction).

5. The indefinite adverb of manner **как-нибудь** is frequently used as an indefinite adverb of time:

Надо будет **как-нибудь** к ним пойти.
We should go and see them sometime.

6. The indefinite adverb of quantity **несколько** is used in a different way from the same word with the meaning of a numeral:

несколько (*numeral*) раз
several times

Он **несколько** (*adverb of quantity*) успокоился.
He has quieted down somewhat.

Predicative Adverbs

This group of adverbs stands quite apart in Russian grammar.* Syntactically, these adverbs express the *predicate* of impersonal sentences. The

* In fact some grammarians (Виноградов, Галкина-Федорук) consider them a separate "category of state"—категория состояния. The Грамматика русского языка АН СССР calls them "предикативные наречия" or "категория состояния."

logical *subject* (when there is one) stands in the dative case. These adverbs may refer to:

1. Nature or surroundings: тепло́—warm; хо́лодно—cold; жа́рко—hot; темно́—dark, etc.

   Сего́дня о́чень жа́рко. It is very hot today.
   В ко́мнате темно́.   It is dark in the room.

2. A physical or emotional state: бо́льно—painful; прия́тно—pleasant; ве́село—gay; ску́чно—boring; гру́стно—sad; жа́лко—sorry; оби́дно—annoying, offensive; доса́дно—annoying, vexing; смешно́—funny; интере́сно—interesting; хо́лодно—cold, etc.

   Им ску́чно, а нам ве́село. They are bored but we are having fun.
   Мне оби́дно слы́шать э́то. It hurts me to hear this.
   Вам хо́лодно? Are you cold?
   Э́то о́чень доса́дно. This is very annoying (vexing).

3. Feelings or personal evaluations: краси́во—beautiful; хорошо́—nice, good; легко́—easy; тру́дно—difficult; далеко́—far; бли́зко—near; ра́но—early; по́здно—late, etc.

   Как здесь краси́во! How beautiful it is here!
   До го́рода дово́льно далеко́. It is quite far to the city.
   Как по́здно! How late!
   Мне тру́дно реши́ть. It is difficult for me to decide.

4. Necessity, possibility, or impossibility: ну́жно—necessary; на́до—necessary; необходи́мо—(absolutely) necessary; мо́жно—possible; невозмо́жно—impossible; пора́—time (to); нельзя́—impossible, forbidden, etc.

   Вам на́до отдохну́ть. You should have a rest.
   Де́тям пора́ идти́ в шко́лу. It's time for the children to go to school.
   Здесь нельзя́ кури́ть. One must not smoke here.

 Notes:

(*a*) A few nouns may be used adverbially in the same constructions as other predicative adverbs. For instance: **лень**; **охо́та**; **грех** (*lit.*, *laziness*; *wish, inclination*; *sin*).

Мне лень вставáть.	I feel too lazy to get up.
И охóта вам ходи́ть к ним!	And why do you really wish to see them (to go and visit them)?
Грех так дýмать.	It's a shame to think so.

(b) The largest class of predicative adverbs includes those which coincide in form with short neuter adjectives: **теплó**, **прия́тно**, etc. These adverbs may form a comparative degree:

Здесь теплée.	It is warmer here.
Там прия́тнее сидéть.	It's more pleasant to sit over there.

Usage of Some Predicative Adverbs

1. Predicative adverbs may also express the *past* and the *future*—with the auxiliary verb **быть**:

Вчерá бы́ло теплó.	Yesterday it was warm.
Всем бы́ло грýстно.	Everybody was sad.
Зáвтра бýдет хóлодно.	Tomorrow will be cold.
Нáдо бýдет узнáть.	We should find out.

Occasionally, another auxiliary verb is used with predicative adverbs:

Present:	Станóвится теплó.	It is getting warm.
Past:	Стáло теплó.	It has become warm.
Future:	Стáнет теплó.	It will become warm.

2. Certain predicative adverbs may govern the accusative case:

Мне нýжно верёвку.	I need a rope.
Отсю́да ви́дно гóрод.	One can see the town from here.
А то не нýжно ли вам кофéйник? (Л. Толстóй)	Perhaps you need a coffee pot?

These sentences are more impersonal than: Мне нужнá верёвка; отсю́да ви́ден гóрод; нýжен ли вам кофéйник.*

---

* Виногрáдов (Совремéнный рýсский язы́к) considers the following expressions conversational or colloquial:

Мне нýжно метр шёлку.	I need one meter of silk.
Нáдо верёвку.	(We) need a rope.

3. A certain ambiguity may arise with the adverbs **надо**, **нужно**, etc. Thus, "Ему надо купить подарок" could mean "We must (one should) buy him a present." or: "He should buy a present." This ambiguity could be partly remedied by reversing the word-order, i.e., "Надо ему купить подарок" would normally mean only the first alternative.

9. PREPOSITIONS

A preposition is an auxiliary part of speech. Prepositions are used with nouns, pronouns, and numerals.

Prepositions may be classified as follows:

1. The original ones (the oldest in the language): **без, в, до, на, о,** etc.
2. Adverbial prepositions (and still used as adverbs): **мимо, напротив, сзади,** etc.
3. Prepositions formed from nouns: **ввиду, в течение, насчёт, навстречу,** etc.
4. A few prepositions formed from verbs: **благодаря, не считая, несмотря на,** etc.

The prepositions, with examples of their usage, are listed in Chapter 3 (Declension of Nouns; Usage of Cases).

The following table gives a recapitulation of prepositions in alphabetical order. Note that most prepositions govern only one case, a few prepositions govern two or three cases, and the preposition **по** governs four cases.

PREPOSITION	CASE	MEANING
без (безо)	Gen.	without
благодаря	Dat.	thanks to, because of
близ	Gen.	near
в (во)	Acc.	into, in, to, at
	Prep.	in, at
в виде	Gen.	as, in the form of, by way of
в продолжение	Gen.	during, throughout
в силу	Gen.	in virtue, on the strength
в течение	Gen.	during
ввиду	Gen.	on account of
вдоль	Gen.	along
включая	Acc.	including
вместо	Gen.	instead
вне	Gen.	out of, outside, beyond
внутри	Gen.	inside

273

PREPOSITION	CASE	MEANING
возле	*Gen.*	near
вокруг	*Gen.*	around
вопреки	*Dat.*	in spite of, against
впереди	*Gen.*	in front of
вроде	*Gen.*	like, similar to
вследствие	*Gen.*	as a consequence, as a result
для	*Gen.*	for
до	*Gen.*	before, until, to
за	*Acc.*	behind, beyond, for (in favor of), during
	Instr.	behind, beyond, for (to fetch), at
	Nom.	(in the expression **что за**)
за исключением	*Gen.*	except, excepting
из (изо)	*Gen.*	from, out of
из-за	*Gen.*	from behind; because of, on account
из-под	*Gen.*	from under
исключая	*Acc.*	excepting, with the exception of
к (ко)	*Dat.*	to, towards, by (*with time expressions*)
кончая	*Instr.*	ending (with, on)
кроме	*Gen.*	besides; except (for)
кругом	*Gen.*	around
между	*Instr.*	between
	Gen.	between (see Isolated Rules, page 277)
мимо	*Gen.*	past, by
на	*Acc.*	on, onto; to; for
	Prep.	on; at
навстречу	*Dat.*	towards
над (надо)	*Instr.*	above, over
назло	*Dat.*	for spite, to displease
накануне	*Gen.*	the day before, on the eve
наперекор	*Dat.*	in defiance, in opposition, against
напротив	*Gen.*	across from
насчёт	*Gen.*	about, regarding
не считая	*Gen.*	excluding, not counting
несмотря на	*Acc.*	in spite of, regardless of
о (об, обо)	*Prep.*	about, concerning
	Acc.	against (*implying shock*)

PREPOSITIONS

PREPOSITION	CASE	MEANING
о́коло	Gen.	near, around; about (approximately)
от (ото)	Gen.	from; because of
относи́тельно	Gen.	regarding, concerning, with regard to
пе́ред (пе́редо)	Instr.	in front of; before (See Isolated Rules, page 277)
по	Dat.	along, on; according to; "each" (*distributive*)
	Acc.	up to
	Prep.	after, upon
	Nom.	"each" (*distributive*). (See Isolated Rules, page 278)
по по́воду	Gen.	in connection with, regarding
по слу́чаю	Gen.	because of, on account of
под (подо)	Acc.	under
	Instr.	under
по́дле	Gen.	near
позади́	Gen.	behind
поми́мо	Gen.	apart from
поперёк	Gen.	across
по́сле	Gen.	after
посреди́	Gen.	in the middle of
посре́дством	Gen.	by means of, with
при	Prep.	at, by, near; with; in the days of, in the presence of
про	Acc.	about
про́тив	Gen.	opposite; against
ра́ди	Gen.	for the sake of
с (со)	Instr.	with; together with
	Gen.	off; from, since
	Acc.	about, the size of
сверх	Gen.	above, over
сза́ди	Gen.	behind
сквозь	Acc.	through
согла́сно	Dat.	according to
снару́жи	Gen.	outside of
спустя́	Acc.	thereafter, after that

PREPOSITION	CASE	MEANING
среди́	*Gen.*	in the middle of; among
у	*Gen.*	near, by, at; from
че́рез	*Acc.*	through, over; in (*with time expressions*)

Variations in the Spelling of Prepositions

1. The prepositions **без, в, из, к, над, от, пе́ред, под,** and **с** may add an **о** to their endings. This takes place in front of a cluster of consonants, and with varying frequency—depending on the preposition.

The most frequently encountered forms are **во, со,** and **ко**:

во вла́сти	in the power
во Фра́нции	in France
со сме́хом	with laughter
со мно́гими	with many
ко мне	to (towards) me
ко дну	towards the bottom

Other forms, such as **изо, надо,** and **подо** occur less frequently (usually, when the first letter of the cluster is **л** or **р**):

изо рта	out of the mouth
надо лбом (ог над лбом)	above the forehead
подо льдом	under the ice

Безо occurs only in front of весь and вся́кий:

| безо всего́ | without anything |
| безо вся́ких разгово́ров | without any arguments (*lit.* conversations) |

Finally, certain prepositions which govern the instrumental case take a final **о** in front of мной (мно́ю) and, optionally, in front of всем, всей, and все́ми:

| надо мной | above (over) me |
| подо мной | under me |

PREPOSITIONS

	пе́редо мной		in front of me
	со мной		with me
на́до всем	or	над всем	over all the, above everything
подо всей	or	под всей	under all the
пе́редо все́ми	or	пе́ред все́ми	in front of everyone, ahead of everyone
со все́ми	(*no variant*)		with everyone, with all the

2. In two compound prepositions (of comparatively infrequent usage) an **о** is added to a **в** preceding a vowel: во и́мя (in the name of), and во избежа́ние (to avoid). These two prepositions govern the genitive.

3. **О** becomes **об** in front of non-jotated vowels:

        об Аме́рике   about America
        об уро́ке   about the lesson

Otherwise it remains as **о**:

        о Япо́нии   about Japan
        о его́ сы́не   about his son

О becomes **обо** in front of мне, and, optionally, in front of всей, всём and всех:

        Они́ говори́ли обо мне.   They spoke about me.
        Она́ обо всём поду́мала.   She thought about everything.

Isolated Rules

1. **Ме́жду** seldom governs the genitive case, and only with similar or identical objects:

    ме́жду дере́вьев or ме́жду дере́вьями   between the trees
        (*gen.*)   (*instr.*)

But only the instrumental would be used in:

    ме́жду дере́вьями и куста́ми   between the trees and the bushes

2. **Пе́ред** and **до** may express the same idea when referring to time:

        пе́ред за́втраком or до за́втрака   before lunch

However, пе́ред implies a shorter period of time:

| Наде́юсь уви́деть вас до экза́менов. | I hope to see you (sometime) before the examinations. |
| Он позвони́л мне пе́ред экза́меном. | He telephoned me (shortly) before the examination. |

3. The usage of **по** in a distributive sense deserves comments.*

(*a*) Оди́н (stated or implied) stands in the dative:

| по одному́ рублю́ | one ruble apiece |
| по килогра́мму са́хару. | a kilogram of sugar each |

Likewise, with the nouns со́тня, ты́сяча, миллио́н, etc.:

| по со́тне папиро́с | a hundred cigarettes each |
| по ты́сяче до́лларов | a thousand dollars apiece |

(*b*) Два, три, четы́ре, дво́е, тро́е, полтора́, полтора́ста, 200, 300, 400 stand in the nominative:

| по три рубля́ | three rubles apiece |
| по два ученика́ за па́ртой | two pupils at each desk |

(*c*) All other numerals stand in the nominative (in conversational Russian) or in the dative:

по пять рубле́й
or по пяти́ рубле́й } five rubles apiece

4. The following prepositions are no longer used as adverbs:

вме́сто; вопреки́; кро́ме; посреди́; сверх.

The following are used very seldom as adverbs:

во́зле; вро́де; о́коло; по́дле.

* The rules given here conform to those given in the Grammar of the Academy of Science, page 385 (Грамма́тика ру́сского языка́. АН СССР). But see Виногра́дов, Совреме́нный ру́сский язы́к footnote, page 128.

Classification and Usage of Prepositions

Primary Meaning

The majority of prepositions pertain to location, motion or time.

Examples:

(a) *Location:* близ; в; вдоль; вне; внутри; возле; вокруг; впереди; за; между; на; около; под; перед; позади; посреди; против; при; снаружи; у; над.
These prepositions normally answer the question где?

    Школа в городе. The school is in the city.

They may also locate a motion or action.

    Мы гуляли в парке. We walked in the park.

(b) *Motion:* в; из; на; к; от; за; под; через; из-под; до; сквозь; мимо
Also, с (meaning *off, from*) and из-за (meaning *from behind*)
These prepositions normally answer the questions: куда?; откуда?; or докуда? and indicate the direction of the motion.

    Я еду в город. I am going to town.
    Мы съехали с горы. We drove down the hill.

(c) *Time:* в; в продолжение; в течение; до; к; между; на; накануне; перед; по; после; от; через; без
Also, за (meaning *during, in*) and с (meaning *starting with*).
These prepositions answer questions, such as: когда?; как долго?; на сколько времени?

    уехать в среду to leave on Wednesday
    приехать на лето to come for the summer

The same preposition may express location, motion, or time:

жить в го́роде	to live in the city
е́хать в парк	to drive to (into) the park
прие́хать в четве́рг	to come on Thursday
гуля́ть за го́родом	to walk in the country (*lit.* beyond the town)
пое́хать за лес	to drive beyond the wood
постаре́ть за год	to age in a year

Many prepositions among those given above have antonyms.

	PREPOSITIONS	ANTONYMS
Location:	у, близ, во́зле, по́дле, о́коло, недалеко́ от	далеко́ от
	в	вне (the meaning is opposite, but the usage is rather limited).
	внутри́	снару́жи (also of limited usage. Used as an adverb)
	впереди́	сза́ди
	впереди́	позади́
	за	пе́ред
	на	под
	над	под
Motion:	в	из
	на	с
	к	от
	за	из–за
	до	от
Time:	пе́ред	по́сле
	от	до
	с	до
	че́рез	за . . . до

Examples:

о́коло го́рода (near the city)—далеко́ от го́рода (far from the city)
в опа́сности (in danger)—вне опа́сности (out of danger)
за до́мом (behind the house)—пе́ред до́мом (in front of the house)

в шко́лу [to (*into*) school]—из шко́лы [from (*out of*) school]
на уро́к (to the lesson)—с уро́ка (from the lesson)
к до́ктору (to the doctor)—от до́ктора (from the doctor)
пе́ред за́втраком (before lunch)—по́сле за́втрака (after lunch)
с утра́ (since the morning)—до утра́ (until the morning)
че́рез час по́сле его́ прие́зда (an hour after his arrival)—за час до его́ прие́зда (an hour before his arrival)

(*d*) *Other relations.* Many prepositions express relations different from location, motion, and time: без, вме́сто, для, кро́ме, о, про, с, etc.

Secondary Meaning

Certain prepositions among the so-called <u>original</u> ones express a variety of relations. The richest in this respect are **в, за, из, на, над, от, про, по, с,** and **у.**

Other original prepositions (без, для, etc.) and especially prepositions derived from adverbs usually keep their concrete, definite meaning.

Among the secondary relations expressed with prepositions are:

(*a*) *Reason*

от :	уста́лый от рабо́ты	tired from work
	мо́крый от дождя́	wet from rain

(A very productive type)

с :	с ра́дости	from joy
	с го́ря	from sorrow

A less productive type; somewhat conversational or colloquial
(In the four examples above, **с** may be replaced with **от**, but not vice versa.)

за :	Не на́до серди́ться за э́то.	One shouldn't be angry for this.
из :	сде́лать из жа́лости	to do out of pity (compassion)
из-за :	опозда́ть из-за дождя́	to be late because of (on account of) the rain
благодаря́ :	благодаря́ его́ по́мощи	thanks to (because of) his help

These last two prepositions indicate an outside reason. They are not interchangeable: when there is nothing to be thankful for, из-за and not благодаря́ should be used:

	из-за плохо́й пого́ды	because of bad weather
по :	отсу́тствовать по боле́зни	to be absent because of (on account of) sickness
	по како́й причи́не?	for what reason?

These constructions suggest an intrinsic reason, contained within the subject.

(b) *Purpose*

в :	сказа́ть в шу́тку	to say in jest
	оста́вить до́ма в наказа́ние	to leave at home in the way of a punishment
на :	е́хать на охо́ту	to go hunting
	пригласи́ть на сва́дьбу	to invite for a wedding
	мате́рия на пла́тье	fabric for a dress
	мя́со на за́втрак	meat for lunch

In these last two examples, на has a slightly different meaning from для (see below). It suggests an amount of something, serving a definite purpose, and perhaps more than is actually needed.

для :	останови́ться для о́тдыха	to stop for a rest
	я́щик для пи́сем	mail box
	пода́рок для неё	a present for her
за :	умере́ть за ро́дину	to die for the fatherland
	боро́ться за мир	to fight for peace.

These constructions (with за plus *accusative*) are characteristic of strong feelings or purpose.

	пойти́ за газе́той	to go for a paper
	пое́хать за ке́м-нибудь	to go and fetch somebody
с :	обрати́ться с про́сьбой	to ask for a favor, to request

Constructions of this type are of limited usage.

от :	лека́рство от ка́шля	cough medicine
про́тив :	сре́дство про́тив морско́й боле́зни	remedy against seasickness

(In this example, про́тив has a meaning similar to от in the example immediately above.)

(c) *Origin, source*

от:	телегра́мма от отца́	a telegram from father
	приве́т от него́	greetings from him
из:	исключе́ние из пра́вила	an exception to the rule
	узна́ть из письма́	to find out from the letter
у:	спроси́ть у них	to ask (to inquire of) them
	заня́ть де́ньги у кого́-нибудь	to borrow money from somebody

(d) *Connection*

от:	пу́говица от костю́ма	a button from a suit
	ключ от чемода́на	the key from the suitcase

(e) *Object or material with which something is made*

из:	вы́резать из бума́ги	to cut out of paper
	сала́т из огурцо́в	cucumber salad

(f) *Object with the aid of which something is performed*

из:	пить из стака́на	to drink out of a glass
	стреля́ть из пу́шки	to fire a gun
в:	смотре́ть в бино́кль	to look through binoculars
с:	есть с ло́жки	to eat from a spoon

(g) *Manner*

на:	прие́хать на парохо́де	to come by boat
	игра́ть на де́ньги	to play for money
по:	называ́ть по и́мени	to call by the first name
	поступи́ть по зако́ну	to act according to law
	говори́ть по телефо́ну	to speak on the telephone
в:	сиде́ть в молча́нии	to sit in silence
	жить в бе́дности	to live in poverty

(h) *Extent*

на:	изве́стный на весь мир	known the world over
	гото́вить на всю семью́	to cook for the whole family
в:	весь в крови́	all covered with blood
	лоб в морщи́нах	a forehead all in wrinkles
по:	по всему́ све́ту	all over the world

(i) Comparison, size, weight, distance

с :	величино́й с дом	as large as (the size of) a house
	подожда́ть с мину́ту	to wait for about a minute
в :	длино́й в два ме́тра	two meters long
	ве́сом в то́нну	weighing one ton
	жить в трёх ми́лях от го́рода	to live three miles from the city
	в два ра́за бо́льше	twice as large
	кварти́ра в три ко́мнаты	a three room apartment
на :	на пять лет ста́рше	five years older
	отойти́ на де́сять шаго́в	to move ten paces away

(j) Occasion

за :	за за́втраком	at lunch, during lunch
	за рабо́той	at work, while working
на :	на сва́дьбе	at the wedding
при :	при встре́че	meeting, upon meeting

(k) Exchange, replacement, reward, payment

за :	рабо́тать за това́рища	to work for (instead of) a friend
	расписа́ться за кого́-нибудь	to sign for someone (in his stead)
	меда́ль за хра́брость	a medal for bravery
	благодари́ть за по́мощь	to thank for help
	приня́ть за ру́сского	to take (mistake) for a Russian
	заплати́ть за биле́т	to pay for the ticket
на :	купи́ть на три рубля́	to buy three rubles worth
	прода́ть на пять до́лларов	to sell five dollars worth

(l) Specification, limitation

по :	специали́ст по де́тским боле́зням	a specialist in children's diseases
	това́рищ по шко́ле	a school friend
на :	хи́трый на вы́думки	smart as far as inventions (tricks)
	о́стрый на язы́к	sharp-tongued

The last two examples belong to a limited class.

в : твёрдый в при́нципах — with strong principles (adamant in principles)

сме́лый в спо́рах — bold in arguments

(m) Distribution
по : вы́пить по стака́ну ча́я — to drink a glass of tea each
получи́ть по рублю́ — to get a ruble each
на : разре́зать на две ча́сти — to cut in two parts
разби́ть на куски́ — to break into pieces

(n) Limit, saturation
до : довести́ до слёз — to bring to tears
люби́ть до безу́мия — to love madly
рабо́тать до изнеможе́ния — to work until completely exhausted

Current Expressions with "Verb + Preposition" Construction

Many verbs combine with a few prepositions to express the so-called objective relations ("объе́ктные отноше́ния"). Frequently, a noun related to a particular verb may convey a similar idea:

ответить на письмо́ — to answer a letter
отве́т на письмо́ — an answer to a letter

A list of examples follows.

в + ACCUSATIVE :
ве́рить в побе́ду — to believe in victory
стреля́ть в цель — to shoot at a target
игра́ть в ша́хматы — to play chess
игра́ть в футбо́л — to play soccer
стуча́ть в дверь — to knock at the door
смотре́ть в окно́ — to look through the window
преврати́ть в пусты́ню — to turn into a desert
броса́ть камня́ми в кого́–нибудь — to throw stones at somebody

в + PREPOSITIONAL:

уча́ствовать в спекта́кле	to take part in a play
нужда́ться в деньга́х	to be short of money
призна́ться в преступле́нии	to confess to a crime
убеди́ться в чём-нибудь	to become convinced of something
уверя́ть в любви́	to give assurance of love
сомнева́ться в результа́тах	to doubt the results
отдава́ть себе́ отчёт в э́том	to realize this
разочарова́ться в ко́м-нибудь	to become disappointed in somebody
упрека́ть в тру́сости	to reproach cowardice
ка́яться в греха́х	to repent one's sins
обвиня́ть в кра́же	to accuse of theft
отказа́ть в про́сьбе	to deny a request
ошиби́ться в счёте	to make a mistake in a bill (account)
подозрева́ть в преступле́нии	to suspect of a crime
помога́ть в рабо́те	to help in work, to assist

за + ACCUSATIVE:

беспоко́иться за него́	to worry about him
ра́доваться за неё	to be glad for her
держа́ть за́ руку	to hold by the hand
держа́ться за верёвку	to hold on to a rope
схвати́ть за́ ногу	to grab by the leg

за + INSTRUMENTAL:

смотре́ть за больны́м	to look after a patient
присма́тривать за ребёнком	to look after (to watch) a child
наблюда́ть за поря́дком	to keep order

к + DATIVE:

гото́виться к экза́мену	to prepare for an examination
относи́ться к де́лу	to treat (consider) a matter
стреми́ться к сча́стью	to strive towards happiness
привы́кнуть к э́тому	to get used to this
пригласи́ть к себе́	to invite to one's home
принадлежа́ть к па́ртии	to belong to the party

PREPOSITIONS

приставáть ко всем	to annoy (nag) everybody
придирáться к помóщникам	to find fault with one's helpers
призывáть к восстáнию	to incite to insurrection
пришúть пýговицу к рубáшке	to sew a button on (*lit.*, to) a shirt
приде́лать рýчку к я́щику	to fix a handle to a box (drawer)
приучúть к послушáнию	to train to be obedient

на + ACCUSATIVE:

полагáться на дрýга	to rely upon a friend
надéяться на пóмощь	to hope for help
согласúться на предложéние	to agree to a proposal
рассчúтывать на негó	to count on him
решúться на э́тот шаг	to decide to take this step
отвечáть на вопрóс	to answer a question
жáловаться на ученикá	to complain about a pupil
сердúться на письмó	to be angry at a letter
негодовáть на всех	to inveigh against everybody
ворчáть на сосéдей	to grumble at the neighbors
клеветáть на когó-нибудь	to malign (to libel) somebody
злúться на погóду	to be mad at the weather
переводúть на рýсский язы́к	to translate into Russian
спешúть на пóезд	to hurry for (to catch) a train
смотрéть на лунý	to look at the moon
взглянýть на неё	to glance at her
кричáть на детéй	to shout at the children
помнóжить на пять	to multiply by five
разделúть на четы́ре	to divide by four
влия́ть на собы́тия	to influence events
обúдеться на письмó	to get offended at a letter
обратúть внимáние на э́то	to pay attention to this
опоздáть на пóезд	to miss a train
произвестú впечатлéние на всех	to make an impression on everyone
походúть на отцá	to be like one's father
(*more often:* похóж на отцá)	

на + PREPOSITIONAL:

настáивать на своём	to insist upon one's own (opinion, etc.)

осно́вываться на фа́ктах	to base (one's opinion) on facts
отрази́ться на результа́тах	to reflect upon results
игра́ть на скри́пке	to play the violin
говори́ть на трёх языка́х	to speak three languages
жени́ться на америка́нке	to marry an American

над + INSTRUMENTAL:

ду́мать над че́м-нибудь	to think over something
шути́ть над дру́гом	to make fun of a friend
смея́ться над ке́м-нибудь	to laugh at somebody
издева́ться над враго́м	to ridicule an enemy
рабо́тать над прое́ктом	to work on a project
труди́ться над диссерта́цией	to work on a thesis

по + DATIVE:

суди́ть по слу́хам	to judge by rumors
узна́ть по го́лосу	to recognize by the voice
скуча́ть по бра́ту	to miss one's brother
тоскова́ть по ро́дине	to long for (to miss) one's country

Note: With скуча́ть and тоскова́ть, по is sometimes followed by the prepositional. This happens:

(a) with some pronouns

  Скуча́ть по вас (по нас, по ком.)   To miss you (us, whom.)

(b) rarely with nouns, and only if these are in the singular.

  скуча́ть по бра́те.   to miss one's brother.

Idiomatic Usage

Finally, there is a large group of set expressions or idioms, many of which cannot be conveniently classified into any type discussed above.
Moreover, many among them are characterized by a limitation in their usage. Thus **на чёрный день** (for a rainy day) has no parallel expression. **Изо дня в день** (day after day) has the parallel form **из го́да в год**, but no similar construction exists with the nouns **ночь, неде́ля, ме́сяц**.
Expressions such as **за со́рок** (over forty), **под шестьдеся́т** (in the late fifties) are used only with a mature age.

Current Expressions and Idioms

(In alphabetical order, according to the prepositions.)

без ума́ (от неё)	madly in love (with her)
люби́ть без па́мяти	to love madly
без зазре́ния со́вести	without any compunctions
без сомне́ния	without doubt
без го́ду неде́ля	a very short time (*lit.*, a week minus a year)
сло́во в сло́во	word for word
во что бы то ни ста́ло	at any cost
(знать) в лицо́	(to know) to face
(сказа́ть) в глаза́	(to say) to someone's face
(е́хать) в о́тпуск	(to go) on leave
взять в долг	to borrow (money)
в конце́ концо́в	finally
в наде́жде	in the hope of
в том числе́	including
Они́ в ссо́ре	They have quarrelled
крича́ть во все го́рло	to yell at the top of one's lungs (*lit.*, throat)
В чём де́ло?	What is the matter?
де́ло в том	the point (matter) is
вдоль и поперёк	criss-cross
вокру́г да о́коло	to beat around the bush
для ви́ду	for appearance sake
до сих пор	up to now, so far
до тех пор	up to then, until
До чего́ она́ мила́!	How nice she is!
до свида́ния	good-bye
Что до меня́, то я гото́в.	As far as I am concerned, I am ready.
до поры́ до вре́мени	for a while, for some time
за и про́тив	pro and con
за пятьдеся́т	over fifty (years of age)
Что за исто́рия!	What kind of a story is this!
она́ за́мужем за	she is married to

она́ вы́шла за́муж за	she married (someone)
сло́во за ва́ми	your turn to speak
за тридевять земе́ль	very far (*lit.*, beyond 39 lands)
за глаза́	behind someone's back
за ва́ше здоро́вье	your health
за исключе́нием	excepting
изо дня в день	day after day
из го́да в год	year after year
Из э́того ничего́ не вы́шло.	Nothing came of it.
к сожале́нию	unfortunately
к сча́стью	fortunately
к тому́ вре́мени	by this time
к тому́ же	besides, in addition
У меня́ к вам про́сьба.	I have a favor to ask you.
к чему́	what for
к ва́шим услу́гам	at your service
приня́ть к све́дению	to note, to keep in mind
лицо́м к лицу́	face to face
ме́жду про́чим	by the way, among other things
ме́жду тем	in the meantime, meanwhile
ме́жду на́ми	between us
На ней краси́вое пла́тье.	She is wearing a pretty dress.
взять на себя́	to take upon oneself
он жена́т на	he is married to
он жени́лся на	he married
хрома́ть на одну́ но́гу	to limp on one foot
на чёрный день	for a rainy (black) day
на мои́х глаза́х	in my presence
сиде́ть (оста́ться) на боба́х	to be frustrated, to end up with nothing
На здоро́вье.	You are welcome. (in answer to спаси́бо—thank you)
на зло	for spite
все на лицо́	"all present"
тяжело́ на душе́	feeling gloomy, depressed
на его́ со́вести	on his conscience
на беду́	unfortunately
на свобо́де	free, liberated

на моё счастье	fortunately for me
на этот раз	(for) this time
на своём веку	in his lifetime
на всякий случай	just in case, in case something is needed
подарить на память	to give as a remembrance
сесть на поезд	to board a train
ехать на запад	to go west
Она на всё способна.	You can expect anything from her.
чек на моё имя	check written out to me
от всей души	with all my heart (soul)
от всего сердца	with all my heart
письмо от десятого марта	a letter of March tenth
Мне стыдно перед ним.	I feel ashamed (to face him).
Мне неприятно перед вами.	I feel badly (on account of what I did to you).
извиниться перед кем-нибудь	to beg somebody's pardon
по-моему	in my opinion, "I think, I believe"
под Москвой	near Moscow
под командой	under the command
под предлогом	under the pretext
под вопросом	uncertain, questionable
под вечер	towards the evening
под утро	towards the morning
под Новый Год	on New Year's Eve
Всё под рукой.	Everything is handy (within reach).
взять под руку	to take by the arm
под наблюдением врача	under the doctor's care (supervision)
под арестом	under arrest
отдать под суд	to take (somebody) to court
под надзором	under surveillance
под пятьдесят	close to fifty (years of age)
ни под каким видом	by no means
У меня нет при себе денег.	I have no money with me.

при слу́чае	whenever possible, when the occasion arises
при усло́вии	under the condition, stipulation
при жела́нии	if one wishes
при всём жела́нии	no matter how much one would like to
при пе́рвой возмо́жности	at the first opportunity
при́ сме́рти	near death
ду́мать про себя́	to think to oneself
с одно́й стороны́	on one hand, from one angle
с э́той то́чки зре́ния	from this point of view
Что с ва́ми?	What is the matter with you?
брать приме́р с кого́-нибудь	to emulate someone's example
с ва́шего разреше́ния	with your permission
Ско́лько с меня́?	How much do I owe?
С меня́ хва́тит	That will do for me, that's enough.
пло́хо с деньга́ми	money troubles, lack of money
мы с жено́й	my wife and I
со вре́менем	eventually
со дня на́ день	any day now
с каки́х пор	since when
с тех пор	since then
с пра́здником	(best wishes) for the holiday
с Но́вым Го́дом	Happy New Year
с Рождество́м Христо́вым	Merry Christmas
у себя́	at home
Как хорошо́ у вас.	What a nice place you have, how nice to be here.
Он живёт у нас.	He is staying with us.
У меня́ пропа́л аппети́т.	I have lost my appetite.
У него́ боли́т голова́.	He has a headache.
У неё боля́т зу́бы.	She has a toothache.

Remark:

It is not unusual for the *stress* to shift from the noun to the preposition: на́ берег, на́ гору, на́ зиму, на́ лето, на́ ночь, на́ пол, за́ ноги, и́з лесу. (Side by side with на бе́рег, на ле́то, из ле́са, etc.)

PREPOSITIONS

Frequently, the stress will vary depending on the type of relation, i.e., purpose *vs.* motion, place *vs.* manner, etc.

Мы дрáлись **за гóрод**.	We fought *for the town*.
Мы поéхали **зá город**.	We drove *out of town* (in the country).
Дéрево упáло **на дом**.	The tree fell *on the house*.
брать рабóту **нá дом**.	to take work *home*.
не обращáть внимáния **на смех**.	to ignore *the laughter*
поднимáть **нá смех**	to ridicule, to make *fun* of
смотрéть **на мóре**	to look *at the sea*
поéхать **нá море**	to leave *for the seashore*

In some expressions the stress *always* remains *on the preposition*.

прѝ смерти	near death
Час о́т часу не лéгче.	It's getting harder all the time (*lit.* with every hour).

10. CONJUNCTIONS

Conjunctions are auxiliary parts of speech which express a connection between words, groups of words, or sentences:

перо́ **и** каранда́ш	a pen *and* a pencil
па́чка папиро́с **и** коро́бка спи́чек	a pack of cigarettes *and* a box of matches
Я не знал, **что** он уе́хал.	I did not know *that* he left.

Conjunctions are divided into two groups, one expressing co-ordination, and the other subordination.

A. Co-ordinate conjunctions join words or sentences which are equally important in the speaker's mind:

брат и сестра́	the brother and the sister
Он там, а она́ здесь.	He is there and she is here.

Co-ordinate conjunctions have various functions:

1. They join words or sentences.
2. They express contrast or opposition.
3. They express choice or alternation.
4. They have an explanatory meaning.

B. Subordinate conjunctions join two clauses. One of these (the *Main Clause*) prevails in importance:

Я не иду́ на рабо́ту, потому́ что я себя́ пло́хо чу́вствую.	I am not going to my work because I don't feel well.
Мо́жно ему́ позвони́ть, хотя́ бою́сь, что его́ нет до́ма.	We could telephone him, although I am afraid he is not at home.

Subordinate conjunctions may express or help to express:

1. Reason or cause.
2. Purpose.
3. Consequence.
4. Condition.

5. Concession.
6. Comparison.
7. Time or Temporal Relations.
8. Ideas or Feelings.

Conjunctions are divided into *simple*, such as **и** (and); **но** (but); **и́ли** (or), and *compound*, such as **потому́ что** (because); **как то́лько** (as soon as); **для того́ чтобы** (in order to).

Classification and Usage of Conjunctions

Coordinate Conjunctions

1. Coordinate conjunctions joining words or sentences

и—and

день и ночь	day and night
рабо́тать и учи́ться	to work and to study
Он опозда́л, и мы се́ли обе́дать без него́.	He was late, so (*lit.* and) we sat down for dinner without him.

и may mean *as well*:

Он и мне написа́л.	He wrote me as well.

и is occasionally repeated with enumeration:

Гром пу́шек, то́пот, ржа́нье, стон,	Canon thunder, trampling of horses, neighing, moans,
И смерть и ад со всех сторо́н. (Пу́шкин)	And death and hell from all sides.

а—and

Посиди́м немно́го, а пото́м пойдём.	Let us sit for a while, and then we shall go.
В саду́ де́рево, а о́коло него́ ска́мейка.	There is a tree in the garden, and near it a bench.

да—and

Щи да ка́ша—пи́ща на́ша. Cabbage soup and (buckwheat) gruel—that's our food.

(Of comparatively limited usage, and characteristic of colloquial speech, as in the saying given above.)

Notes:

(*a*) The conjunction **да** is used sometimes when identical words are repeated:

спо́ры да спо́ры arguments and arguments
А он всё пи́шет да пи́шет. And he keeps on writing and writing.

(*b*) The conjunction **а**, when simply joining two clauses, may have a meaning close to **и**:

Жена́ пое́хала в го́род, а че́рез час я пое́хал за ней. My wife went to town, and an hour later I went to fetch her.

However, **a** is more frequently used to express contrast or opposition. (See page 297.)

то́же—also

Лю́ди си́льно проголода́лись, ло́шади то́же нужда́лись в о́тдыхе. The men were quite hungry, the horses also needed a rest.*

та́кже—as well, also

Класс реши́л зада́чу; я та́кже реши́л её. The class solved the problem; I also solved it.†

Note: То́же and та́кже are usually adverbs. The examples above show their rather infrequent usage as conjunctions. In contrast with other conjunctions of the same type, they do not stand at the beginning of the second clause.

* Example from Грамма́тика ру́сского языка́ АН СССР. Том 2. Си́нтаксис.
† Example from Методи́ческие разрабо́тки по грамма́тике. Под реда́кцией С. Г. Бархуда́рова.

CONJUNCTIONS

не то́лько . . . но и—not only . . . but

Я говори́л не то́лько с ним, но и с ней.	I spoke not only with him, but also with her.

ни . . . ни—neither . . . nor

ни он, ни я	neither he nor I

и . . . и—both . . . and

и он и я	both he and I

2. Coordinate conjunctions expressing contrast or opposition

Those most currently used in this group are:

а—but, and (*also:* while, on the contrary)
но—but (*also:* however, on the other hand, just the same)

Both these conjunctions express opposition.

А introduces a contrasting idea (including antonyms), or simply a different idea:

Э́то не перо́, а каранда́ш.	This is not a pen but a pencil.
Вам ве́село, а мне гру́стно.	You are having fun but I feel sad.
Здесь река́, а там о́зеро.	Here is a river and there's a lake.

Но expresses a stronger opposition, or an idea which is not a logical consequence of the first one expressed:

Я ему́ предложи́л пое́хать, но он реши́л оста́ться до́ма.	I offered him to go but he decided to stay at home.
Мы вы́ехали по́здно, но прие́хали во́время.	We left late but we came on time.

Но may also introduce a shade of limitation or compensation:

Рестора́н дорого́й, но он о́чень хоро́ший.	This restaurant is expensive but it is very good.

The following examples will further illustrate the difference between these two important conjunctions:

Мой автомоби́ль здесь, а ваш там.	My car is here and yours is over there.

Сегодня погода хорошая, а вчера погода была плохая.	Today the weather is fine, but yesterday it was bad.
Он живёт в городе, а не в деревне.	He lives in the town (and) not in the village.
Костюм не новый, а старый.	The suit is not new, but old.
Мой автомобиль здесь, но я иду пешком.	My car is here, but I am going on foot.
Сегодня погода хорошая, но холодная.	Today the weather is fine, but it's cold.
Он живёт в городе, но я не знаю его адреса.	He lives in town, but I don't know his address.
Этот костюм не новый, но хороший.	This suit is not new, but it's good.

A comparison between the examples above shows that those containing **a** could be re-written without this conjunction:

Мой автомобиль здесь. Ваш там.
Сегодня погода хорошая. Вчера погода была плохая.
Он живёт в городе. Он не живёт в деревне.
Костюм не новый. Он старый.

This would *not* be possible with the examples containing **но**. The logical continuity would be broken.

Additional Rules:

(*a*) The conjunction **a** may also express an unexpected result by joining two sentences, the second of which is not a logical consequence of the first. This happens with the adverbs **уже** and **ещё**:

Уже поздно, а вы всё работаете.	It is already late and you are still working.
Сейчас одиннадцать часов, а он ещё спит.	It is eleven o'clock and he is still asleep.

(*b*) Sometimes, either conjunction **a** or **но** may be used, or either one may be omitted. This would merely correspond to a stylistic difference.

Examples:

Ле́том здесь жа́рко, а зимо́й хо́лодно. — In the summer it is hot here, and in the winter it is cold.

(*A contrast in statements*)

Ле́том здесь жа́рко, но зимо́й хо́лодно. — In the summer it is hot here but in the winter it is cold.

(*A stronger contrast, with* зимо́й *emphasized in speech*)

Ле́том здесь жа́рко, зимо́й хо́лодно. — In the summer it is hot here, in the winter it is cold.

(*A simple succession of statements, said casually, with no particular emphasis*)

Ле́том здесь жа́рко—зимо́й хо́лодно. — In the summer it is hot here—in the winter it is cold.

(*A contrast emphasized in speech by a pause in place of the dash*)

Other conjunctions may express contrast or opposition:

одна́ко—however

Он сказа́л, что он напи́шет, одна́ко до сих пор не написа́л. — He said that he would write; however, he has not written yet.

Note: Одна́ко is stronger than но:

Он серьёзно бо́лен, одна́ко наде́жда есть. — He is seriously ill; however, there is hope.

а то—otherwise

Ты сего́дня же до́лжен поговори́ть с отцо́м, а то он бу́дет беспоко́иться о твоём отъе́зде. — You should talk with father today, otherwise he will be worrying about your departure.*

же—whereas, but, and

Ра́ньше мы ви́делись ча́сто, тепе́рь же вида́емся о́чень ре́дко. — Before we saw each other often, but now we see each other very seldom.

* Example from Грамма́тика ру́сского языка́. Том 2. Си́нтаксис.

Же, unlike **а** or **но**, *follows* the contrasting word.

всё же—yet, just the same

Я зна́ю, что э́то тру́дно—всё же на́до постара́ться э́то сде́лать.	I know it is difficult, yet we must try to do it.

зато́—on the other hand, but (then)

Кварти́ра дорога́я, зато́ она́ о́чень удо́бная.	The apartment is expensive, but (then) it's very comfortable.

The statement following зато́ compensates the preceding one.

да—but, but then

Я б пошёл, да уже́ по́здно.	I'd go, but it's too late.

Да is close to но but it is not used as widely. It is also somewhat colloquial.

3. Coordinate conjunctions expressing choice or alternation

и́ли—or; or else; otherwise

тепе́рь или никогда́	now or never
Он до́лжен уе́хать, и́ли я поги́бла. (Турге́нев)	He must leave, otherwise I am lost.
Они́ говори́ли по-италья́нски и́ли по-испа́нски.	They were speaking Italian or Spanish. (*Choice:* Not knowing the language, I could not tell.)
До́ма мы говори́м по-ру́сски и́ли по-англи́йски.	At home we speak Russian or English. (*Alternation:* Sometimes English, at other times Russian.)

и́ли . . . и́ли—either . . . or

Он уезжа́ет и́ли в конце́ ию́ля, и́ли в нача́ле а́вгуста.	He is leaving either at the end of July or at the beginning of August.

ли́бо—or

This conjunction is used less frequently than и́ли (and not in the meaning of "otherwise"). It is currently used in the compound form:

ли́бо . . . ли́бо—either . . . or

| По вечера́м мы ли́бо чита́ем, ли́бо слу́шаем му́зыку. | In the evenings we either read or listen to the music. |

то . . . то—now . . . then

| Стра́нная пого́да: то жа́рко, то хо́лодно. | Strange weather: now it's hot, then it's cold. |

То . . . то expresses alternation, precluding simultaneity.

не то . . . не то—either . . . or

| не то снег, не то дождь | either rain or snow |

Не то . . . не то expresses choice, *not* alternation.

4. Coordinate conjunctions having an explanatory meaning

то есть (abbreviated to т. е.)—that is, i.e., "I mean"

| Он уезжа́ет в сре́ду, то есть че́рез три дня. | He is leaving on Wednesday, that is in three days. |
| Сейча́с четы́ре часа́, то есть две мину́ты пя́того. | It is now four o'clock, I mean two minutes past four. |

не то что—not, not really

| Не то что хо́лодно, но всё же прохла́дно. | Not really cold, but just the same cool. |

и́менно, а и́менно—namely, to be exact.

| В то вре́мя, а и́менно два го́да тому́ наза́д, мы рабо́тали вме́сте. | At that time, namely two years ago, we worked together. |

Subordinate Conjunctions

It may be recalled that subordinate conjunctions join two clauses of a complex sentence. These sentences express various relations:

1. *Reason or Cause*

потому́ что—because

| Я закры́л окно́, потому́ что ста́ло хо́лодно. | I closed the window because it became too cold. |

оттого́ что—because, for the reason that

| Он похуде́л, оттого́ что он о́чень ма́ло ест. | He has lost weight because he eats very little. |

так как—because, since

| Я до́лжен встать ра́но, так как по́езд отхо́дит в семь часо́в. | I have to get up early because the train leaves at seven o'clock. |

Так как, in contrast to **потому́ что,** may frequently begin a complex sentence:

| Так как он опозда́л, мы начнём без него́. | Since he is late, we shall start without him. |

ввиду́ того́ что—since, on account of, because of (the fact)

| Ввиду́ того́, что вы отка́зываетесь уплати́ть э́ту су́мму, нам придётся обрати́ться в суд. | Since you refuse to pay this sum, we will have to take the matter to court. |

благодаря́ тому́ что—thanks to, due to the fact that

| Благодаря́ тому́, что опера́ция была́ сде́лана во́время, всё обошло́сь благополу́чно. | Due to the fact that the operation was performed on time, all turned well. |

и́бо—because, for (considered obsolete)

2. *Purpose*

что́бы—to, in order to, so that*

Что́бы is followed by the predicate verb in the past tense when the subjects of the main and the subordinate clauses are different:

| Я дал ему́ де́нег, что́бы он купи́л себе́ пальто́. | I gave him some money to buy himself an overcoat. |

Or, in impersonal sentences:

| Мы откры́ли окно́, что́бы не́ было так жа́рко. | We opened the window, so that it would not be so warm. |

* See also usage of что́бы, type 8, page 310.

CONJUNCTIONS

Чтóбы is followed by the verb in the infinitive when both predicates refer to the same subject:

Я идý в гóрод, чтóбы купи́ть газéту.	I am going to town to buy a paper.

Or, in impersonal sentences when both clauses imply the same subject:

Чтóбы получи́ть ви́зу, нáдо обрати́ться в кóнсульство.	To get a visa you have to apply to the consulate.

для тогó чтóбы—in order to, so that

Для тогó чтóбы поступи́ть в вуз, нáдо сдéлать слéдующее: . . .	In order to enter a university, one must do the following: . . .

This conjunction emphasizes the purpose. There would be no necessity in using для тогó чтóбы with a simple purpose, expressing an ordinary event:

Я идý напрóтив, чтóбы купи́ть папирóс.	I am going across to buy cigarettes.

3. *Consequence*

так что—so that

Он ещё не отвéтил, так что я не могý вам ничегó сказáть.	He has not answered yet, so I can't tell you anything.

4. *Condition*

éсли—if

Éсли вы не понимáете, я объясню́ вам.	If you do not understand, I will explain to you.

Note: The English "if," meaning "whether," is not translated by éсли, but by **ли**

Я спрошý её, получи́ла ли онá письмó.	I will ask her if (whether) she received the letter.

éжели (if) is considered obsolete

раз—if, since

Зачéм вы говори́те э́то, раз вы не знáете?	Why do you say it if you don't know?

Note: When the subordinate clause precedes the main one, **éсли** and **раз** are frequently complemented by **то**:

Éсли вы не понимáете, то я вам объясню́.	If you don't understand, I will explain it to you.
Раз вы не знáете, то зачéм вы э́то говори́те?	Since you don't know, why do you say it?

5. *Concession*

хотя́ (**хоть**)—although, though

Бы́ло прия́тно пойти́ погуля́ть, хотя́ бы́ло хо́лодно.	It was nice to go for a walk, although it was cold.

When **хотя́** begins the complex sentence, it is frequently complemented by **но**.

Хотя́ водá былá холо́дная, но мы реши́ли пойти́ купáться.	Although the water was cold, we decided to go swimming.

Note: When хотя́ or хоть are followed by **бы** they form an emphatic particle of quite a different meaning: "at least," "if only."

Ну, хотя́ бы позвони́те ему́.	Well, at least telephone him.
Хоть бы кто́-нибудь пришёл!	If only somebody would come!

несмотря́ на то что—in spite of (the fact)

Несмотря́ на то что экзáмены бы́ли тру́дные, он прошёл их.	In spite of the fact that the examinations were difficult, he passed them.

пусть (**пускáй**)—let (it be)

Пускáй э́то ску́чно, но идти́ нáдо.	Let it be boring, we have to go.

рáзве что—unless

Я ему́ всё скажу́, рáзве что вы сáми хоти́те поговори́ть с ним.	I will tell him everything, unless you want to talk with him yourself.

The conjunction **рáзве что** is perhaps more characteristic of conversational Russian than of businesslike speech.

впро́чем—however, but then

Мы мо́жем пойти́ пешко́м; впро́чем, как хоти́те.	We can go on foot, but then as you wish.

как . . . ни—no matter how (much)

Как он ни стара́ется, ничего́ не выхо́дит.	No matter how much he tries, nothing comes out of it.

пра́вда . . . но—true . . . but

Пра́вда, я забы́л, но и вы мне не напо́мнили.	It is true that I forgot, but you did not remind me (either).

6. *Comparison*

чем—than (used with the comparative degree)

Эта кни́га интере́снее, чем та.	This book is more interesting than the other one.

A number of conjunctions are used to express *as*; *like*; *as if*:

как	as, like
как бу́дто	
как бу́дто бы	
бу́дто	as if
бу́дто бы	
как бы	
то́чно	as if, as, like
сло́вно	as if, as, like

Как expresses a close comparison:

Он говори́т как ру́сский.	He speaks like a Russian.
Служи́те мне, как вы ему́ служи́ли. (Пу́шкин.)	Serve me as you served him.

Sometimes, the comparison is more remote:

Вода́ как зе́ркало.	The water is like a mirror.

Как бу́дто, как бу́дто бы clearly express a hypothetical comparison.

Вы говори́те, как бу́дто вы ничего́ не зна́ете. (present)	You are speaking, as if you did not know anything.

Вы говори́те, (как) бу́дто вы не по́няли, что он сказа́л. (past)	You are speaking, as if you did not understand what he said.
Вы говори́те, как бу́дто бы вы не могли́ реши́ть. (either present or past)	You are speaking as if you could not decide (now). *Or:* You are speaking as if you could not have decided (then).

Бу́дто бы may be used in the example above. Бу́дто has another quite different meaning (see page 313).

Как бы also is used to express a hypothetical idea:

Он останови́лся, как бы не зна́я, что де́лать.	He stopped as if he did not know (as if not knowing) what to do.

Note here the characteristic usage of the Russian gerund after **как бы**.

Further examples may illustrate the differences between **как** (in the first meaning: *close comparison*), **как бу́дто**, and **как бы**:

Вы говори́те **как** францу́з.	You speak *like* a Frenchman. (implying that your French is perfect)
Вы говори́те, **как бу́дто** вы францу́з.	You are speaking *as if* you were a Frenchman. (referring to ideas or feelings on a subject)
Он отве́тил нам по-францу́зски, **как бы** жела́я показа́ть, что он понима́ет наш разгово́р.	He answered us in French, *as if* wanting to show that he understood our conversation.

То́чно and **сло́вно** may express a more or less close comparison:

Вода́ то́чно (сло́вно) зе́ркало.	The water is like a mirror.

(In this example they have the same meaning as **как**.)

Or, they may express a hypothetical comparison:

Вы говори́те, сло́вно вы не зна́ете, в чём де́ло.	You are speaking as if you did not know what it was about.

In the above example, **словно** has the same meaning as **как бу́дто**.

Note: Точно and сло́вно are more colloquial than businesslike.

насто́лько . . . наско́лько—as . . . as

Он насто́лько же умён, наско́лько (и) образо́ван.	He is as clever as he is well educated.

не так . . . как or **не насто́лько . . . наско́лько**—not as . . . as

Он не так умён, как образо́ван.	He is not as clever as he is well educated. (He is more educated than clever.)

чем . . . тем—the . . . the

Чем ра́ньше вы придёте, тем лу́чше.	The earlier you come the better.

7. *Time (Temporal Relations)*

There are many conjunctions in this class. The principal ones are listed below, in groups, according to their meaning.

(*a*) **когда́** and **как** both mean *when*

когда́

Я поступи́л в шко́лу, когда́ мне бы́ло во́семь лет.	I entered school when I was eight years old.

Note: When both predicate verbs are perfective, the action expressed by the clause containing когда́ comes chronologically first:

Когда́ он вошёл в ко́мнату, все вста́ли.	When he entered the room, everyone got up.

With imperfective verbs, it is not necessarily so:

Когда́ он вхо́дит в ко́мнату, все встаю́т.	When he enters the room, everyone gets up.
Когда́ он рабо́тает, он ни о чём друго́м не ду́мает.	When he works he does not think of anything else. (Indicates simultaneity)

как (as a temporal conjunction) is used seldom and only colloquially:

| Ну, как приедем туда, там и поужинаем. | Well, when we'll arrive there, we shall have dinner. |

(b) **Едва́, лишь (лишь то́лько), чуть (чуть то́лько), как то́лько**—all mean: *as soon as; no sooner than; the moment* . . .
These conjunctions normally express an immediate succession of events.

едва́

| Едва́ мы вы́шли, (как) пошёл дождь. | No sooner we went out, it started to rain. |

Лишь and **чуть** are often characteristic of poetic speech:

| По си́ним волна́м океа́на, Лишь звёзды блесну́т в небеса́х . . . (Ле́рмонтов) | On the blue waves of the ocean The moment (as soon as) the stars begin to glisten in the skies . . . |

Как то́лько has a wider usage than **едва́, лишь**, and **чуть**. It may express an immediate succession of events, or simply a close one:

| Как то́лько мы вы́шли, пошёл дождь. | As soon as we went out, it started to rain. |
| Как то́лько он попра́вился, он на́чал иска́ть рабо́ту. | As soon as he recovered, he began to look for a job. |

Как то́лько, in contrast to the conjunctions mentioned above, is used not only in conversational or poetic language, but also in business speech:

| Мы вам дади́м знать, как то́лько полу́чим ну́жные све́дения. | We will let you know, as soon as we get the necessary information. |

(c) **Пока́, пока́мест, покуда, в то вре́мя как, ме́жду тем как**—all mean *while*:

Пока́

| Пока́ мы вас жда́ли, я всё рассказа́л ему́. | While we were waiting for you, I told him everything. |

CONJUNCTIONS

Пока́ . . . не means *until*:

Не де́лайте ничего́, пока́ я не напишу́ вам.	Don't do anything until I write you.

Покуда and **покамест** are used instead of пока́ mainly in colloquial speech.

В то вре́мя как and **ме́жду тем как** have additional meanings: *whereas* and *yet*, respectively.

Он уже́ уе́хал в о́тпуск, в то вре́мя как я до́лжен ждать до конца́ ме́сяца.	He has already gone on vacation whereas I have to wait until the end of the month.
Она́, повидимому, ничего́ не слы́шала, ме́жду тем как во всех газе́тах об э́том писа́ли.	She apparently has heard nothing, (and) yet all the papers wrote about it.

(ещё) не . . . как—no sooner . . . when; hardly . . . when

This so-called "inversive conjunction" pertains to two actions, one of which starts before the other has ended:

Не успе́л я войти́ в ко́мнату, как все на́чали меня́ расспра́шивать.	Hardly had I entered the room, when everybody began to ask me questions.

(d) **по́сле того́ как**—after

По́сле того́ как он уе́дет, я вам всё скажу́.	After he leaves, I will tell you everything.

пе́ред тем как, до того́ как, пре́жде чем—all mean: *before*

Он уе́хал до того́ как (пе́ред тем как; пре́жде чем) мы верну́лись.	He left before we returned.

с тех пор как—since

С тех пор как мы прие́хали, мы ни ра́зу не́ были в теа́тре.	Since we arrived here, we have not been a single time to the theater.

8. *Ideas* or *Feelings*

   что and **чтобы**

The usage and comparison between что and чтобы is illustrated with a few examples.

Что (that) primarily states a fact:

Они написали, что он приехал.	They wrote that he has arrived.
Я не верю, что он это сделал нарочно.	I don't believe that he did this on purpose.
Видно, что все поняли.	It is obvious that everybody has understood.
Очень важно, что он согласился прийти.	It is very important that he has agreed to come.
Боюсь, что мы опоздаем.	I am afraid that we will be late.
Это такая трудная задача, что её нельзя решить.	This is such a difficult problem, that it is impossible to solve it.
Сейчас так холодно, что лучше надеть пальто.	It is so cold, that it's better to put on an overcoat.

Note: **Что** with настолько (so) or до того (so *emphatic*) is used in sentences similar to the last two examples:

Сейчас настолько холодно, что я не хочу выходить.	It is so cold, that I don't want to go out.

Чтобы means "that," or else is translated into English using the "assumed subject" (such as: I want *him* to come).

Чтобы is used primarily to express *wish, desire, request, command* (or to express the opposite: unwillingness, undesirability, etc.). It is used with such verbs as: хотеть (to want); желать (to wish); просить (to ask); требовать (to demand); приказывать (to order), also with: не хотеть, etc.

Я хочу, чтобы вы поняли.	I want you to understand.
Он попросил вас, чтобы вы позвонили ему.	He asked you to call him up.
Он потребовал, чтобы все ушли.	He demanded that everybody leave.

CONJUNCTIONS

Она́ не хо́чет, что́бы ей помога́ли.	She does not wish that anybody should help her.

In addition to expressing wish, command, etc., **что́бы** may express a conjecture, a doubt, a personal opinion, an eventuality.

The following examples illustrating the usage of **что́бы** may be compared with the corresponding ones given with **что** on page 310.

Они́ написа́ли ему́, что́бы он прие́хал.	They wrote him to come.
Я не ве́рю, что́бы он сде́лал э́то наро́чно.[1]	I can't believe that that he could have done it on purpose.
Необходи́мо, что́бы все по́няли э́то.	It is absolutely necessary that everyone understand it.
Очень ва́жно, что́бы он согласи́лся прие́хать.	It is very important that he agree to come.
Бою́сь, что́бы (как бы) мы не опозда́ли.[2]	I am afraid that we might be late.
Это не така́я тру́дная зада́ча, что́бы её нельзя́ бы́ло реши́ть.	It is not so difficult a problem that it can't be solved.
Сейча́с не так хо́лодно, что́бы надева́ть пальто́.[3]	It is not cold enough to put on an overcoat.

Notes: on sentences (1), (2), and (3).

(1) Что́бы is used with negated sentences which express a doubt or a conjecture, after не ду́мать (not to think); не слы́шать (not to hear); не по́мнить (not to remember), and also сомнева́ться (to doubt):

Я никогда́ не слы́шал, что́бы о нём так говори́ли.	I never heard anybody say that about him.
Я сомнева́юсь, что́бы они́ верну́лись до у́жина.	I doubt that they will return before supper.

(2) Что́бы + не is used with verbs expressing fear and worry: боя́ться (to fear); опаса́ться (to fear, to apprehend); беспоко́иться (to worry).

(3) Что́бы is used in similar constructions with не тако́й (not such, not so); не насто́лько (not so, not that much); не доста́точно (not enough), and доста́точно (enough, sufficient).

When two clauses are joined together by что or чтобы the main clause may or may not contain the pronoun **то**:

Я уве́рен, что он говори́т пра́вду.	I am sure that he is telling the the truth.

Or:

Я уве́рен в том, что он говори́т пра́вду.	I am sure (of the fact) that he is telling the truth.

The sentence in the second example may be more complete or clarified, but it is also more bookish or formal.

Sometimes the pronoun **то** *has to be* inserted. Thus, there is a difference between:

Я ду́мал, что она́ приезжа́ет за́втра.	I thought that she was arriving tomorrow.

And

Я ду́мал о том, что она́ приезжа́ет за́втра.	I was thinking about her arriving tomorrow.

In the last example, the "theme" of thoughts or reflexions is stressed.*

The use of **то** is also compulsory with a few verbal constructions clearly calling for a certain case:

нача́ть (с чего́-нибудь *Genitive*)—to begin (by something).
ко́нчиться (чём-нибудь *Instrumental*)—to end (by something).
состоя́ть (в чём-нибудь *Prepositional*)—to consist (in something).

Examples:

Он на́чал с того́, что прочита́л нам телегра́мму.	He began by reading us the telegram.
Ко́нчилось тем, что они́ поссо́рились.	It ended by their quarreling.
Тепе́рь труд её состоя́л в том, чтобы научи́ть други́х хорошо́ труди́ться.	Now her work consisted in teaching others to work well.†

* . . . ука́зывается предме́т, "те́ма" размышле́ний—Грамма́тика ру́сского языка́, АН СССР, Том 2, Си́нтаксис.
† Example from *op. cit.*

CONJUNCTIONS

ли—whether, if

(*a*) This conjunction is used in sentences which express a desire to find out something. It is used with verbs such as: спроси́ть (to ask); узна́ть (to learn); вы́яснить (to find out), and also with хоте́ть знать (to want to know). For example:

Он спроси́л, пришли́ ли пи́сьма.	He asked whether the letters had come.
На́до вы́яснить, мо́жно ли рассчи́тывать на него́.	We have to find out whether one can depend on him.
Я хочу́ знать, есть ли здесь гара́ж.	I want to know if there is a garage here.

(*b*) Ли also indicates *doubt, uncertainty*. It is used with many negated verbs.

Не зна́ю, сто́ит ли писа́ть об э́том.	I don't know whether it is worthwhile writing about it.
Я не по́мню, говори́л ли я вам.	I don't remember if I told you.
Она́ не пи́шет, приезжа́ют ли де́ти.	She does not write whether the children are coming.

(*c*) Ли is used after: неизве́стно (not known); непоня́тно (not clear, incomprehensible); нея́сно (not clear); интере́сно (interesting).

Неизве́стно, ко́нчилось ли заседа́ние.	We don't know whether the meeting has ended.
Интере́сно, понра́вился ли им фильм.	I wonder if they liked the film.

Бу́дто—that, that supposedly, as if

Бу́дто implies *doubt, uncertainty, disbelief*.

Он говори́т, бу́дто его́ то́же пригласи́ли.	He says that he has also been invited. (He has also been invited—so he says.)
Я слы́шал, бу́дто они́ поссо́рились.	I have heard that supposedly they have quarrelled.

Бу́дто is frequently used with the following verbs: каза́ться (to seem); слы́шать (to hear); сни́ться (to be dreamt of); притворя́ться (to pretend); воображáть (to imagine).

Мне показа́лось, бу́дто он оби́делся.	It seemed to me that (possibly) he was offended.
Она́ притворя́ется, бу́дто она́ лю́бит его́.	She pretends that she loves him.

Note: In the examples above **бу́дто** could be replaced with **что**, but the implication would be different. The sentence would state a fact.

Я слы́шал, что они́ поссо́рились.	I heard that they have quarreled.
Мне показа́лось, что он оби́делся.	It seemed to me that he was offended.

Как means *how*, or else it is rendered into English by using the participle (such as: *I saw him playing*). Как is used when the predicate verb of the main clause expresses perception, i.e., after ви́деть (to see); смотре́ть (to look); слы́шать (to hear); слу́шать (to listen); заме́тить (to notice), etc.

Я ви́дел, как он вошёл в ко́мнату.	I saw how he came into the room (I saw him come in).
Они́ слу́шали, как она́ пе́ла.	They were listening to her singing.
Я смотре́л, как они́ игра́ли.	I watched them playing.
Мы заме́тили, как он положи́л де́ньги в карма́н.	We noticed how he put the money in his pocket.

Notes:

(*a*) The verbs ви́деть, слы́шать and заме́тить may express a shorter action or the result of one. They are then followed by **что**:

Я уви́дел, что он вошёл в ко́мнату.	I saw that he came into the room.
Мы заме́тили, что он положи́л де́ньги в карма́н.	We noticed that he put the money in his pocket.

(*b*) Similar constructions are used with ви́дно, слы́шно, заме́тно:

Отсю́да ви́дно, как они́ игра́ют в футбо́л.	One can see from here how they are playing soccer.
Бы́ло слы́шно, как сосе́ди спо́рили.	One could hear the neighbors arguing.

CONJUNCTIONS

Conjunctive Words

These words (conjunctions, adverbs, pronouns) not only establish a relation between the main and the subordinate clauses, but also refer specifically to one word of the main clause, even if sometimes this word is only implied:

Я знаю город, где они живут.	I know the town where they live.
Я слышал (то), что вы сказали ему.	I heard *what* you told him.

The difference between a conjunctive word and a conjunction proper may be illustrated by comparing the last example above with:

Я слышал, что вы сказали ему всё.	I heard *that* you told him everything.

The conjunctive words **который** and **какой** agree in gender and number with the word to which they refer. They do not agree in case—or else only fortuitously. (The case is governed by the structure of the subordinate clause.)

Вот дом (*masc.*, *sing.*, nom.), в котором (*masc.*, *sing.*, prep.) он живёт.	Here is the house in which he lives.
Видите девочку (*fem.*, *sing.*, acc.) которая (*fem.*, *sing.*, nom.) читает?	Do you see the girl who is reading?
Я нашёл книгу (*fem.*, *sing.*, acc.), которую (*fem.*, *sing.*, acc.) вы искали.	I found the book you were looking for.
Там такие высокие дома (*plur.*, nom.), каких (*plur.* gen.) вы здесь не увидите.	There there are tall houses such as you won't see here.

11. PARTICLES

Particles are auxiliary words which impart an additional shade of meaning either to one word or to the whole sentence:

    Да́же он не зна́ет.   Even he does not know.

Here the particle **да́же** pertains to and emphasizes **он**.

    Ра́зве вы не чита́ли сего́дняш-   Haven't you read today's paper?
    нюю газе́ту?   (Do you mean to say that . . .
        Is it possible that . . .)

Here the particle **ра́зве** pertains to the whole sentence.

Note: Some particles, such as **да́же, не,** have a clearly indicated meaning, and are readily translated into English. Others, such as **ра́зве** or **же,** do not lend themselves easily to translation. They are often rendered by the proper intonation.

General Remarks

1. Occasionally a particle or a combination of particles, may be quite independent, and may form a meaningful sentence. This happens namely in conversation:

    —Вы уезжа́ете за́втра?   —Are you leaving tomorrow?
    —Вряд ли.   —I doubt it. (It is improbable)

    —Он рассерди́лся и ушёл.   —He got angry and left.
    —Ну, и пусть.   —Well let him.

2. Particles are closely tied to other parts of speech (conjunctions, adverbs, etc.). Actually, the same word, depending on its function, can be a particle, an adverb, a pronoun, etc.* For example:

    Он всё чита́ет.   He reads everything.
    Он всё чита́ет.   He keeps on reading.

* Виногра́дов in "Совреме́нный ру́сский язы́к" refers to some of them (почти́, приблизи́тельно) as "adverbs-particles."

А вы всё рабо́таете и рабо́таете.   And you keep on working and working.

In the first example, всё is a pronoun. In the last two examples всё is a particle; it carries no stress in the intonation.

3. Particles may precede the word to which they refer:

Ну и пого́да!	What weather! (Some weather!)
Пусть он сам ска́жет.	Let him tell it himself.

Or, they may follow the word in question:

Вы же опозда́ли, не я.	You were late (weren't you), not I.
Зна́ет ли он об э́том?	Does he know about it?

Some particles have no fixed position in a sentence:

Ведь вы не зна́ете его́?	
Вы ведь не зна́ете его́?	You don't know him, do you?
Вы его́ ведь не зна́ете?	

4. Certain particles are joined to the word in question by a hyphen:

Кто́–то пришёл.	Somebody has arrived.
Пойдёмте-ка на пляж.	How about going to the beach?

Classification and Usage of Particles

Particles are divided into the following classes:

1. *Demonstrative*

Вот (here is, there is, here's, there's, here are, there are), as a general rule, refers to something or somebody in close proximity—at least when compared to **вон** (there is, there's, there are):

Вот ва́ша кни́га.	Here's your book.
Вон лети́т самолёт.	There's an airplane flying.

Вот is of a more current, and also wider usage than вон. In some instances, вот does not imply any close proximity:

(a) It may mean the emphatic *that* in sentences such as:

Вот кому́ на́до помо́чь.	That's someone whom one should help.

It attracts attention to a word logically emphasized:

Вот в чём де́ло.	(Now) that's the thing; That is the point.
Вот кто здесь!	(Look) who is here!
Вы е́дете в Ита́лию? Вот куда́ я хоте́л бы пое́хать!	Are you going to Italy? That's where I would like to go!

(b) Вот is frequently found in narratives:

Вот иду́ я по у́лице и вдруг ви́жу —идёт ко мне навстре́чу мой ста́рый прия́тель.	Well, (there) I was going down the street, and suddenly I see my old friend coming towards me.

Note: The particles вот and вон are used in the same way as the French "voici" or "voilà." They do not function in the same way as the adverbs здесь and там, which indicate location:

Вот рестора́н.	Here's a restaurant. (Pointing—if not literally—to it)
Здесь рестора́н, а там банк.	Here is a restaurant, and there is a bank.
Рестора́н здесь.	The restaurant is here.

Это is emphatic (and usually is not rendered in translation).

Кто э́то пришёл?	Who came?
Куда́ э́то вы спеши́те?	(Now) where are you hurrying?

When preceding a predicate noun, э́то may be translated *this is, it is*:

Ум—э́то си́лища. (Го́рький)	Intelligence—this is (great) strength.

PARTICLES

А по-мо́ему, совреме́нный теа́тр —э́то рути́на, предрассу́док. (Че́хов)

And I think that modern theater it is routine, prejudice.*

2. *Limitative*

то́лько—*only, just*

    Я то́лько на мину́ту.   I (have come) just for a minute.

Лишь (**лишь то́лько, то́лько лишь**) may be considered synonymous with то́лько. However, то́лько has a wider usage, it is found in poetry, conversation and business speech.

    Remark: То́лько and лишь have clearly different meanings—when they function as particles, or as conjunctions:

(*Conj.*)	Лишь звёзды блесну́т в небеса́х . . .	No sooner the stars begin to glisten in the sky . . .
(*Part.*)	Лишь одна́ звезда́ видна́. (slightly stressed)	Only one star is seen.
(*Conj.*)	То́лько он прие́хал . . .	No sooner he arrived . . .
(*Part.*)	То́лько он прие́хал. (stressed)	Only he arrived.

Хотя́ бы ; хоть ; хоть бы all of which mean *if only, at least*.

Пое́дем хотя́ бы на три дня.   Let us go, if only for three days.
Ну, хоть вы мне скажи́те.   Well, at least you tell me.

3. *Emphatic*

Да́же and **и** mean—*even*. Да́же is usually stronger than и.

А, ваш брат прие́хал? Я и не знал.   Oh, your brother has arrived? I (even) didn't know.
Я да́же не знал, что он здесь.   I even did not know he was here.

At the beginning of a sentence, **и** may carry a strong emphasis.

И зачем э́то ну́жно?   And why is it necessary?
И я ещё винова́т!   And I am to blame! (On the top of everything.)

---

* Example from Совреме́нный ру́сский си́нтаксис. Под реда́кцией Е. М. Га́лкиной-Федору́к.

Же and **ведь** are both translated as *but, why* . . ., *after all*—or are frequently rendered by expressions such as *didn't I, don't you know*, etc:

Я же (ведь) вам сказа́л!   But I told you! (I told you, didn't I?)

Ведь has no fixed place in a sentence. Же is always enclictic.

Ведь банк закры́т сего́дня.	Why, the bank is closed today.
Он ведь ско́ро приезжа́ет.	He is coming soon, don't you know?

With interrogative parts of speech, же is often translated as *then*.

Кому́ же вы написа́ли?	To whom did you write then?
Когда́ же они́ верну́тся?	When are they coming back (then)?

Note: In an interrogative construction, ведь cannot be substituted for же.

Да—*but* (at the beginning of a sentence) may express impatience, even annoyance. A great deal, however, depends on the tone:

Да не хочу́ я идти́ туда́!	But I don't want to go there.
Да я вам э́того никогда́ не говори́л!	But I never said that to you!

Notes:

(a) **Да нет** means *not at all*; *oh, no*; *by no means*.

(b) Да may be used in questions, sometimes in combination with же.

Да почему́ вы мне не сказа́ли?	But why did not you tell me?
Да когда́ же они́ жени́лись?	But when did they marry then?

Ну—*well* is usually mildly emphatic, but this again depends on the tone:

Ну, я не зна́ю.	Well, I don't know.
Ну, хорошо́.	Well, all right.
Ну, приходи́те в пять, е́сли хоти́те.	Well, come at five, if you wish.
Ну, дово́льно!	Well (now) that's enough!

Уж—*well, really* often carries only a mild emphasis:

Это не так уж до́рого.	This is really not so expensive.
Я уж не зна́ю.	Well, I really don't know.

PARTICLES

Note: Here again the tone plays a role. Lermontov's (Borodino) "Уж мы пойдём ломи́ть стено́ю." ("We will go, breaking through like a wall.")—is not mildly emphatic.

With the imperative mood, уж usually mollifies the order or the request:

Вы уж пойди́те са́ми.	(Look) you better go yourself.
Уж не забу́дьте, пожа́луйста.	Please don't forget (will you?).

4. Definite

Some of these particles are very close to adverbs, and may be classified as such.

Именно—namely, just

Все произошло́ и́менно так.	Everything happened just so.
Кому́ и́менно вы написа́ли?	To whom did you write namely?

Как раз—just

Это как раз то, что я слы́шал.	That is just what I heard.

Почти́—almost, just about

Он почти́ всегда́ до́ма.	He is almost always at home.

Приблизи́тельно—approximately, about

приблизи́тельно в час	at about one o'clock

Про́сто—simply

Она́ про́сто о́чень ми́лая.	She is simply very nice.

Чуть не—almost

Я чуть не забы́л.	I almost forgot.

5. Affirmative

Да—*yes* is the most widely used affirmative particle.

Note the variants:

Ну, да—well, yes; yes, of course

—Это дово́льно до́рого.	—This is rather expensive.
—Ну, да.	—Yes, of course.

Да, да—oh, yes; surely; yes, yes.

    —Надо бы написать им.   —We (really) should write them.
    —Да, да.   —Yes, yes.

Ещё бы—of course; naturally; I should say so; indeed; by all means.

    —Он прошёл экзамен?   —Did he pass his examination?
    —Ещё бы!   —Of course!

Есть—right! aye aye. (Characteristic of military speech)

    —Полный ход!   —Full speed!
    —Есть!   —Right!

6. *Negative*

Нет—no. This particle may also have an independent meaning of a whole sentence:

    —Вы кончили ваш доклад?   —Did you finish your report?
    —Нет.   —No.

At the beginning of a sentence, it emphasizes the negation: Нет, не кончил—No, I haven't (finished). At the same time, and said in the proper tone, this construction is more polite than the laconic нет.

Нет not only denies a sentence, but has an independent value of its own. Compare, for example, the same answer to two different questions:

    —Вы куда-нибудь едете?   Are you going anywhere?
    —Нет.   No.

    —Вы никуда не едете?   You are not going anywhere?
    —Нет.   No.

Не—not. Usually precedes the predicates, and thereby negates the whole sentence:

    Я не говорил с ним.   I did not speak with him.

Otherwise, не may negate another word of the sentence by immediately preceding that word:

    Я не с ним говорил.   I did not speak with *him*. (It wasn't he with whom I spoke).
    Не я с ним говорил.   *I* did not speak with him. (It wasn't I who spoke with him).

PARTICLES

Remark: The double usage of не makes the statement affirmative—yet of a different shade of meaning, compared to a simple affirmative:

| Не могу́ не пора́доваться. | I can't help being happy. |
| Он не мог не знать. | It would be impossible for him not to know. |

As compared to:

| Могу́ ра́доваться. | I can be happy. |
| Он мог знать. | He could know. |

Ни—not a. Ни normally combines with не in negative sentences:

| Мы не получи́ли ни одного́ письма́. | We did not receive a single letter. |
| Она́ не сказа́ла ни сло́ва. | She did not say a word. |

In impersonal sentences, ни alone can carry the negation:

| Ни сло́ва! | Silence! (Not a word!) |
| Ни с ме́ста! | Don't leave your place. |

Even in this type of a sentence, не is implied (не говори́те ни сло́ва.).

Remark: After certain pronouns and adverbs, ни loses its negative character, and imparts a generalization to the statement:

| Куда́ он ни пойдёт, всю́ду ему́ ску́чно. | No matter where he goes, he is bored. |
| Кого́ ни спро́сишь—никто́ не зна́ет. | Whomever one asks—nobody seems to know. |

7. Interrogative

Ли—not translated into English (unlike the conjunction ли which means *whether, if*).

Ли follows the word which is being questioned:

Зна́ете ли вы?	Do you know?
Прие́хал ли до́ктор?	Has the doctor arrived?
Вы ли э́то?	Is that you?

This construction is most frequently replaced by the positive statement said with the proper interrogative intonation:

Вы зна́ете? Прие́хал до́ктор? Это вы?

Note: In a few set expressions, ли loses its interrogative meaning: видите ли (you see); шутка ли (it's no joke); то ли дело (it's a different matter, how can one compare?); мало ли (there are many things, I don't care what . . .), etc:

Не нравится мне здесь. То ли дело жить в деревне!	I don't like it here. How can it compare with life in the country?
Мало ли что он говорит.	I don't care what he says.

а?—(informal) *what?*, means *eh?* or the French ''n'est ce pas?''
The usage of this particle is often characteristic of individual speech:

—Англичанин хвастает . . . а? . . .—говорил Анатоль. (Л. Толстой)	—The Englishman is boasting . . . eh?—Anatole was saying.

Разве and **неужели** mean *is it possible that*; *do you mean to say that*; *why*, . . . They are frequently omitted in translation and expressed by reversing the English word order and optionally adding ''really'':

Разве он русский?	Is he Russian?
Разве вы не знаете? Неужели вы не знаете?	Don't you really know? (Do you mean to say you don't know?)

Both these interrogative particles express doubt, disbelief, or surprise—the latter is especially characteristic of неужели.* Here, the surprise may be mixed with different—in fact fully opposite—feelings or emotions. Thus:

Неужели они приезжают завтра?	Are they really coming tomorrow?

may express surprise coupled with joy as well as with displeasure. On the other hand, sentences such as

Разве они приезжают завтра?	Do you mean to say they are coming tomorrow?
Разве почта на этой улице?	Why, is the post office on this street?

are usually more matter of fact.

* See Частицы by М. В. Ушаков. Методические разработки по грамматике. Под редакцией С. Г. Бархударова.

PARTICLES

Remarks:

(*a*) Ра́зве is often used in interrogative-negative sentences:

—... Я всё ви́жу. Ра́зве ты тако́й был полго́да наза́д? (Л. Толсто́й)	"... I see everything. Were you like this half a year ago?"

Here the speaker (Lise Bolkonsky) herself already knows the *negative* answer to her question.

(*b*) Неуже́ли frequently, (but not always) expresses the opposite:

"... Что э́то за лю́ди?—всё ду́мал Росто́в ...—Неуже́ли францу́зы? ... Заче́м они́ бегу́т? Неуже́ли ко мне?" (Л. Толсто́й)	"Who are these people?" Rostov kept thinking, "... Are they Frenchmen? ... Why are they running? Could it be towards me?"

Here the speaker actually cannot doubt that these *are* French soldiers running towards him.

8. *Exclamatory*

Ну и—what (a, an); certainly, "sure":

Ну и день!	What a day!
Ну и уста́л я!	I'm certainly tired!

Про́сто—simply, just. More emphatic that the definite particle про́сто, given above:

Я про́сто не могу́ поня́ть!	I simply can not understand!

Ведь is both, exclamatory as well as emphatic; It is discussed above (page 320).

9. *Indecisive*

Indecisive particles, introduced into a sentence, express doubt, uncertainty:

Вря́д ли—unlikely, I doubt, etc.

Они́ вря́д ли до́ма.	I doubt that they are at home.

Едва́ ли—hardly

    Этому едва́ ли мо́жно пове́рить.   One could hardly believe this.

Пожа́луй—I suppose, "I guess," maybe.

    Ну, я, пожа́луй, пойду́.   Well, I suppose I will go.

Чуть ли не—just about, practically.

    Это чуть ли не са́мый дорого́й рестора́н в го́роде.   This is just about the most expensive restaurant in town.

10. *Comparative*

The comparative particles **бу́дто, как бу́дто, как бы, сло́вно** have the same meaning as the corresponding conjunctions. They express a comparison between similar notions, or may refer to something hypothetical:

Он как бу́дто пра́вда уе́хал.	It seems as if he really has left.
Вы сло́вно не понима́ете, что я говорю́.	(You act) as if you did not understand what I am saying.
Он как бы не знал, что отве́тить.	(It seemed) as if he did not know what to answer.

11. *Auxiliary Particles*

Auxiliary particles may form new words or new verbal constructions.

    Particles forming new words

    (*a*) The particles **-то, -нибудь, -либо, кое-**, serve to express indefiniteness when combined with interrogative pronouns or adverbs.

    Examples:

кто́-то	somebody
что́-нибудь	anything
когда́-либо	ever
кое-где́	here and there

(See Indefinite Pronouns and Indefinite Adverbs, pages 116, 267.)

The word **уго́дно** (when functioning as a particle) may be added to the same pronouns or adverbs:

кто уго́дно	whoever you wish (one wishes)
когда́ уго́дно	whenever you wish (one wishes)

PARTICLES

(b) The particles **ни, не** express negation. For example:

    никто́   nobody
    ничто́   nothing
    ника́к   in no way
    нигде́   nowhere
    не́где   nowhere (to . . .)

(See Negative Pronouns and Negative Adverbs, pages 113, 267.)
The particle **не** is widely used in forming antonyms, such as небольшо́й—small (not large); недалеко́—near (not far).

(c) The particle **ся (сь)** is used in the formation of reflexive verbs:

    мы́ть**ся**   to wash: мо́ю**сь** . . . мо́ют**ся**
    одева́ть**ся**   to dress: одева́ю**сь** . . . одева́ют**ся**

Particles forming new verbal constructions

(a) **Бы** combined with the past tense forms the conditional (or subjunctive) mood; combined with the infinitive **бы** is sometimes used to express a wish:

Я пошёл бы, е́сли не́ было бы   I would go if it were not so late.
так по́здно.
Хорошо́ бы отдохну́ть!   It would be nice to rest!

(b) **Пусть** and the less emphatic **пуска́й** combine with the third person to form the equivalent of an imperative. The same applies to the particle **да**, the usage of which is limited to a few expressions:

Examples:

Пусть он придёт в де́вять.   Let him (He should) come at nine.

Пуска́й они́ игра́ют здесь.   Let them play here.
Да здра́вствует!   Long live!
Да бу́дет вам изве́стно.   Let it be known to you.

(c) **Быва́ло**—formerly; used to; sometimes . . . would. This particle may be used with the present, past, or future—however, it always refers to an action which happened, at intervals, in the past:

Быва́ло, сиди́м мы у реки́.
Быва́ло, сиде́ли мы у реки́.   We used to sit near the river (in those days).
Быва́ло посиди́м мы у реки́.

12. INTERJECTIONS

Interjections are non-inflected parts of speech. With few exceptions, they are devoid of any grammatical characteristics.

Interjections often have no intrinsic meaning, especially the primary ones (*see below*). In other words, the same interjection may express various—in fact, fully opposite—feelings, depending on the intonation, the gesture, the situation, etc.

So great a role does the intonation play that in written language it may be impossible to determine the meaning of the interjection, without knowing more about the situation. (Thus "A" in -**А,—сказа́л он** may express a variety of feelings.)

Conversely, even a man who does not understand Russian may determine the meaning of an interjection by simply noting the tone or the facial expression of the speaker.

Classification of Interjections

Interjections are divided into the following groups:

1. Primary
2. Secondary
3. Idiomatic
4. Foreign-borrowed
5. Imitative

1. *Primary*

Primary interjections usually consist of one syllable, sometimes of one letter.

Examples: **а**—ah, oh; **ой**—oh.

2. *Secondary*

Secondary interjections are derived from meaningful words—but are only remotely connected with them as far as meaning. Examples:

Ба́тюшки!	—Dear me! (*lit.* Father! Daddy!)
Поми́луйте!	—Oh, no! How can you! (*lit.* Have mercy!)

INTERJECTIONS

Брось (бро́сьте)!	—stop, quit (*lit.* throw)
По́лно	—enough, stop (*lit.* full)
Здра́вствуйте	—good morning, good day, hello (*lit.* be well, be healthy)
Спаси́бо	—Thank you (*originally:* God save you.)

3. *Idiomatic*

Another group is composed of idiomatic, or set, expressions which function as interjections. For example:

Вот оно́ что!	So that's what it is!
Вот так–так!	That's something! What do you know!
Вот те (тебе́) раз!	Well, I never! What do you mean?
Была́—не была́.	Come what may.

The borderline between these interjections and other parts of speech is not always clear.

4. *Foreign-borrowed*

To another group of interjections belong words borrowed from foreign languages. For example:

Алло́.	Hello (answering a telephone, only).
Стоп.	Stop (with traffic).
Бра́во.	Bravo!
Бис!	Encore (at a theater)!
Ура́!	Hurrah!
Ба!	Well!?

5. *Imitative*

Some words which imitate actions (such as laughing, whistling) or sounds made by animals or objects are classified as interjections:

Ха-ха-ха	Ha-ha-ha (laughter)
мя́у-мя́у	Meow-meow (miauling)
Бум!	Boom!
Бах!	Bang!

Usage of Interjections

Interjections are divided into two classes:

1. those which express feelings,
2. those which express inciting, prompting.

1. Interjections which express feelings

The principal interjections which express feelings are listed below.

А! Ах! О!	Ah! Oh!
Ага́!	Ah! Oh! Well! See!
Ой! Ай!	Oh! Ouch!
Эх!	Ah! Oh! Alas! (reproach, regret)
Ох!	Ah! Oh! (pain, grief, complaint)
Увы́!	Alas!
Фу! Фуй!	Phew! (disgust, annoyance)
Бра́во!	Bravo!
Бис!	Encore!
Ура́!	Hurrah!

Some interjections have only one, clearly indicated meaning; the feeling or reaction expressed may be positive (with **бра́во, бис, ура́**) or negative (with **ох, увы́, фуй**).

Other interjections, especially **ах**, **а**, and **о**, have quite a variety of meanings. A few examples will illustrate the diversity of feelings expressed by these, although it is, of course, impossible to express here the various shades of intonation.

Ах, как хорошо́!	Oh, how wonderful!	(joy)
Ах, как жаль!	Ah, what a pity!	(pity)
Ах, как мне стра́шно!	Oh, I'm so afraid!	(fear)
Ах, пожалу́йста, приезжа́йте!	Oh, please do come!	(emphatic request)
Ах, заче́м вы э́то сде́лали?	Oh, why did you do it?	(reproach)
Ах! Вот кто пришёл!	Oh, look who came!	(surprise)

INTERJECTIONS

Ах, здра́вствуйте!	Oh, hello!	(somewhat casual joy or surprise)
Ах, как оби́дно.	Oh, that's too bad.	(vexation, disappointment)
Ах, како́й трус!	Oh, what a coward!	(indignation)
А, вот что он хо́чет сказа́ть.	Oh, that's what he means.	(guess, conjecture)
А, э́то вы?	Oh, is that you?	(surprise)
А, здра́вствуйте.	Oh, hello.	(slightly casual tone in greeting)
—А!—А!—закрича́л он.	"Ah! Ah!" he yelled.	(terror, pain)
А, не говори́те мне.	Oh, don't tell me that.	(displeasure, annoyance)
А, тепе́рь вы бои́тесь!	Ah, now you are afraid!	(mockery; threat)
А, подожди́-ка!	Oh, just wait now!	(threat)
А, я вас не по́нял.	Oh, I didn't understand you.	(mild regret, apology)
О, моя́ дорога́я!	Oh, my dear!	(love, admiration)
О, како́й у́жас!	Oh, how awful!	(grief)
О! о!	Oh! Oh!	(pain)
О, несча́стный челове́к!	Oh, poor man!	(strong pity)
О, э́то дли́нная исто́рия.	Oh, that is a long story.	(emphatic—but without any special feeling)
О, э́то я зна́ю.	Oh, this I do know	(confident assurance)

2. Interjections which express prompting, inciting

The principal interjections which express prompting or inciting are the following:

Эй!	Hey! Hey you!
Ау́!	O-eh! (calling out)

Ну!	Well! Come on!
На! Háте!	Here! Take it!
Вон!	Out!
Марш!	March!
Стоп!	Stop! Halt!
Алло́.	Hello!

Sounds as Interjections

Finally, there are certain words or sounds—some of them easier to pronounce than to spell—which may be classified as interjections. To mention a few:

ым?	what?
ым	no
ыхым	yes
ым—ым	no, no
тсс and шш	quiet

These "words" are undoubtedly many milleniums old and probably the oldest in the language—going back to the days of Primitive Man.